MW00773663

ALIYA

4/24/06

Dear Selma,

Best Wishes,

LIEL LEIBOVITZ

ALIYA

THREE GENERATIONS OF AMERICAN-JEWISH IMMIGRATION TO ISRAEL

ST. MARTIN'S PRESS
NEW YORK

 For information, address St. Martin's Press, 175 Fifth Avenue, New York, N.Y. 10010.

www.stmartins.com

Library of Congress Cataloging-in-Publication Data

Leibovitz, Liel.

Aliya : three generations of American-Jewish immigration to Israel / Liel Leibovitz.

p. cm.

Includes bibliographical references (p. 261).

ISBN 0-312-31515-5

EAN 978-0-312-31515-3

1. Jews, American—Israel—History. 2. Immigrants—Israel—History. 3. Levin family. 4. Ginsberg family. 5. Kalker family. 6. Israel—Emigration and immigration. 7. United States—Emigration and immigration. I. Title.

DS113.8.A4L45 2005

929'.2'095694—dc22

2004051299

First Edition: January 2006

10 9 8 7 6 5 4 3 2 1

To my parents, for their support, and to Lisa,
the light of my life, for giving me the warmth, love,
and encouragement without which this book
could never have been written

CONTENTS

INTRODUCTION

The Billigs, it seemed, had everything. They were my American cousins, and in 1986, a few months short of my tenth birthday, my mother and I spent two weeks in their spacious home on the southern New Jersey shore. It should be noted right away that the lasting impression that trip made on me wasn't due to radical class differences; on the contrary: I was fortunate enough to be born to an affluent Israeli family and live most of my life in relative comfort. But the Billigs, I thought then, occupied a different planet. Whereas back home in Israel I had one television channel, showing mainly educational programming and aged British dramas, the Billigs had a plethora of televisual entertainment, ripe with cartoons and comedies. In lieu of the fast food back home, falafel in pita bread soggy with runny tahini sauce, the Billigs went to McDonald's; the twin golden arches were, for me, a gate to a new world, offering a cornucopia of fun food, free of the heavy and familiar scents of the Middle East. When Alan and Amalia Billig, who were only a year or two older than I, spoke of the future, they spoke of graduating from high school and going on to college; I had three years of mandatory service in the Israel Defense Forces to look forward to. For all these reasons, I considered the Billigs to be the luckiest people on earth.

Several months later, my mother picked me up from school one day and, with a toothy smile, said she had some exciting news: the Billigs were making aliya, the term used to describe Jewish immigration to Israel. Instead of sharing my mother's joy, I was dumbfounded. Why were the Billigs leaving their New Jersey oasis? Furthermore, why were they leaving it for dull and dusty Israel, where there's war and terrorism and not even a single shopping mall? I had so many questions, but felt awkward. There must be, I thought, grand reasons behind my cousins' decision, reasons which only grown-ups knew, reasons that I could not possibly understand.

The search for these reasons is at the heart of this book.

Foremost, and perhaps most obviously, one must ask why would Jews leave behind a nation which has arguably provided them with more assurance, acceptance, and affluence than any other nation in modern history, choosing instead to move to a distant land plagued by violence, poverty, and petulant politics? While this is, of course, an exaggeration of both the virtues of the United States and the vices of Israel, the fundamental question remains valid: Why do American Jews make aliya?

One way to examine this question is by looking at the traditional sociological explanations for immigration. These usually differentiate between "push" and "pull" factors, the former providing an impetus to consider life elsewhere and the latter providing incentives to emigrate.

In the case of American Jews, push factors are virtually nonexistent. According to the National Jewish Population Survey, published in 2002 by the United Jewish Communities, the Jewish population in the United States is wealthier and better educated than the national average. For example, 55 percent of Jews, according to the survey, hold an undergraduate degree, as opposed to the national average of 29 percent. Also, at $50,000, the median annual income for Jewish households exceeds the national median, $42,000, by almost 30 percent. Another way to examine the stature of Jews in the American community is to look at the pervasiveness of Jewish artists, entertainers, educators, and leaders in the American landscape. While this is a more intuitive gauge, one must still admit that Lawrence Summers's appointment as Harvard's first Jewish president, Joseph Lieberman's nomination as the first Jew on a major presidential ticket, and Jerry Seinfeld's success in introducing words like *babka* to a national audience are all signs of a vibrant American-Jewish community, comfortable in its cultural skin and content with its choices.

The other end of the equation, Israel's "pull" appeal, hardly offers concrete rational reasons for immigration. With a major war erupting, on average, every seven years, with constant violence, economic insecurity, and social instability, Israel is hardly a haven. Rather, it is a country demanding great sacrifice from its citizens, from the mandatory military service to the constant anxiety of exploding buses. It is enough, perhaps, to recall the story of Kobi Mandell, a fourteen-year-old youth who made aliya with his parents, moving from Maryland to the West Bank Jewish community of Tekoa.

In May 2001, Mandell and a friend, propelled by youthful wanderlust, skipped school to hike in the Judean desert. By chance, they came upon a group of Palestinian cattle rustlers, who attacked them, bludgeoning their skulls with rocks and sticks and fists and then hiding their bodies in a nearby cave, using the boys' blood to write anti-Semitic screeds on the cave's walls. The next day, a New York tabloid ran Mandell's picture, a smiling teenager wearing a New York Yankees baseball cap. A former colleague of mine, an American-Jewish woman in her midforties, saw the newspaper with Mandell's picture on my desk and burst into tears. She hadn't, she told me between sob and gasp, known the boy or his family; neither was she appalled by the sheer brutality of the murder or by the young age of the victims. What killed her, she said, using unintentionally ironic terminology, was that Mandell could have been her son, an all-American kid with nature hikes on his mind and a baseball cap on his head. The Mandell story, in its extremity, is the manifestation of every nightmare anyone considering aliya must face: the possibility of primeval brutality, the sense of looming tragedy, the terrible tally of the dead.

It is rather clear, then, that the traditional and rational reasons for immigration are null and void in the case of aliya, the only mass movement of emigration *from* the United States. We must, therefore, search elsewhere, in the more ephemeral realms of spirituality, religiosity, and Zionism.

Jewish history and lore, of course, are filled with yearnings for the Holy Land. Ever since the destruction of the temple by the Romans in 70 CE, followed by the end of Jewish sovereignty in the land of Israel and the dispersal of the Jewish population to a two-thousand-year exile across the globe, Jews have remained, in thought and practice, focused on Zion. Daily prayers, for example, are recited facing east, toward Jerusalem, and the Haggadah, the religious text read during the Passover Seder ceremony, ends with the calling "Next year in Jerusalem!" Rabbi Shimon Hadarshan, a medieval compiler of Talmudic tales, relates the following story in his collection, *Yalkut Shimoni,* proving just how strong Zion's appeal has remained even in exile: "It happened that Rabbi Yehuda ben Beteira, Rabbi Matia ben Cheresh, Rabbi Chanina ben Achi, Rabbi Yehoshua and Rabbi Yonatan were walking in the Diaspora and reached Flatus and remembered *Eretz Israel.* They lifted their eyes, shed their tears, rended their clothes, and read this verse: 'And you shall possess it and you shall dwell therein. And you shall observe to do all the statutes . . .' (Deut. 11:31–32). They said, 'Dwelling in *Eretz Israel* is equal to all of the commandments in the Torah.'"

While European Jews approached the issue of Eretz Israel—the Land of Israel—from a religious and messianic perspective, later replaced by active Zionism that set emigration as a major goal, American Zionism was, from its inception, different. Faced with tidal waves of Jewish immigrants arriving at Ellis Island in the early twentieth century, the fledgling American-Jewish community at the time was forced to focus more on absorbing the newly arrived masses than on dispatching its own members to an uncertain fate in Palestine. Therefore, as historian Ben Halpern notes, most early American Zionist organizations functioned mainly as social groups, as "lodges and fraternal orders or . . . *landsmanshaften* composed of fellow-townsmen from abroad," organizing balls and picnics and lectures. This vision of the shtetl, the little Jewish town, was reimagined in America, leaving little room for Zion; Jews were seeking refuge in the New World, and America, with its promise of liberty and justice for all, was *Der Goldeneh Medineh,* the Golden Country.

It is only logical, then, that American Zionism largely diverted from the basic idea imagined by Theodor Herzl. Herzl proposed to solve the Jewish problem by creating a national Jewish homeland in Eretz Israel; his vision portrayed Zionism as an essentially nationalistic movement and viewed immigration to Zion as the main currency with which Jews would one day be able to buy back their fatherland. American Jews, however, were themselves an immigrant community struggling for self-definition, a tiny ethnic peninsula in a nation composed of a hodgepodge of races, colors, and creeds. Like many western European Jews in the late nineteenth century, American Jews came to view their nationality and their religion as two distinct features that coexisted more or less happily, pledging allegiance to both. They were in no hurry to leave.

The yearning for Jerusalem, however, was not lost, and the American-Jewish community soon began investing portions of its wealth in aid of their struggling kin in Zion. One of the earliest recorded examples of this practice dates back to 1761, when Rabbi Chaim Muddahy from Safed, a center of Jewish mysticism, traveled to New York to raise funds for victims of the earthquake that devastated much of his city the previous year.

While this arrangement seemed to work for a long while, prompting Israeli leaders to embark on fund-raising tours of

American-Jewish locales, a fundamental chasm began opening between Israeli and American Jews. While the latter were mostly comfortable with their contributions, proud that their generosity helped fund everything from soldiers' socks to missile silos, most Israelis were led by characteristic national machismo to develop a different view of American Jews, that of "the American cousin."

The American cousin is a proverbial American Jew who, while not necessarily having any blood relatives in Israel, feels for his deprived Israeli kin, showering them with luxury items and expensive gifts before returning to his convenient life abroad. Israelis were brought up to seek the American cousin and mock him at the same time. Sure, went the common perception, the goods are wonderful, but we are tough and proud; we actually risk our lives for the future of this country. American Jews, on the other hand, just use Israel as an ethnic insurance policy, a refuge they must support from afar, just in case an English-speaking Hitler ever comes to power in Washington, D.C.

As Israel was becoming more independent, both politically and financially, this attitude grew even stronger. In 1994, the brusque Ezer Weizman, then Israel's president, told a group of American-Jewish leaders that Israel was no longer a tiny, needy country. "We've already had our Bar Mitzvah," Weizman said, adding that what Israel really needed was not American-Jewish dollars but American-Jewish immigrants. The Jewish leaders, appalled, told Weizman that for the majority of American Jews, this simply was not an option.

Both sides at that meeting seemed to be talking different languages much stranger than Hebrew and English. Shortly after that meeting, Natan Sharansky, the famed Soviet refusenik and at times Israel's minister of immigration and absorption, wrote an op-ed for the *Jerusalem Report,* claiming that both sides were plagued by paternalism. The Israelis, he wrote, perceived the American Jews as having an attitude focused, essentially, on "saving the 'poor, tired, huddled masses,'" while the Americans may have felt that the Israelis looked at them as "minor assistants in the writing of Jewish history, while demanding funding for political intrigues at the same time."

This debate, obviously, raises many issues, some of which are much too voluminous to address here. While we ask ourselves why the American Jews who decide to make aliya do so, we must also consider the majority who choose not to, asking some questions fundamental to the future of the Jewish people: Can there be a thriving Jewish Diaspora coexisting side by side with Israel? Or was Israel's first prime minister, David Ben-Gurion, right when he wrote in an article in an American Labor Zionist magazine that in the Diaspora, "Jews as Jews are human dust"? Can there exist a Zionist movement that, for the first time in two thousand years, is able to fulfill the calling "next year in Jerusalem," yet chooses not to, yearning for Zion while safely staying stateside?

While these questions have no definite answers, they all have one thing in common: aliya. The approximately one hundred thousand American Jews who made aliya since 1947, while still few, are a window onto the largest, most influential Jewish community in modern times, the first Jewish state in two thousand years, and the tumultuous relationship between the two. Their experiences and decisions portray the evolution of both American Jews and Israel, a history rich with violence and healing, crisis and comfort, demise and rebirth.

This book, therefore, will not offer lengthy comments on Jewish theology; neither will it be a documentation of recent Jewish history. It will provide neither sociological analyses nor political commentary. Instead, it will tell the stories of three American Jews who, each at a different point in time and for different reasons, made aliya. It will tell the story of the 1947 generation, who rushed from the fronts of World War II to the shores of Palestine in order to help build the nascent Jewish nation. It will tell the story of the soul-searching generation of the late 1960s who, following Israel's glorious triumph in the Six-Day War, moved there to assert their ethnic identity. Finally, it will tell the story of the men and women who, obeying their religious beliefs, moved to

Jewish communities in the West Bank and the Gaza Strip, often at great personal risk and followed by wide-ranging criticism, often from fellow Jews.

Several years after that eerie conversation in which I was told that my cousins, the Billigs, were leaving New Jersey and moving to Israel, I was walking down a Tel Aviv street on a particularly sweltering summer day. By then I was a soldier, a proud member of the army's spokespersons' unit, and was on my way to one meeting or another. Summer in Tel Aviv being a conspiracy of heat and humidity, targeted at halting all rational thought, I was rather numb when I heard a loud, deep baritone call out that quintessentially Israeli greeting: "Hey! *Chayal!*"—the latter the Hebrew term for soldier.

I stopped and looked around. Israel being what it is, I was sure that I wasn't the only soldier walking around the street at the time. Was the greeting directed at me? Again the voice spoke, even deeper than before: *"Chayal! Bo, bo hena!"* Come here, soldier.

Examining my surroundings more scrupulously, I saw a smiling young man in an army uniform standing behind me. I turned around and approached him slowly, determined to use every second I had to decipher who this mysterious stranger was. I took a closer look: neatly cropped blond hair, sun-bitten skin—complete with the familiar army tan lines that are common to all Israeli males, those semicircular marks where the military-issued tank top ends—dark shades, a smug expression.

I took another step. This is tough, I thought; this guy looks so generic, just like any soldier I've ever met. Did we go to the same high school? Is he a friend from the Scouts? Have I dated his sister?

Then, the soldier, probably sensing my discomfort, spoke again, this time in English, his voice carrying nothing of the army bravado which had engulfed his greetings in Hebrew.

"Liel," he said, "it's me, Alan."

Alan Billig, my American cousin, now a paramedic in the paratroopers, now indistinguishable from any other Israeli soldier on the street. Here was my American cousin, nothing like that proverbial figure who gives gifts and then hurries back home to America. Here was my American cousin, with an M-16 rifle slung across his shoulder and boots caked with mud, a testament to sleepless nights spent training for action. Here was my American cousin, reassuring me with a silent smile that maybe "them" and "us" can become "we," if only for a brief moment, if only long enough to consider seriously all the tough questions detailed above.

This book is my first step.

ALIYA

PROLOGUE

At 11:00 a.m. on a May morning in Israel, 2003, a siren goes off. Unusual for a country in which the unexpected is the only routine, the siren is scheduled, and once it arrives, searing the air with its monotonous shrill, the people are prepared. It marks Yom Hazikaron, Israel's Memorial Day, and is observed with a moment of silence. Israeli drivers, on any other day darting down lanes as fast as they can, hear the siren and stop their cars on the side of the road. They get out of their cars and, for one minute, lower their heads and remember those who have fallen while fighting Israel's wars. It is not a theoretical exercise; almost every Israeli has been personally touched by loss, has experienced firsthand the unbearable grief for a life ended too soon. On the streets and in shopping malls, in army bases and on college campuses, in elementary schools and gyms and coffee shops, everywhere, the country stops, its citizens standing silent.

The siren dies down, but life refuses to return to normal. It is a day in which Israelis, so many of them, go to military cemeteries, so many of them as well, to lay little pebbles, as is the Jewish custom, on the tombstones of their friends or relatives. Looking at the tombstones, one is struck by the terror of sheer math: this one, whispers the legend on a tombstone, was born in 1976 and died in 1995, and another tells of a life begun in 1955 and ended in 1973. Here, the dead are all young, and those who visit them are older, sometimes feeling guilty for having survived, always mindful of the fact that they could easily have been the ones covered in earth and their friends the ones walking away, black yarmulkes on their heads and tears in their eyes. On television, a special channel broadcasts slides with the names of every fallen soldier; even allotting just five seconds for each slide, the list still takes more than a full day to run in its entirety. Every year, new names are added. Other channels broadcast documentaries, mainly stories of sacrifice, and on the radio a playlist of several dozen sad songs repeats itself, sending listeners into a ghostly state of moroseness.

As the day unfolds, a few Israelis in particular are pondering their lives. Like all Israelis, they, too, are overcome by melancholy, taking the day to reflect on friends who have died. Like many Israelis, they were born elsewhere, choosing, at different times in their lives and for different reasons, to make aliya, to immigrate to Israel. Unlike most immigrants, however, they arrived in Israel not out of necessity, not having been persecuted by malicious regimes, but out of choice; they were all born in the United States, and all led lives of relative comfort before moving to Israel, where they endured hardships and even risked their lives.

In Jerusalem, Marlin and Betty Levin are at home. Their house is in the Nayot neighborhood, which they helped found forty years ago, along with a group of other American-Jewish immigrants. Then, they orchestrated a massive artificial landfilling, creating just enough space to form two rows of homes on the newly created hill. Now, overlooking the valley below, the Levins' house is shrouded in memories. For six decades, Marlin has been working as a journalist, keeping every single one of his stories filed. He is an amateur photographer, and when he and Betty came to Palestine in 1948, he was the only person in the region to possess a camera with color film, taking thousands of pictures, all of which are now stored, in perfect order, in rusty filing cabinets cluttering his house. He is also an avid painter, and his drawings, which cover the walls, show the progression of the artist as well as that of the man. In the late 1940s, Marlin drew cheery portraits of young men and women, bubbling with robust colors and broad brushstrokes; in the late 1990s, he drew a scene of a stormy night in Jerusalem, black on gray, dark and ominous.

Talking to the Levins, one would be hard-pressed to guess their age. They are both octogenarians, and as such are afflicted, naturally, by the scars of time. But as they talk to each other—teasing, cooing, tenderly touching—they appear to be just as old as they were when they came to Israel, two people in their twenties, spending their honeymoon on a crowded boat to Palestine, eager to quench the burning of their ideology. None of that passion was lost; now it is simply directed elsewhere, toward other goals. For Betty, it's her garden, a splendid blanket of pink and violet and green; she spends hours toiling over her flowers, forgetting herself, her age, and sometimes even her husband, who from the porch above begs her to come on in already and have tea with him. For Marlin, it's his painting, and writing, and Betty. Once or twice a week, they get into their tiny, antiquated car, drive through the serpentine streets of Jerusalem, and go out to a restaurant or a show. They live in the present, but they cannot escape their past.

Their past is filled with the dead. On Yom Hazikaron, they go for a drive. They drive past the hospice across from the Old City wall and remember their friend Moshe, who fell there after being struck by a Jordanian sniper. Another place reminds them of Hannah, a young and enthusiastic acquaintance who was a nurse and died tending to her patients. Even in the city center, bustling as it is with traffic and shoppers, teeming with the hubbub of humanity, they remember those who were killed in explosions that happened here many years ago, those who were gunned down, those who were stabbed and burned and crushed. Death, they realize, has been their constant companion in the city, and on every street it has left its mark, a token to remember it by.

They return home. They turn on the radio, and the sad songs pour out. Marlin and Betty, energetic even in their eighties, are affected; it is the only day of the year on which they allow themselves to slow down, to slow down and think.

Across the country, on Israel's border with Lebanon, about a four-hour drive north of the Levins' home, Mike Ginsberg is in his command room. As director of security for kibbutz Misgav Am, where he has lived for the past thirty years, moving there shortly after he came to Israel in 1969, he is in charge of operating the kibbutz's siren, to announce to the members the moment of silence observed on Yom Hazikaron. Elsewhere in Israel, most communities are served by regional sirens, which automatically go off at the same time and alert everyone at once. Misgav Am, however, is too far away from other cities and towns, and the sound of the regional sirens fades and dissipates before arriving at the hilltop on which the kibbutz is built. So Mike operates a local device, the same siren used to alert members to rocket attacks launched by Lebanese terrorists based several dozen feet away, across the border. At 11:00 a.m. sharp, he pushes the button.

Then, a minute later, he pushes it again. The siren winds down and dies, and Mike joins the rest of the kibbutz members in the cemetery. The cemetery is located to the northeast of the kibbutz, so close to the border that Mike loves to joke and tell everybody that the cemetery is really inside Lebanon itself. The joke, however, is partially true: the cemetery lies just outside the kibbutz's fence, and in 2000, as the Israel Defense Forces ended an eighteen-year military presence in southern Lebanon and a new borderline was designed, Mike had to fight with army officials to guarantee that the cemetery remained under Israeli control.

There are approximately twenty-five graves in the cemetery. Only half of those buried there, however, were fortunate enough to die of natural causes; the rest died in military actions or in terrorist attacks. Here is the tombstone for Yoav Gross, who died as a soldier fighting the battle for Jerusalem in 1967, and here lies Mike's friend Schori, who fought with him in the desert peninsula of Sinai in 1973 and was killed there by Egyptian artillery shelling. Some, however, died as civilians; Mike passes by the grave of Sami Shani, the kibbutz's secretary who was killed when a cell of terrorists infiltrated the kibbutz in 1980, taking over the children's house. Sami saw them, tried to stop them with his body, fought them with his bare hands; he was killed on the spot, shot at point-blank range. Next to him lies Eyal Gluska, who died in the same attack. He was two and a half years old at the time of his death, his skull crushed with the butt of a rifle because he wouldn't stop crying. To relieve himself from the burden of memory, Mike looks up at the view. This is his favorite piece of scenery in the world: here, he can see the snowy Mount Hermon, and south Lebanon, all the way to the Mediterranean. He made some calculations once, and found that the cemetery offers a 270-degree view. He looks at the verdant Saluki River valley below, and at the Lebanese village of El Adaisa on the opposite hill, not more than a few feet in aerial line. He looks at the Israeli town of Metula to the northeast, where the official border passage between Israel and Lebanon—called, with some irony, the Good Fence—used to be. He feels as if he were hovering, not quite in the sky but no longer on earth.

Then the ceremony starts. There's a black plastic bucket containing red roses, and each member takes one. On the ground, in the middle of the cemetery, is a military steel helmet, turned upside down. In it there's a torched rag, a makeshift memorial flame. There's also a flagpole, and today the flag is at half-mast. The kibbutz members are not religious Jews, so no Bibles are to be found. Instead, someone carries a black folder labeled *Takanon Avlut,* Hebrew for mourning procedures. The procedures include a few well-known poems, the most famous of which speaks of the fallen soldiers as the silver platter on which the State of Israel was handed over to the Jewish people. They also include the reading of the names of the kibbutz's fallen soldiers and victims of terrorist attacks; with each name read, some of the members walk silently to the gravesides, laying down their roses. Shortly thereafter, the ceremony is over.

In central Israel, approximately halfway between Jerusalem and Tel Aviv, another ceremony begins. It is held in Hashmonaim, a small settlement just miles east of the Green Line, the much-contested demarcation between Israel and the West Bank. Hashmonaim is home to several hundred families, many of whom are newly arrived immigrants from the United States, most of whom are Orthodox and politically committed. One such family is the Kalkers; Sharon and her children Rachel and Michael are standing, along with their neighbors and friends, in Hashmonaim's basketball court, watching as local residents take turns reflecting on the meaning of the day. Although the Kalkers arrived from New York not long ago, in 2001, they have already, like all their friends, experienced firsthand the ravages of violence. Ever since the autumn of 2000, when the second Palestinian intifada (Arabic for uprising) started, thousands, on both sides, have lost their lives. The Jewish settlers in particular have been a convenient target: like Hashmonaim, all the settlements are isolated dots engulfed by Palestinian villages. Given the hilly topography of the West Bank, settlers have often found themselves like ducks in a shooting gallery, driving their cars on angry roads, snipers aiming from above. Many have died that way, including some of the Kalkers' friends.

But even to the west of the Green Line, inside Israel proper, violence is rampant. Rachel, taking the bus every day to her high school in Jerusalem, realizes that one day she, too, may fall victim to the murderous wrath of a Palestinian suicide bomber, dozens of whom have blown themselves up on Jerusalem's buses, in its cafés, and on its streets. She knows some who were wounded, and knew others who lost their lives. Standing silent as the siren's wail culminates in a grating screech, the Kalkers, new Israelis, are already intimately acquainted with death.

All throughout Israel ceremonies are held, and people listen to the same songs on the same radio stations. Like most Israelis, Marlin and Betty, Mike, and the Kalkers mourn, but gradually a soothing calm envelops their minds; soon, they know, Yom Hazikaron will be over, and at that exact moment Yom Ha'atzmaut, Israel's Independence Day, will begin, a magical transformation, a ceremonial reminder that freedom was never possible without sacrifice, that in Israel, redemption is always preceded by sorrow.

PART I

FROM HARRISBURG TO JERUSALEM, 1947

CHAPTER ONE

If there could be said to exist a certain look, a peculiar demeanor, which is ideal for journalists, then Marlin Levin chose the right vocation. Even as an octogenarian he is still a striking man, with a mane of white hair and a handshake whose firmness betrays nothing of the feebleness inflicted by the passing years. He is handsome, yet his looks belong to the nonthreatening variety, the kind possessed by generations of Hollywood supporting actors, pleasant enough to get people to open up and talk yet not overwhelming, the perfect equilibrium for someone dedicated to enticing others to tell their stories while himself remaining on the outside, a dispassionate observer of events. His thick-rimmed glasses seem to magnify his stare, a gaze so powerful that one feels almost compelled to reveal, instantly and without provocation, all the content of one's soul. And should one do so, Levin would listen, keeping the stare strong throughout the confession, never once letting go, engulfing his conversational partner in attentiveness until the very end. When he finally responds, his parlance is expressive, weaving staccato one-liners with slow, almost arrested, pensive bouts. As are all seasoned journalists, he is a man who has had a lot of conversations over the years with a lot of different people, and he is able, in the most natural and unpretentious way, to alter his speech almost entirely to suit and seduce whomever he happens to be talking to. And it was this oratorical talent he was invoking on Saturday night, January 12, 1946, in a dismal little cafeteria in Harrisburg, Pennsylvania, not to an interviewee but to a blue-eyed girl named Betty.

Recently released from the army, Marlin returned to Pennsylvania on New Year's Day of 1946 after having served in the Intelligence Corps as a cryptographer, a position that allowed him to experience both the Pacific and European theaters. His return home, he thought, especially on such a symbolic date as January 1, marked the end of all that he had seen in combat, the horrors of war and the atrocities of the European death camps. In Europe, he had seen the sunken eyes of Jewish survivors, the ghostly encampments, the horrible order of destruction. It was a sight seared in his mind's eye, an experience he rarely talked about yet would never forget, carrying the burden of memory like a medallion, close to his heart. He politely refused an offer to sign on to the army's reserves, collected a 10 percent disability pension for an injury he had sustained during the war, pinned the six ribbons he had received to his chest, and returned home to small-town Harrisburg, to resume the life he had before the war, as a journalism major at Temple University. This, he thought, was what life would be about: complete his studies, get a job, and join the millions of his peers as they moved to the suburbs, started their own families, and basked in the warmth of the economic boom of the postwar years. Yet, two or three days after returning home, boredom descended on Marlin.

It was not that he, like some of his friends, missed the adrenaline rush of military life, the nearly anarchic excitement of battle, or the unique camaraderie among men who risk their lives for one another on a daily basis. It was just that, having fought a battle he conceived as being an Armageddon-like struggle between good and evil, adjusting to routine—any kind of routine—was an uneasy task. The war gave him meaning; he was fighting the Nazis and their allies, a well-defined mission with obvious stakes. Civilian life, on the other hand, offered nothing but self-advancement, a métier in which Marlin had never been steeped. He knew he wanted to be a journalist, a vocation he had always been committed to, but he needed—had always needed—a bigger reason, a common cause, something larger than his own self to strive for. And Harrisburg, or any other town for that matter, offered none of that, nothing but long careers and programmed lives.

Restless, Marlin wandered about. He passed his time with some of his childhood friends, also recent returnees from combat. His parents, though thrilled to spend time with their son after not having seen him for several years, sensed his ennui, and a gray cloud of discontent descended on the Levin household. Marlin sought to escape his home by spending as many hours as he could out of doors, going to movies, playing tennis, basketball, and baseball, driving around in his father's Pontiac, and trading war stories with his friends—in short, trying to think about any subject other than himself. Which is why, on the Saturday night of January 12, 1946, he responded with quick enthusiasm when a friend offered an otherwise mundane plan to spend the evening together: again a movie, again dinner in the only cafeteria in town, again empty talk of the good old days followed by an anticlimactic return home to another sleepless night. The two met up early in the evening, chatted briefly, saw some forgettable film, and then headed up to the cafeteria, a bleak institution yet the only place of entertainment open at that time in a town where most businesses shut their doors at seven and most people were sound asleep by ten.

Entering the cafeteria, Marlin's friend noticed two young women sitting at a nearby table. "I know the one to the right," the friend said. "I'll sit next to her. You take the one on the left." The two men quickly injected themselves with a healthy dose of bravado and swaggered toward the two women, no longer dispassionate. Marlin didn't wait long to start his conquest.

"I know a match trick," he told the girl on the left as soon as he sat down beside her, uninvited. He took out a box of matches and arranged some of them on the table. "No one," he said in his best macho voice, "no one has ever been able to figure out how I do this." Certain that the blue-eyed young woman wouldn't succeed where his hardened army comrades had failed, he proceeded to show her his trick, a riddle involving replacing one match in order to change the entire structure. She, in turn, smiled gently and solved the riddle effortlessly. His ego stricken, Marlin nonetheless looked at the woman with newfound admiration; suddenly, she was no longer just a girl in a cafeteria, a pickup for the night. She had suddenly become enveloped in an aura reserved for those few and far-between objects of mad infatuation.

In a softer, more respectful tone, Marlin asked the woman question after question about herself. He wanted to know everything, he said. She told him that her name was Betty. She said that she was top of her class in math at high school, which is why his riddle was no real challenge for her. He smiled humbly, pushing for more details, more information. She was a Brooklyn girl, she said, who had ended up in Harrisburg almost by mistake. A friend of hers was invited by a local rabbi to teach Hebrew at his day school, and Betty joined her, thinking that someone needed to teach Hebrew to those hicks in small-town Pennsylvania. On that Saturday night, she and her friend were sitting, having coffee, reminiscing about how exciting life was in New York, the life they had left behind to come to Harrisburg.

As she spoke, Marlin looked at her intently, half listening, transfixed by her eyes; for the first time in many days, he was genuinely excited. He remembered an old dictum of his grandmother's, who used to tell him that a good woman needed only three things: clear eyes, straight teeth, and strong legs. Applying his grandmother's wisdom to Betty, Marlin was secretly pleased: Her legs were strong and slender, the result of many years of dancing, some of them under the tutelage of the famous Martha Graham. Her teeth were white, well aligned, and glistening. And her eyes, her eyes were what had attracted Marlin in the first place, soft blue pools that exuded warmth, attractive yet soothing.

The conversation carried on for a little while, then dwindled and died. That night, Marlin returned home and went right to sleep, no longer haunted by indecision and anxiety, full with the promise of that evening's chance encounter. The next morning, he went down to the breakfast table with a grin. Meekly, and with a mouth full of toast, he said to his mother, "Last night I met the girl I'm going to marry." His mother, accustomed as she was to her son's impetuousness, just smiled.

Armed with a new cause, Marlin was now more energetic, better prepared to carry on with life. He informed his university of his intention to resume his studies, and was offered his old position as the editor of the school's newspaper. Most of the writing he did, however, was directed at one reader: Betty. He wrote her long letters, trying his best to overcome his inclination toward wisecracking and bad punning, desperate to prove to her that despite being a self-proclaimed puny farm boy from nowhere, despite having none of her worldly charm and big-city sensibilities, despite being quick with a joke or a prank, he was a suitable spouse. A year later, he was graduated with honors, distinguished as one of the university's ten most outstanding students. Unlike some college graduates, he had no doubts concerning the future: he knew that he wanted to be a journalist, and he knew that he wanted Betty by his side. He channeled most of his energy into wooing her, often using his way with words to one-up one of Betty's other suitors. Still, he could no longer postpone the inevitable; the time had come for him to join—as he was fond of saying yet terrified of thinking—the rat race.

One day soon after graduation, Robert L. Johnson, president of Temple University, summoned Marlin to his office. He liked Marlin's writing and the way he edited the school's paper, and wanted him to pay a visit to his friend in New York, Henry Luce, who was looking for young talent to come and work for his magazine, *Time*. Yet, Marlin respectfully refused. He told Johnson that he preferred learning the trade not in a revered institution such as *Time*, where reporters were called upon to cast their wide lens and present a weekly summary of the world, but at a daily of some sort, where one had the chance to witness everyday life in all its glory. Leaving behind a baffled Johnson, Marlin exited the president's office, still himself uncertain whether turning down an offer considered to be the Golden Fleece of his profession was a liberating act or sheer foolishness. He was offered a job as news editor of the local radio station, WFIL, and prepared to settle down. Several months later, however, he resigned, as Betty announced that she was going back to New York. Still determined to win her over, Marlin followed her there in December 1946. Shortly after his arrival, he accepted a position as an associate editor of the trade paper *Women's Wear Daily,* writing about the retail fur market.

The job was all Marlin could hope for. Every morning he arrived at the office, located on Fourteenth Street in Manhattan, at around nine. Some coffee, some discussion of the day that lay ahead, and he was off to Fifth Avenue, interviewing fur buyers at such stores as Saks Fifth Avenue or Bergdorf Goodman. Then, at 3:30 p.m., when Betty got off from her job teaching Hebrew at the elite Ramaz day school, the two would meet for a nonalcoholic drink, after which Betty would go to classes at the Teachers Institute or to dance rehearsals, and Marlin back to the office to write his stories for another several hours. Marlin found this routine rewarding. First, it allowed him the time and energy to pursue Betty with even more zeal then before, wooing and charming her as best he could; her defenses, he could sense, were giving in. Second, the job allowed Marlin ample opportunities for the type of creative mischief he was so fond of. One time, for example, bored beyond relief, he deliberately sparked a controversy between those of New York's leading fur buyers who preferred stoles and those who preferred fur capes. His uneventful beat also provided Marlin with an opportunity to hone his skills of observation: interviewing a fur buyer at the upscale Bergdorf Goodman one day, he witnessed a raggedy-looking middle-aged woman with straggly hair, no makeup, and a cheap, well-worn cloth coat walk into the store and, after seeing cheaper alternatives, insist on a $40,000 fur coat. To the utter astonishment of both Marlin and the store's salesman, the woman's check was honored; it was only a week later that Marlin learned that the woman was the wife of a local New York mafia don. Such moments filled him with joy; he reported these stories like a Damon Runyon in a department store, making his articles for the seemingly mundane trade publication teem with observation and insight.

Still, for all the fun there was to be had and all the freedom that Fairchild, the parent company of *Women's Wear Daily,* was willing to grant Marlin in choosing his own subjects, something fundamental was missing. In his mind, Marlin could not resist accelerating his progression, asking questions as he went along: he could see that his current job would lead to a better one, and from there, perhaps, to an editorial position, to serious pay and professional credit, to a marriage with Betty and a house in the suburbs and . . . But that was enough. He knew enough to realize that this was not the life he desired, not the future he was willing to sacrifice his time and energy for. Again, he became restless. This time, however, it was not vague ennui haunting him, but a singular, clear plan.

Throughout 1946 and 1947, Marlin read with great interest as events in Palestine rapidly unfolded. Because he had had a modicum of Jewish education as a young boy, and the memory of witnessing the smoldering ashes of European Jewry was still fresh, he became increasingly interested in the fate of the Jewish community vying for independence in Palestine. He eagerly consumed every news story of the Jewish underground movements, the Haganah and the Irgun and the Lehi, all fighting both the British, who by force of a UN mandate were the legal custodians of Palestine, and the Arabs, the land's other inhabitants, who were rapidly organizing and increasingly belligerent. He was fascinated by every bit of information about the ongoing events in Palestine, followed the UN's fervent discussions regarding the future of the much-contested swath of land just west of Jordan, hoped for some sort of swift resolution which would birth the first independent Jewish state in millennia. As 1947 rolled in, the pace of developments increased dramatically, and Marlin listened intently as the radio spat out an *allegro non tropo* of breaking news: the British government announcing that it would terminate its mandate in Palestine, the British government referring what it called the "problem of Palestine" to the UN, the UN forming an eleven-member committee to decide the fate of Palestine. Especially captivating were the reports by the famed newspaperman Homer Bigart, writing in the *New York Herald-Tribune*, the first reporter to witness the secret induction of Jewish youth into the underground movements fighting for independence.

Learning of these developments, Marlin was struck by a series of small epiphanies. The Second World War, he realized, had been a fight between good and evil on a global scale, and he had participated, had fought on the side of good, had helped deliver the world from malice. The struggle for a Jewish homeland, on the other hand, was also a seminal event on a global scale, albeit one for which he was gradually beginning to feel personally responsible. How could he, he thought, throw off his life, study, prospects, to go to war with Germany and Japan, to fight for an ephemeral and enticing idea, freedom, yet not budge when his own people were standing trial? How could he who had listened to his grandmother haltingly tell stories of pogroms in her native Russia, he who had witnessed the aftermath of the Holocaust, not join the struggle to ensure that such atrocities were never again committed against the Jewish people? In his heart, the cause was growing bigger every day.

And possibly it was a new adventure, one as removed from the suburbs as could be. Staying in the army reserves and fighting a war that had already been won was futile, but joining the one about to begin was not. He could be a journalist anywhere, he thought, only instead of furriers and haute couture he would cover bombings and shootings and moonlit raids, finally fulfilling his dream of becoming a foreign correspondent. This appealed to the romantic in him, inspired him to put behind the safety of stateside life. There was only one matter he had to attend to prior to boarding the boat to Palestine: his blue-eyed love.

A Hebrew teacher by profession, Betty was even more immersed than Marlin in the constant concern over the progression of events in Palestine. She, too, felt drawn to the Jewish cause, having herself emigrated from Estonia to Latvia and from there to the freedom offered by the United States. Her father had traveled to the United States in 1923 with his oldest son, with the intention of bringing the rest of the family with him shortly thereafter. Just then, however, Congress passed a law requiring immigrants to become citizens before granting them the right to bring over their families, which meant that Betty, her mother, and her three siblings had to wait for five years, fatherless, every day asking their mother if the *shif's carta,* Yiddish for ship ticket, had arrived. Palestine, then, represented the promise of an independent Jewish state, a state where Jews would never again have to wait for others to decide their fate. She realized the risks, of course—when reading the news one was burdened with images of carnage—yet thought them all trivial compared to the goal at stake. She also had Marlin, at that point already rather adamant about going, and she trusted his good judgment, his amicable ways, and his savvy character. When he proposed, in June of 1947, she accepted. Whether out of awareness of her future husband's modest means or out of a spartan upbringing, she refused his offer of a traditional diamond-studded engagement ring. Instead, he bought her a gold watch, on the back of which he had engraved, in Hebrew, "She whom my soul loved, I found," a variation of a traditional canticle. Betty told him she couldn't have been happier. They both decided not to wait too long; they would celebrate their honeymoon, they agreed, on a ship en route to the port of Haifa, Palestine.

Which left the minor responsibility of telling their family, friends, and employers. Some, the more practical ones, showered them with fact upon fact, each carefully selected to dissuade them from leaving. Palestine, they said, was no-man's-land, a war zone where three peoples and countless different sects clashed over incoherent and ever-shifting political goals. It was a land where bombs just went off, reaping lives with no warning. Others focused on shaking the couple's confidence; they reminded Marlin that the only three words of Hebrew he spoke were *shalom, Bar Mitzvah,* and *hallelujah,* none of which were likely to come in handy for a reporter wishing to cover the ongoing battle for Jewish independence. You know no one there, they would say, and nobody guarantees that you will find a job, a home, a circle of friends. Others tried a more cautious approach, supporting the couple's decision, yet trying to persuade them to wait just a little while longer, until things clear up just a little bit. The United Nations, they would repeat time and again, were deliberating on the matter. Wait until they're done. Wait until the state is established. Wait until the violence quells. Just wait.

Yet wait was precisely what Marlin and Betty were disinclined to do. Young, in love, and lacking, as so many young people so often do, a clear sense of their own mortality, they brushed all doubts and concerns aside. There was only one important thing, they patiently explained to their families and friends, and that was to participate in building the Jewish homeland. With a wink, Marlin would add that he had defeated the mighty Nazis and Imperial Japanese, so the Arabs of the region should prove absolutely no problem for him. Getting a visa to Palestine, however, did: wanting to stay longer than the few short months a tourist's visa permitted, Marlin and Betty considered applying for an immigration visa, a nearly impossible task considering the tens of thousands of displaced persons, living in squalor in detention camps all across Europe, anxious to resettle in the Holy Land. Fearing a change of demographics in the region, and wishing to avoid the wrath of the more numerous and better-organized Arab nations, the British published a series of documents known as the White Papers, setting severe limitations on the permissible quotas of Jewish emigrants to Palestine. Feeling apprehensive about taking permits away from European Jews who had survived the

Holocaust, Marlin and Betty sought an alternative, a pretext to convince the British government to grant them long-term visas. Unable to find any recourse, Betty, who was the national chairwoman of Junior Hadassah, the national women's organization, had previously signed up for a trip to Palestine with several of the organization's leading activists. Now that she was married, however, going by herself seemed inappropriate.

In the meantime, Marlin realized that his service in the United States Army granted him, as it did his peers, a period of postgraduate studies at any accredited university, under the auspices of the law commonly known as the GI Bill of Rights. Among the universities recognized by the American government was the Hebrew University in Jerusalem: established less than twenty years before, the university was, in 1947, graduating into international prominence. Its original board of governors, which had included such luminaries as Albert Einstein, Sigmund Freud, and Martin Buber, catapulted the nascent academic institution from a peripheral campus to a global intellectual center. With the help of generous donations, the university's student body mushroomed exponentially, numbering more than one thousand by the late 1940s, taught by two hundred faculty members. Marlin submitted an application and, aided by a Jewish Agency official named Avraham "Abe" Harman, who would years later become one of Israel's first ambassadors to the United States as well as the chancellor of the Hebrew University, was granted the desired visa. As Betty had already obtained her visa through Junior Hadassah, the two were ready to go.

With his visa in hand, Marlin had only to resign his position at *Women's Wear Daily*. His boss, Fred Eichelberger, was the embodiment of the newspaperman stereotype, complete with rumpled fedora, staccato speech, and an abundance of cynicism. When Marlin informed him of his intention to quit in order to move to Palestine, Eichelberger didn't think long before responding. "You're mad!" he growled at Marlin. "You're not only mad, you're crazy. You have a good future here with America's top trade daily and you're going out there? You'll get yourself killed." Then, after a short pause, he smiled and offered Marlin a one-third increase in pay, thinking the whole Palestine bit a clever ruse aimed at extracting extra wages. Marlin, however, refused politely, reiterating his decision once again. "If that's what you want," Eichelberger sighed, "you can do some articles for us on the fur market." Amused by the concept of reporting on the fur market in subtropical Palestine, which conjured images of Jewish Eskimos inhabiting the desert, Marlin jovially agreed. "I'll be glad to, Fred," he told the older man, and with that he stood up and shook his editor's hand, said good-bye, and left the building, knowing that his decision was truly final.

Having removed all the major obstacles in their way, Marlin and Betty scheduled their departure for August 14, 1947, leaving themselves two short months to prepare for their new life. Their knowledge of Palestine limited mainly to Bigart's reports, Marlin and Betty sat down to imagine what their new home would be like. The result was a combination of Marlin's romanticism and Betty's realism, a land which was one part battlefield and one part Wild West, a desert with barracks and camels and horses. So they set out to shop accordingly. One day in early August, in the midst of one of the hottest spells in recorded history, with the mercury in the midnineties, Marlin and Betty rummaged around the East Side, going from store to store, searching for suitable provisions to take to Palestine. Betty insisted on utensils, as well as mosquito nettings, linen, and books. Marlin, on his end, was infatuated with an army surplus two-way Hallicrafter radio. Although he had neither the intention nor the technical ability to take advantage of the radio's transmission capabilities, Marlin was tempted by its cheap price, shortwave bands, and, perhaps more than anything else, its look. Designed by renowned industrial designer Raymond Lowey, the Hallicrafter SX-42 was the first electronic device ever to win an international design award from New York's Museum of Modern Art. Its relatively slim black casing and shiny metallic surface endowed it with a futuristic look that producers of 1950s science fiction movies such as *Cat Women of the Moon* were captivated by, often placing the radio as a seminal prop in their movies. Its symmetrical rows of knobs, buttons, and switches, all in uniform black, and spherical dials in pale, backlit green, made the radio appear at once the pinnacle of contemporary craft and an object sent back in time, more than enough to get the average man, even one such as Marlin with little technological savvy, excited. Armed with their radio, a Kodak 35-mm camera with the relatively new Kodachrome color film that Marlin had purchased, some survival gear, and other bric-a-brac that they picked up on a whim, the newlywed Levins were as prepared for the journey as they would ever be. They contacted Santini Brothers, a well-known Queens-based shipping company, and had their few belongings crated and ready to go.

On August 14, 1947, the same day the British left both India and Pakistan, granting the two countries their independence and relinquishing what was considered the crown jewels of the decaying British Empire, Marlin, Betty, and a small band of family members and friends drove to Manhattan's Pier 84 to board the ship to Palestine. Pictures taken that day show two youths, Marlin and Betty, beaming with excitement, and a host of older, more reserved family members doing their best to conceal their utter dread of the imminent departure, yet not entirely able to control their emotions. In the pictures, Marlin and Betty are the only ones smiling; Marlin's mother, on the other hand, looks terrified, gazing at the camera with a blank stare, as if unaware that her picture is being taken; and Betty's father, a tall, slender, goateed, and impeccably dressed man, just frowns, a result, maybe, of an attempt at smiling gone sour.

Perhaps the heat was to blame: that morning, the temperature climbed to seventy degrees before 7:45 a.m., continuing its ascent with every hour that passed. By the time Marlin and Betty arrived at the harbor, the temperature was ninety-five degrees, aided and abetted by a devastating 93 percent humidity. It was one of the hottest days in years, the newspapers reported, one of those muggy New York summer days that slowly subdue both body and mind, and all present were succumbing to the heat, to their emotions, to the imminent moment in which Marlin and Betty would board the ship and disappear.

The ship, a navy vessel converted for civilian use, was called the *Marine Carp*. Together with its twin, the *Marine Jumper*, it was one of the Second World War's unsung vessels, 523 feet of unimpressive metal capable of carrying up to 3,451 soldiers in its belly. It was launched in July of 1945, and so missed the war's glorious naval battles. Unlike its senior sisters, the carriers and destroyers and battleships, it bore no arms, having been designed primarily for transportation purposes, a floating school bus of sorts designated to haul troops and equipment over long distances. It was briefly used in the Pacific war theater before being returned stateside in 1946. It then enjoyed a five-year run as a civilian vessel, was docked, put out of service in 1957, and sold ten years later to a private operator, largely forgotten by all but the most staunch of naval enthusiasts. To the Levins, however, standing at the dock on that hot August day, the *Marine Carp* was both a mighty vessel, a luxurious ocean liner, and their own personal *Mayflower* to carry them across the ocean and into the Promised Land. They boarded the ship, waved their brief good-byes, and disappeared amid hundreds of other young men and women, most of whom were recently released soldiers, some Jewish and others of Arab descent, all headed to the Middle East for adventure, ideology, or a concoction of both.

Still staffed by the U.S. Military Transport Administration, the same authority responsible for transporting soldiers overseas during the war, the *Marine Carp* had not, at the time of Marlin and Betty's journey, completely shed its former military identity. The officers and crew members who operated the ship were in uniform, and despite the innately civilian nature of their journey still adhered to strict military decorum. Every morning an early inspection of the ship's quarters was conducted, an inspection that did not take into consideration any expectation of privacy on the part of the ship's female passengers; it was only on the third or fourth day that Betty and the rest of the women on board learned to remain in their bunk beds until the officers stormed by en route to another pointless exercise in army styling. The protomilitary nature of the ship, however, was not entirely without benefits: having become familiar with similar vessels during the war, Marlin knew the innards of the ship inside and out, and could make such wise choices as picking a bunk in the upper tier, in a corner under a fan, where air circulation was maximal and the heat the least oppressive.

And so, sans privacy but with unhinged excitement and a nervous sense of accomplishment, Marlin and Betty spent their honeymoon. While the days were usually long and hazy, hours upon hours filled with idle conversations and inedible food, the nights awarded the newlyweds with plenty of opportunities to escape the panoptical gaze of their shipmates, to find a remote corner somewhere on the far end of the deck and take solace in each other. Usually the two would limit themselves to the main deck, where the noxious odors of diesel and the whiffs of rotting food emanating from the kitchen had little hold. Holding hands, they would sit and watch the fiery stars reflected in the smooth ocean, enjoying the late-summer breeze and the transcendental tranquillity of looking at the horizon and seeing the sea and the sky melt into one another in a thousand hues of frowning blue. Sometimes they would sing, especially the Yale Glee Club's renowned "Whiffenpoof Song." Though neither Marlin nor Betty had attended the university, the song's lyrics were too poignant to ignore: "We're poor little lambs who have lost our way," the song went, followed by a joyous bleating, "Baa, baa, baa." Then it would conclude: "We're little black sheep who have gone astray, baa, baa, baa." Bleating at the top of their lungs, the two would burst out laughing. New York seemed very far away, and so did Palestine. For the moment, they were poor little lambs who had lost their way, and they were making the most out of their situation.

Others were there to help them along. Boarding the ship, Betty discovered that Jack Cohen, an acquaintance of hers from her days studying at the Jewish Theological Seminary in Manhattan, and his wife, Rhoda, were also on board. So were the wife and son of Moshe Brilliant, a reporter for the Jerusalem-based English newspaper *The Palestine Post,* as well as a nice young woman who later turned out to be one of Jerusalem's earliest and most industrious prostitutes, and Zerach Werhaftig, a Russian Jew who was immigrating to Palestine via the United States, and who would later become one of the signatories of Israel's Declaration of Independence, a member of Knesset with the National Religious Party, and a cabinet minister in several consecutive governments. Placed in such close quarters for two weeks, unable to escape each other's company, the group became a coterie. The modest meals provided on board were quickly supplemented by an assortment of foodstuffs brought from home, a minuscule cornucopia of canned goods. The dreary days were filled with laughter and card games and chatter, with Marlin, Betty, and their circle of friends now visibly reclusive from the others, distinguished by their private language and encoded jokes. Yet the nights remained the domain of romance, a time for reflecting, under the moon's yellow glare, on all that was about to happen.

As the days went by, more and more landmarks appeared on the horizon, each marking the nearing of the end. First was the Rock of Gibraltar, then the Athenian port of Piraeus, followed two days later by the harbor in Beirut, Lebanon. Eager to get off and catch their first glimpse of Middle Eastern grandeur, Marlin, Betty, and some of their peers were informed that they had better stay on board; Jews were not welcome in the city of Beirut. A day or so later, on a bright Saturday morning, Marlin and Betty stood on deck as the ship approached Haifa, watching with awe the hazy blue of Mount Carmel protruding from the calm sea, with white buildings planted across the mountains' slopes, reflecting the brilliance of the Mediterranean sun. Never in his life, Marlin thought, had he seen a port city so immaculate, so enticing.

Having arrived on a Saturday, the men and women aboard the

ship became engrossed in heated discussions concerning the feasibility of disembarking on the Sabbath. After much radio traffic between ship and shore, it was decided that the more observant Jews on board, Marlin and Betty among them, could wait until the following morning. The two were relieved; the extra day on board would allow them, they thought, some time to get used to the idea of their new homeland, to calm down from the voyage, to relax.

The first disturbance occurred shortly after the ship's docking. As soon as the ship's motors shut down, a series of underwater discharges went off, each of them powerful explosions, violently rocking the *Marine Carp.* Chaos ensued: startled by the commotion, the people on board were convinced, if only for a short minute, that they were coming under attack. The identity of those responsible for the attack, however, differed depending on the beholder: the Jews on board were convinced the blast was the result of Arab terrorism, while the Arabs suspected the Haganah, the Jewish underground movement, was the perpetrator. Neither was right: the discharges were part of an official policy executed by the British police and meant to deter illegal Jewish immigrants, mainly Holocaust survivors who were interned at displaced persons' camps and were desperately trying to enter Palestine, from jumping overboard and swimming to shore in a dashing attempt to avoid the British authorities. This was quickly explained to the befuddled people on board, and Marlin and Betty were shocked to learn that the British, America's allies in fighting against the Nazis, could execute such a cruel policy. Yet, they had a big day ahead of them, and finally, overcome by excitement, they fell asleep.

The following day, Sunday, August 31, 1947, was a crucial date for the hopeful Jewish community in Palestine. That day, the special committee formed three months earlier by the United Nations to study the conditions in Palestine and recommend long-term plans submitted its report to the UN's secretary-general, Trygve Lie. The committee, which consisted of eleven member states, convened at the UN headquarters in Lake Success, New York, studying documents and interviewing experts, witnesses, and interested parties. The committee's findings were unequivocal: unanimously, it recommended that Great Britain terminate its mandate and grant Palestine independence at the earliest possible date. Even more important, seven out of the eleven nations voted in favor of a partition plan, slicing the country into two separate states, one Jewish and the other Arab.

The historical significance of the day, however, was largely lost on Marlin and Betty, both of whom were focused on their own personal history in the making. Early in the morning, eager to head down the gangplank, the two heard a voice come on the public announcement system, asking a Mr. Levin to report to the quarterdeck. In his mind, Marlin was entertaining a hundred doomful scenarios, ranging from the plausible to the absurd. The call, it wasn't difficult to tell, was ominous, a sign that his arrival in Palestine would not be a smooth one. But why? The best explanation he could come up with concerned his vocation: the mighty British government must have found out that he was a journalist and, upset by unfavorable reporting by some American newspapermen, had decided to bar Marlin from entry. Was he destined, like Moses, to witness the Promised Land yet never enter it?

The officious, mustachioed British officer in knee-length socks and khaki-colored shorts curtailed his stream of consciousness. "Mr. Levin?" he asked.

"Yes, sir," Marlin responded. "I'm Levin. What is it?"

"Are those yours?" the officer said, pointing to a stack of cases in the center of the deck, surrounded by British soldiers with rifles and menacing looks.

Marlin was at a loss. "Well," he said, "I don't know. I suppose if they have my name on them, they are mine." Having entrusted the packing process to Santini Brothers, neither Marlin nor Betty had seen the actual crates containing their belongings.

Marlin's hesitation unnerved the British officer even further. British officials were targets of both Jewish and Arab violence, both sides eager to end the mandate and drive the British Empire away from Palestine's shores. After a prolonged series of hangings, bombings, and assassinations, the British police weren't taking any chances. Still, Marlin wondered why he was being questioned. Did they fear scurrilous reporting concerning the tight relations between the mandate's higher echelons and the Arab leadership? The British officer didn't betray a thing; he just motioned for Marlin to approach closer to the crates. When he did, he nearly fainted; the crates all bore his name alongside clearly stenciled descriptions of the crates' contents: BOMBS, FUSES, MORTARS.

Marlin shuddered. Who could be sending ammunition in my name? he wondered. What was going on here?

Again, the British officer interrupted his thoughts. "Open them up!" he ordered his soldiers, all the time staring at an increasingly pale Marlin. "Open them up!"

Once opened, the crates revealed their true contents: pots, pans, books, and records, all of Marlin and Betty's earthly possessions, all of the things that the two had left with Santini Brothers. The company, Marlin realized, used surplus ammunition crates from the Second World War to pack innocuous items. He explained as much to the officer, who was not amused. "Some joke!" he said indignantly, calling off his troops and leaving a smiling Marlin behind, ready to head off for his first day in Haifa, in Palestine, in the Holy Land.

CHAPTER TWO

As they stepped off the plank and into the port of Haifa, Marlin's and Betty's senses were assaulted on every front. First there was the commotion, the droning din of many languages reverberating simultaneously, bouncing off one another, vying for prominence in the open air. Then there were the smells: the salty sea, the sweaty stevedores, the steaming asphalt. There were also the sights: all those white buildings that Marlin had spotted from aboard the *Marine Carp,* those minuscule white constructions with their clean lines and protruding angles, were now upon him, engulfing him, like a forbidden city entered for the first time, glistening and enchanting, foreign yet somehow familiar. Most of all, however, Marlin was struck by one realization: everyone around him, from foreman to forklift operator, was Jewish. He watched with amazement as a dozen or so men, dressed in grubby khaki shorts, their muscles bulging from their stained tank tops, formed a human chain and unloaded the ship's cargo, all the while shouting, cursing, and conversing in Hebrew. It was not the Hebrew taught in Manhattan's day schools, tinted by eastern European pronunciation, at once foreign and familiar, the language of prayer and scholarship. Instead, it was a living organism, rolling on the tongues of the men, throaty and guttural, ripe with consonants that seemed impossible to pronounce, like the rolling *r*'s or the unfamiliar *ch* sound that seemed to emanate from the bowels and spurt out with force, cleansing the insides of the vocal cords. There was no doubt about it: these were New Jews.

But for all of the port city's beauty, Marlin and Betty were eager to leave Haifa. They were headed for Jerusalem, where, they were told, much bureaucracy awaited before they could quietly settle down in Palestine. One of their first stops, their friends and acquaintances all said, should be the Jewish Agency's Tourist Information Center on Ben Yehuda Street, a major vein of business, commerce, and entertainment. There, Marlin and Betty were presented with a formal letter intended to ease their passage along some of Palestine's more contested roads, as well as to open the doors and hearts of the often suspicious Jewish population. "To whom it may concern," the letter read, in a formal tone very uncommon to the local mentality, "it gives us great pleasure to formally introduce to you two American-Jewish students who have just arrived from the United States in order to study at the Hebrew University in Jerusalem. The aforementioned two desire now, before the academic year begins, to tour the country in order to closely observe the various facets and achievements of our settlements. We would be grateful if you would provide them with help should they happen to need it, whether by guiding them around or by putting them up for a day or two, according to what is possible for you. The names of the guests: Moshe and Batya Levin."

Marlin and Betty were now Moshe and Batya. The sudden change, the automatic Hebraization of names applied to all arriving Jews, was reflected in the host of identity cards Marlin was issued by the British authorities, most of which identified him as Moshe. The cards were numerous: some merely contained basic information about their holder, others specified which areas of Jerusalem were permitted or prohibited for one's entry, some spoke of one's vocation, while yet others determined one's allotted food rations. As time and events progressed, new cards replaced old ones, each poignantly reflecting the reality of life in Jerusalem at the time, where one's identity had to be described as accurately as possible, where one was categorized, analyzed, and assessed, marked as friend or foe.

To understand why identity played such a predominant part in determining a resident's prospects, one need only glimpse at a map of Jerusalem circa 1947. Unlike other cities, governed by a sense of coherent geographical continuity, the map of Jerusalem resembled a modernist painting, with an assortment of paint blotches, seemingly distributed at random, each representing a different nationality, different sensibilities, restrictions, and regulations. In its construction, Jerusalem was truly history's city. It was not designed, like most modern capitals, by urban planners, starting with a grid of streets and avenues and building their way up. Instead, each of its neighborhoods represented a different historical period: the Old City of biblical days, the Arab neighborhoods built during the Ottoman Empire's rule, the newer neighborhoods constructed since the beginning of the British Mandate in 1917, each neighborhood standing alone, each occupying a different part of the city, each connected to the others by a disorderly system of tortuous roads, fathomable only to the initiated and senseless to the accidental traveler wishing to commute from one place to another. Traveling between neighborhoods was, therefore, less traveling in space and more traveling in time. Although the city's changing governances throughout the ages had enforced regulated construction which stressed a similar facade using only Jerusalem stone, a rose-hued and pockmarked rock unique to the area's quarries, each neighborhood, however similar in appearance, differed nonetheless in the silent energies it exuded. Walking down the cavernous alleyways of the Old City, for example, one could not help but feel time looking over one's shoulder, quietly reminding the awestruck traveler that a certain street was once trodden by the ancient Hebrew kings or that a certain house once bore witness to some of the dramas depicted in the Bible. Even the newer neighborhoods, bereft of historical grandeur, were nonetheless monumental, their two- or three-story buildings with high ceilings and hidden backyards a testament, concomitantly, both to time's progress and to its basic irrelevance in a city that had seen so much transpire over so many centuries. While other cities moved forward in time, Jerusalem moved around, from neighborhood to neighborhood and from decade to decade, its stony face recording history yet betraying none of its upheavals.

The regions surrounding the city were almost entirely under Arab control, and were dotted with villages such as Deir Yassin, Beit Tzafafa, and A Tur, which controlled the main lines of transportation to the city, including the only major intercity road and the only existing railroad track. To the far west lay the Jewish neighborhood of Motza, the outermost boundary of the city; just southeast of Motza lay a finger-shaped peninsula encompassing three Jewish neighborhoods: Beit Vagan at the very tip, Beit Hakerem in the middle, and Kiryat Moshe at the end, connected almost seamlessly to the Arab neighborhoods of Upper Lifta and Sheik Bader. The three Jewish neighborhoods were dubbed Jerusalem's "Garden Suburbs"; in the early 1920s, Jewish Jerusalemites eager to escape the city's confined quarters and narrow, serpentine streets decided to adopt a British style of neighborhood development known as the garden suburb, consisting of single-family dwellings in the center of a plot of land surrounded by greenery, complete with tree-lined avenues and, wherever possible, central landscaped islands. Richard Kaufmann, a renowned German-Jewish architect who immigrated to Israel, was instrumental in developing those neighborhoods; to avoid Jerusalem's strict building codes, demanding that each house adopt the same facade, Kaufmann and his developers built the first suburbs just outside of the city's municipal limits. Instead of the antiquated, heavy, local Jerusalem stone, they erected staples of modern architecture, all built in the Bauhaus, or International, style, with clean lines and straight angles.

The original garden suburbs proved so appealing, however,

that soon others were being constructed within Jerusalem itself, just east of the original suburbs, neighborhoods such as Rehavia and Talpiot. Each of the neighborhoods attracted, for some unclear reason, disproportionate numbers of certain professions; Rehavia, for example, was where the clerks, or the officials, as they were then known, lived, as the neighborhood was home to a large number of Jewish Agency employees, while Talpiot was home to the city's bankers. With the influx of Jewish immigration from Germany in the mid-1930s, many architects arrived in Jerusalem, expanding the Bauhaus movement in the city, making its skyline more cubic.

Moving farther to the east was the neighborhood of Romema, which bordered the British Camp Schneller. Once known as the Syrian Orphanage because it housed blind Arab children, the camp was used as the bureaucratic nerve center of the British government in Palestine. It was in Camp Schneller, a cobbled courtyard surrounded by stone barracks, that paychecks were disbursed and motions were filed and records were kept, all watched over by a large contingent of clerks dedicated to bringing order to the disheveled land. Because of its importance and because its guardians were largely undertrained young corporals, Camp Schneller was often the target of choice for random attacks, mostly perpetrated by members of the more zealous Jewish underground groups.

Engulfing Camp Schneller to the north, east, and south was the main block of Jewish neighborhoods: the ultra-Orthodox Mea Sha'arim, Talbieh, Beit Israel, and a host of other, smaller neighborhoods making up the bulk of Jewish Jerusalem. For many of that area's residents, exiting the safe confines of the Zone, as the area came to be known, was a rarity, as harassments by the British police and random acts of violence by Arab gangs were almost guaranteed. As political events unraveled, and as the British Mandate in Palestine neared its end, the unmarked borders of the Zone turned from ephemeral to concrete, rendered visible by bursts of machine-gun fire and showers of stones. For those living in the Zone, the world became smaller with each day that passed.

East of the Zone lay the main swath of British presence in the city, marked by the Allenby Camp in the south and the King David Hotel in the center, both fortified British camps housing the higher echelons of the mandate's forces, as well as the Russian Compound to the north. Originally funded by the czar in the late 1800s, the compound was to be the epicenter of a vast fiefdom overseen by the Greek Orthodox Church in Jerusalem. The church owned most of the lands surrounding the compound, controlling, in essence, the lion's part of the city's center. The compound was designated as a terminal for receiving the thousands of Orthodox pilgrims streaming into Jerusalem each year. With the outbreak of the First World War, however, the czar's funding slowly decreased, coming to an abrupt end with the October Revolution of 1917. Having lost its sole patron, the Greek Orthodox Patriarchate of Jerusalem auctioned off most of its possessions, providing the premises for the single most important territorial expansion in the city's history; in the 1920s, on lands purchased from the church, neighborhoods such as Rehavia, Talbieh, and Talpiot were built. The Russian Compound itself, however, was not sold but rented out to the British authorities and reinvented as a punitive megalopolis, containing the police headquarters, numerous courthouses, and Jerusalem's central prison. The once-inviting terminal was surrounded by barbed wire, prisoners replaced pilgrims, and the compound quickly became the symbol of all that was hated about the often oppressive British colonial rule. In the Jewish parlance of the time, it was known as "Bevingrad," after Ernest Bevin, Great Britain's foreign minister who was known for his staunch anti-Semitic positions and rigid policies meant to deflect Jewish efforts at gaining independence in Palestine. To the east of the British territory lay another isolated isle of Jewish neighborhoods, such as Ramat Rachel, and to its east, clearly visible yet largely unapproachable, was the Old City, mostly Arab save for a small contingent of Jews holed up in the ancient Jewish Quarter.

It was into this patchwork that Marlin and Betty arrived on the first day of September 1947. Because they came from a country where state lines carried little significance and interneighborhood rivalries consisted mainly of good-hearted banter, the reality of passage permits and forbidden areas was hard for the two to swallow. Even harder to swallow was the local cuisine; in a letter the two sent to their relatives in the United States shortly after arriving in Jerusalem, they complained not so much about belligerent Arabs or boisterous bureaucracts as about Palestine's food. "We also had to avoid drinking water," the two confessed, "since newcomers suffer with *shilshul* (a mean case of diarrhea). We were advised not to eat too much fruit, sweets, or raw vegetables. In spite of all the care you take you are bound to experience a case of *shilshul* anyway. Besides, you don't really know Palestine unless you do have it. But, believe us, when it finally does get you, your idealism flies out of the window and you think of the good old United States. At this point, however, you can't get to the U.S. since it isn't safe to walk more than five steps out of your bed without having an accident. By the time you are well again—a day or two—you don't want to leave."

Yet, despite the cheery tone of the letter, walking around the city with sore feet and stricken bowels, Marlin was overcome by a gray mist of silent disappointment. Without admitting it, he was devastated by the discrepancy between his expectations of Jerusalem and the reality of the city itself. He had come with images in mind, visions of the eternal capital of the Jewish people, a regal city with stone buildings like citadels, and instead he had found narrow, soot-covered streets and aging houses. He imagined sun-kissed men and exotic women, and instead found a city nearly rotted with dirt and mold and grime, littered with pushcarts and beggars, with merchants hawking feeble-looking goods and children selling newspapers, with none of the variety of commerce and entertainment that even the most remote of American towns could effortlessly offer. This, Marlin thought while feigning enthusiasm for the city's sights and smells, this was the fabled capital? Yet he remained silent, determined to learn to love the city he had traveled thousands of miles to inhabit.

Slowly, neighborhood by neighborhood and street by street, Marlin and Betty found themselves starting to fall in love with Jerusalem. It began with Ben Yehuda Street, where they visited the Jewish Agency building to collect their letter of reference. The hilly street was the city's spine, both literally and metaphorically; it ran through the almost exact geographical center of Jewish Jerusalem, and it was the first, and only, place where one could go to find anything from coiffeurs to coffee shops. Yet, despite its central location and cardinal position in the life of Jerusalem, the street was cloaked with a humble air of provinciality. An accidental tourist stumbling onto Ben Yehuda Street would never have guessed it to be the Champs-Elysées of Palestine, as there were no flashy storefronts or flashing neon signs, hardly any advertising, and nothing but a desultory traffic of customers shopping out of necessity rather than desire. The most modern of stores went as far as displaying marble facades or slanted windows, yet those were few and far between. For the most part, customers avoided window-shopping, considered to be in poor taste, discreetly sliding into stores and emerging moments later with inconspicuous packages, plainly wrapped, tucked underneath their arms.

Accustomed to the dazzling department stores of Manhattan, Marlin came to find Jerusalem's attitude toward commerce utterly refreshing. Not much of a socialist, he nevertheless appreciated the utilitarian modesty of the city and its people. This, he thought, was the perfect answer to all that had pained him back home; no one in Jerusalem seemed to be obsessed with disposable income or property values or career advancement, concentrating instead on the imminence of Jewish independence. Marlin also admired the fact that the city, walled off for centuries, vigorously adopted progress and was constantly in the process of being built anew. In an article he wrote shortly after his arrival, he quoted a fellow American tourist who said, "Throw a brick at someone here, and they pick it up to start a building." More than anything, however, Marlin and Betty were struck by the direct nature of the population. Although Jerusalem's residents hailed from a multitude of national origins, once underneath the Mediterranean sun they all seemed to shed their customs, refer to complete strangers with the empathy reserved for kin, and feel free to meddle in affairs not their own. Sitting in outdoor cafés, men in unbuttoned short-sleeved shirts would shout out greetings at passersby, and women in unsophisticated dresses would quip and laugh, seemingly unconcerned with the ladylike decorum, demanded at the time, of women throughout most of the rest of the world. In a city where strangers were virtually nonexistent, Marlin and Betty began feeling at home.

The next step, naturally, was to search for an apartment and jobs. Concerned, the two began asking around; for the first time, Betty put her Hebrew to use not to teach biblical stories but to determine availability and negotiate rent. Fairly quickly the Levins found an affordable and accommodating place; they rented an apartment in a three-story house in Talbieh owned by an Arab doctor named Jamal, a well-known figure in the local Christian community, a slim and handsome man of fine manners and winsome conversation. A middle-aged German-Jewish immigrant, Mrs. Rothstein, lived alone on the top floor. The Levins shared an apartment on the ground floor with Rhoda and Jack Cohen, their fellow voyagers on the *Marine Carp,* creating, in effect, a microscopic urban kibbutz, limited to one apartment and four members. The two couples shopped together and ate together, shared stories and advice and morsels of gossip about mutual friends, each couple drawing on the other for comfort, company, support. On the second floor lived a couple of Jewish immigrants from Yugoslavia, who were renowned locally for being the proprietors of Chic Parisienne, one of Jerusalem's only establishments for European-style haute couture. In the small courtyard of the building there was a well, which served all of the building's residents, and a towering stone wall, covered with shrubbery, which protected the house from the gaze of neighbors and onlookers. Although the apartment was sparsely furnished (and the high ceilings, tiled floor, and arched windows made the dearth of furniture even more noticeable) and often poorly heated, and though they had to use *mazut,* a substance made of cow dung, to heat water, the newlyweds nonetheless adored their first real home as husband and wife.

The second task, that of finding gainful employment, proved just as uncomplicated for the two. On their first Saturday night in Jerusalem, the two took a walk downtown to see what the center of the city looked like. On Jaffa Road, Betty bumped into a young man she knew from the Jewish Theological Seminary in New York, who told her he was working for the *Palestine Post,* the country's only English-language newspaper. The man asked Marlin what he did, and when Marlin replied that he was a journalist, the man, without saying a word, grabbed him by the arm and pulled him straight up to the *Post*'s Hasolel Street offices.

Run by the famed Gershon Agron, the *Post* was part paper of record and part media organ of the Jewish establishment in Palestine, often used to convey official Jewish positions to the English-speaking international readership, especially in Great Britain and the United States. Agron had achieved legendary status almost instantaneously; a short, stout, and meticulously dressed man, he possessed the poise and polite parlance of the seasoned diplomat, which made him a welcome guest in the highest echelons of both British and Jewish leadership. He was very much of Jerusalem, a terrific achievement for a man born in the Ukraine who immigrated with his family to the United States at an early age. In 1920 he moved to Palestine to volunteer in the British army's Jewish Legion. When he was released, he served as the spokesman for the Jewish community in Palestine and, in 1924, became a journalist, reporting for such papers as the *Times* of London and the *Manchester Guardian.* Troubled by the scattered and skewed reporting of the conditions in Palestine, on December 1, 1932, Agron established the *Post*. Already well connected to the senior cadre of Jewish luminaries, Agron deftly combined his career as the paper's editor in chief with another, diplomatic one, and was in the late 1930s sent on behalf of the Jewish Agency to a League of Nations convention in San Francisco. There were also hushed rumors that Agron was somehow connected to the Haganah, though in what capacity few were sure.

Those who worked under Agron at the *Post* remember it as a journalistic oasis. Unlike most of Palestine's newspapers at the time, fiercely partisan organs of their respective parties, the *Post* adopted a Western, and particularly American, modus operandi. While it occasionally allowed a whiff of sentimentality or a touch of patriotism, it adhered to strict ethics, shunning the common practices in the Jewish press of the day of hyperventilating hyperbole, slanderous stories, and overwrought emotionality. In his personal behavior, Agron did his best to emulate what he imagined to be the quintessential editor, crusty and cynical but also, when the occasion merited, kind and encouraging to his staff. For the excitable and enthusiastic young reporters who flocked to him, most of whom, like Marlin, were recent immigrants with some experience and unlimited rations of goodwill, Agron was just the father figure they needed in both their personal and professional lives. Around Agron's cluttered desk congregated talented youth from around the world; there were Mordechai Chertoff and Mike Eskolsky from Pennsylvania, Leah Ben Dor from London, and Eugen Mayer from Berlin. Agron, whose own life had taken him from Europe to America to Jerusalem, knew just enough to appeal to each reporter's cultural background, addressing him or her on familiar terms, then somehow pulling them all together into one bundle of Jewish nationality focused on the struggle for Jewish independence.

As he entered the *Post* for the first time, the twenty-six-year-old Marlin knew little of what to expect. He began by presenting his credentials to a sour-looking Agron, who was busy reading galleys and smoking a cigarette using a long cigarette holder. Marlin never finished his sentence; breathless and impatient, Agron muttered at him, "Get into the newsroom and start working." Marlin asked his new boss for a short deferment so that he and Betty could travel and see the rest of the country. Agron agreed to three weeks. "As soon as you come back to Jerusalem," he told Marlin, "come in and start working."

Armed with a backpack, a typewriter, and the Jewish Agency's letter, the two boarded a bus headed north, aching to see Tiberias, swim in Lake Kinneret, and visit a kibbutz. If Jerusalem initially failed to live up to Marlin's expectations, he and Betty found the rest of the country perfectly in accordance with their preconceived romantic notions. Up north they saw vast fields where bare-chested young men pulled plows, and others rode horses in the heat. They saw wizened Arab men in white robes leading donkeys across dusty markets. They saw a wild and fertile land, sparsely inhabited by pioneering people who got up before dawn and worked hard and blended into each other and into the scenery. Marlin was especially taken by the several kibbutzim he and Betty visited; if in Jerusalem people seemed socially inclined toward a certain degree of mutual effort and communal sense of responsibility, the men and women in the kibbutzim were single-mindedly devoted to collectivism, assessing members almost solely according to their inclination for self-sacrifice. Marlin was struck by the joint living quarters, the absence of private property, the egalitarianism carried to the extreme. For all his admiration, however, Marlin could not relinquish the inquisitive and doubting nature of the journalist; self-sacrifice, he observed, was a blessed virtue, yet running rampant it was as perilous and undesired as its opposite. Visiting Sdeh Eliyahu, for example, a small religious kibbutz on the southern skirts of Lake Kinneret, Marlin noted the poor condition of the kibbutz's communal toilets, shallow holes dug in the ground with thin sheets of tin providing minimal privacy; no seat, no flushing mechanism, no sink or any other staple of comfort or hygiene was to be found. Marlin approached one of the kibbutz's members and asked why the dismal condition was allowed to persist. Don't you, he asked, *need* better toilets? Passionately, the kibbutznik recited the oft-practiced and somewhat dogmatic answer: Sure, he said, we need many things. What of it? If we have to stand in line, or crouch when we use the toilets, is that so terrible? How can we consciously tolerate spending money on our personal needs when there is so much left to do around the kibbutz? We have gone by for long enough without decent restrooms, and we can go on without them for a while longer.

Subdued at first by the man's fervor and humbled by his dedication, Marlin became less convinced the more he thought about the issue. In an article published in Sdeh Eliyahu's newsletter shortly after his visit there, Marlin expressed his concerns over the kibbutzniks' blind devotion to the greater good. "The workers of Israel," he wrote, "like workers everywhere in the free world, aspire towards similar ends: shorter workdays, more production of excellent products and a higher standard of living. I imagine that if a higher standard of living is a common goal all over the country, it should be one for kibbutzniks as well. The kibbutznik works more hours, manufactures more, and enjoys his handiwork less than any other worker in the country. It is time for him to feel that by paying more attention to his own, personal standard of living and by expending every effort to raise that standard, the worker serves not only himself but also his kibbutz, elevating the status of Israel in a world that isn't too friendly."

Although Marlin's criticism would prove prescient in the long term, as the kibbutz movement would eventually collapse under the burden of various social and economic factors, it was not well received at the time of its publication. There was no animosity, no blunt exchanges or outright denouncements, but to the members of Sdeh Eliyahu, Marlin was simply not entitled to his opinions. After all, he was a Jew from New York, from the dying Diaspora, gentle and spoiled and hopelessly bourgeois, while they were closer to the biblical Israelites, men and women who worked the land and lived by the sword and shared their fortunes with their brethren. One kibbutz member, who was in Sdeh Eliyahu at the time of Marlin and Betty's visit, remembers having a conversation with a friend shortly after reading Marlin's essay, incensed that someone—an American, nonetheless—dared to call into question the absolute merit of the communal ideal. For him, the man recalled, as for many of his comrades, the lines were clearly drawn: the kibbutzniks, mainly Jews of eastern European descent, were the true *halutzim*, or pioneers, stopping at nothing to guarantee both the establishment of a Jewish homeland in Palestine and the socially just nature of that homeland; the others, the Westerners—Americans, Germans, French—were insufficiently devoted, uncommitted, and egocentric. It mattered little to the kibbutzniks that just as they had done, Marlin, too, had left his homeland behind and chosen to move to Palestine. To them, he was still a Diaspora Jew.

Yet while actually in the kibbutzim, Marlin and Betty were too dazzled for their critical faculties to have any real effect on their initial impressions. In Sdeh Eliyahu, for example, Betty worked in the laundry room, while Marlin got up at 5:00 a.m. to work in the fish ponds. There, he and the other kibbutzniks would line up in the shallow water, stretch a large net across the pond, and drag the bottom of the net backward across the pond to collect the fish. While the kibbutzniks would select the carp and throw away the scavenger fish, Marlin could not bear to see the fish gasping and threw them all back.

Marlin and Betty continued their tour of the country, moving from kibbutz to kibbutz and from town to town, looking at each new person they met with envious admiration. It was hard, several days after arriving in Palestine, not to succumb to the misguided notion that each person they had met was a true and towering exemplar of Zionism at its best. Their spirits rekindled, they returned to Jerusalem determined to begin their own saga of settlement in the Holy Land.

For a brief moment life seemed to Marlin and Betty not much

different than it would have been if the two had stayed stateside. Marlin took the bus every morning to the *Post*'s office, Betty found a job teaching English at a Hadassah-run high school, and the two were looking forward to pursuing some studies at the Hebrew University, the official reason for which they had been granted a visa to Palestine. Despite the vast differences between Jerusalem and Manhattan, their life together had a universal quality shared by so many young couples the world over: humble dwellings, entry-level jobs, that constantly optimistic outlook on life when everything is new, exciting, challenging. The couple made a few friends, learned to appreciate the city, and succumbed, as people everywhere do, to the syncopated rhythm of scheduled routine.

Several months after they settled down in Jerusalem, Marlin wrote an exclusive series of reports titled "Brooklynites in Israel," published by the borough's now-legendary chronicle, the *Brooklyn Eagle.* One story was titled "Life for a Young Housewife Isn't Fancy, but It's Pleasant," and featured a photograph of the slender, shapely legged Betty in a simple checkered skirt, picking oranges from a large crate. Marlin's reportorial strategy was to allow the readers a glimpse into Betty's life by giving them an hour-by-hour account of her daily routine.

"When she's finished at 3:30," he wrote, "she heads for home. But on the way, Betty stops at Yonathan's, the greens grocer (vegetable store), takes her market bag made from colored cord out of her brown plastic handbag and fills it with rations. Into the bag go four pounds of Dutch potatoes, two pounds of Turkish onions, and four pounds of homegrown navel oranges. Betty's bill comes to 240 mils, or 72 cents." Published side by side with articles such as "Mutilated Body of Woman Found in Refrigerator" and a report concerning Soviet misbehavior titled "And Now Reds Blame Us if Kids Smoke," the quaint account of Betty's life continued, describing her wardrobe. "In winter," it read, "she wears skirts and sweaters mainly, and low heeled sports shoes. She has two pairs of high heeled shoes, but she has seldom worn them, because of the hard walking on the rough city streets. As in the States, Betty has had the problem of what to do with her knee-length dresses. For those that she couldn't lengthen she has sewed on borders. In summer she wears solid color cottons, since prints are seldom worn in Jerusalem."

Despite the relatively blissful existence the two had found in their new home, events had been set in motion on an international scale that were destined to have a direct and devastating effect on the lives of all Jews in Palestine, Marlin and Betty included. After years of an ongoing war of attrition waged by Jewish paramilitary movements in Palestine, facing the political pressures applied globally by Zionists calling for a Jewish homeland, and plagued by the implosion of colonialism and the descent of the once mighty empire, Great Britain acknowledged the need to end its mandate in Palestine. In April 1947 Great Britain announced that it intended to terminate the mandate over Palestine that it had received from the League of Nations in 1920, and left the permanent geopolitical solution in the country to the United Nations. An exploratory committee was formed, the United Nations Special Committee on Palestine (UNSCOP), which submitted its report in August 1947. Almost unanimously, the committee supported a solution dubbed the partition plan, which would, in effect, create two states within territorial Palestine, one Jewish and the other Arab, connected by commerce, sharing the internationalized city of Jerusalem. Despite the heavy price of abandoning the hope of establishing a capital in Judaism's holiest city, the Jewish leadership in Palestine supported the plan, considering it an excellent basis from which to negotiate further developments and changes in the status quo. On the other hand, the Arab Higher Committee, the umbrella organization governing a multitude of Arab political parties in Trans-Jordan, refused any solution save for an outright Arab state throughout Palestine.

The members of UNSCOP deliberated throughout the summer, visiting Palestine as well as displaced persons' camps across Europe, summoning a host of leaders, experts, and academics in the futile hope of conjuring a magical formula that would please all. Tackling every issue from the economy to future borders to constitutional guarantees for safekeeping the peace, the committee convened in New York on August 27, 1947, to write the final draft of its report. During the meeting, seven of UNSCOP's eleven member states—Canada, Czechoslovakia, Guatemala, the Netherlands, Peru, Sweden, and Uruguay—endorsed the partition plan, officially titled "The Plan of Partition with Economic Union." Its report read:

> The basic premise underlying the partition proposal is that the claims to Palestine of the Arabs and Jews, both possessing validity, are irreconcilable, and that among all of the solutions advanced, partition will provide the most realistic and practicable settlement, and is the most likely to afford a workable basis for meeting in part the claims and national aspirations of both parties. It is a fact that both of these people have their historic roots in Palestine, and that both make vital contributions to the economic and cultural life of the country. The partition solution takes these considerations fully into account. The basic conflict in Palestine is a clash of two intense nationalisms. Regardless of the historical origins of the conflict, the rights and wrongs of the promises and counter-promises, and the international intervention incident to the Mandate, there are now in Palestine some 650,000 Jews and some 1,200,000 Arabs who are dissimilar in their ways of living and, for the time being, separated by political interests which render difficult full and effective political co-operation among them, whether voluntary or induced by constitutional arrangements. Only by means of partition can these conflicting national aspirations find substantial numerical or political parity between the two population groups.

The report, issued on the very day Marlin and Betty arrived in the port of Haifa, was the first shot in a prolonged battle. In September the UN General Assembly was presented with UNSCOP's recommendations, devoting much of its deliberations to the problem of Palestine. Thus began three shattering months of grandiloquent speeches and petty politics and frantic attempts to persuade different parties of the merits of this position or the other. As the assembly's term waned, the stakes for both warring factions became higher and higher, as the decision was now left up to a handful of disinterested nations. Finally, a vote was scheduled for November 29.

On a dreary day in Flushing Meadows, Queens, residence of the General Assembly's temporary headquarters, cameramen, newspapermen, and radio journalists with oversize microphones all crowded into the building's lobby to cover the momentous decision. With the UN still in its infancy, the decision had the potential to turn the organization into the global peacemaker it aspired to be. Inside the building, delegates and visitors packed the room to capacity. On the podium, three stern-looking men patiently listened to speaker after speaker: Secretary-General Trygve Lie, Assistant Secretary-General Andrew Cordier, and Oswaldo Aranha, president of the General Assembly. A few speeches were scheduled for the day, the last in a three-day-long series of marathon sessions and filibusters and eleventh-hour changes of heart, followed by the actual vote. When the last of the speakers returned to his place, Aranha quietly announced that he intended to call for votes in alphabetical order; Cordier was to repeat each vote out loud. In his nasal drone, Cordier dispassionately read the votes as if they were a transnational grocery list. "Argentina?" he recited, monotonously and mechanically. "Absent. Afghanistan? No. Australia? Yes."

At the time of the vote, the citizens of Jerusalem huddled around the city's few transistor radios, following in silent anticipation the vote which could deliver their independence. Passersby lingered by open windows to listen for a while; friends got together, preparing special meals in anticipation of a resoundingly affirmative resolution; crowds formed spontaneously in public places, eager to share the moment, for better or worse, with others. Marlin, Betty, and a large group of their acquaintances spent the night in the Meir Shfeya Youth Village in Zichron Ya'akov, just south of Haifa, an academic institution and boarding home for young immigrants known for its resplendent beauty and careful landscaping. Tired from the day's traveling, exhausted by the supreme tension of the pending vote, and overcome by a general sense of malaise, Marlin went to sleep.

In the meantime, in Flushing Meadows, the voting continued. Belgium, Bolivia, and Byelorussia voted in favor. Others voted against. When the turn came for France to vote, the French representative said, in a loud and clear voice, *"Oui,"* sending the audience into a frenzy of applause: the vote had already covered more than half the countries present, and the two-third vote necessary for the partition plan to pass was already guaranteed. Aranha suppressed the outburst, and the vote resumed, with Jews in Palestine and the world over still incredulous. When Yugoslavia, the last country to vote, responded with an abstention, Cordier dully summed up the results of the vote over the future of Resolution 181 concerning the partition plan in Palestine. "Thirty-three in favor," he said, "thirteen against, ten abstentions, one absent. The resolution is adopted."

In the UN's lobby, members of the Jewish delegation were hugging and crying, shouting and whispering, unable to recover from the grandeur of the occasion. In Jerusalem, throngs of Jews poured into the streets, dancing the hora and celebrating. Outside of the Jewish Agency building in Rehavia, hundreds gathered to listen to the recitation of the vote, bursting into song and cheers. Golda Meir, then a senior Jewish Agency official and herself an American emigrant, went out to the building's balcony and with a voice stifled by tears managed to say "Mazal tov," good luck. Miles away, alone in his office in Tel Aviv, David Ben-Gurion, leader of the Jewish community in Palestine, sat at his desk, his head buried in his hands. Elated as he was about the major victory of the day, the most important part of the night for Ben-Gurion was not Cordier's counting of the tally but the short and ominous speech delivered by the Arab representative, Azzam Pasha. "The partition line," Pasha said, "shall be nothing but a line of fire and blood." Ben-Gurion realized full well that the vote was not an end but a beginning, the point of departure for a long and gruesome war. He understood that the Arabs would not wait long before trying to reverse the resolution by means of force. He imagined that even at that moment, as people throughout Palestine were celebrating, waves of murderous rage were being unleashed on Jerusalem's Jews.

In Zichron Ya'akov, Marlin Levin was sound asleep. The next morning, he woke to a different reality.

CHAPTER THREE

The Jerusalem Marlin and Betty returned to a day after the United Nations vote, which, in effect, birthed the long-awaited Jewish state, was not the one they had left behind. Prior to November 29—or Kaf Tet Be'November, as the date was referred to by most of the people in Jerusalem at the time, using the Hebrew numeration in an effort to mark the event as not another date on the Gregorian calendar but as something unique, something exclusionary, something entirely Jewish—Jerusalem was a city divided by politics and geography but kept from falling apart by the might of the mandate. It was a geopolitical centrifuge, kept in check by the calm, organized administration of the British authorities. Granted, the British had their weaknesses; they were often accused by Jewish Jerusalemites of favoring the Arab cause, of being numbed by colonial insensitivity. Yet they were there, and that was their major achievement; they were there, keeping the Jews and the Arabs largely at bay. True, they often looked the other way when a sporadic ambush claimed the lives of some or an errant bomb the lives of others, but they always took measures to prevent the imminent explosion of outright war. When they left, as Ben-Gurion realized early and most Jews a short while later, an immense struggle would begin. The Arab Higher Committee had made it abundantly clear that it intended to orchestrate a crescendo of blood and fire to reverse the inclusiveness of the UN resolution. Jewish Jerusalemites needed only to look through their windows to realize that with the outbreak of war, they would be completely isolated, engulfed as they were by Arab villages. After the euphoria of triumph wafted away, smiles slowly became uneasy, and jubilant voices twisted with fear. Marlin and Betty returned to a different Jerusalem, a city preparing for battle, uncertain of what to expect.

Marlin, however, did not have to wait too long to experience the unraveling of peace and order. On his very first day of employment at the *Post,* after the paper went to print, he and his colleague, city editor Mike Eskolsky, went out for some coffee and conversation at one of Ben Yehuda Street's small, cavelike cafés. The two strolled leisurely down the broad and nearly empty street, largely undisturbed by traffic because cars were still uncommon in Jerusalem at the time, enjoying the cool breeze that traveled from the surrounding mountains above. Finally they reached the café, one of many similar institutions that crowded the street, and went in. To the uninitiated, the place could have been described as quaint, romantic, or cozy; but for those, like Marlin, with the reporter's omnivoyant eye, with a knack for subtext and with sufficient understanding of the conditions in Palestine, the seemingly mundane interactions taking place at the small tables covered with red-and-white oilcloths were infused with a whole new meaning. Like actors at a Kabuki theater, the café's patrons and employees all communicated with each other through exaggerated gestures that often carried entirely different messages than those conveyed on the surface level. On any given day one could see, for example, British officers sharing a bottle of locally produced liquor, talking loudly, jovially, eager to appear carefree and confident and controlling, transcendent to the turmoil around them, knights of the empire. Yet, their every movement signaled the contrary; between loud laugh and risqué joke, their eyes would dart to the café's darker corners or to its marbled storefront, searching for assassins. Their hands would caress their short, heavy shot glasses, tipping them restlessly from side to side, as if half expecting, at a moment's notice, to drop the glasses and grab their guns. And their good humor could easily be undone by an undesirable patron entering the café, such as an informant, a known underground leader, or an agitator; more often than not, they would smile at the man, nod their heads or touch the tip of their hats, yet their conversation would go limp and lifeless, their energy now devoted to observing the doings of their unwelcome acquaintance.

Sporadically surrounding the British officers were young Jewish women. Fashionably dressed and impeccably groomed, they would spend their days not at work or at home but at the cafés along Ben Yehuda Street. For some, they were a despicable kind, no better than whores, offering themselves to the British men in hope of being whisked away from the hardships and uncertainties of Palestine and into a life of affluent comfort in Great Britain. Others were more forgiving, understanding that a great many of the coquettish young women prancing about were clandestine spies enlisted by the Haganah, the central Jewish underground movement. Attractive young women, the Haganah realized early on, made for quintessential gatherers of human intelligence. Lonely British soldiers, sitting in cafés and feeling sentimental, would be flattered by the unfailing and ravenous attention suddenly bestowed upon them by these Hebrew Mata Haris and slowly open up to them; inebriated by drink and perfume and the promise of romance, they would talk, divulging schedules and agendas and manpower counts, details that the young women were trained to respond to with utter indifference while concomitantly committing to memory.

Also in the cafés would be the plotters and planners, using the innocuous cover of public places to concoct illicit schemes. For the cognoscenti, these types were the easiest to spot. First, they had a sullen look about them, as if they were horrified that someone would mistake them for mere flaneurs, idly sipping coffee at midday, when, in fact, they were brave young revolutionaries. Second, they would never order much, usually just a single cup of coffee or a small appetizer, unlike the celebratory opulence of the British soldiers. Finally, they spoke in code, usually exchanging bits of surreal dialogue so incomprehensible that it could only be code for some coming clandestine action. A woman who lived in Jerusalem at the time and served as one of the Haganah's seductresses remembers observing two such plotters in an outdoor café one day. Even from the distance of decades, the woman can still quote their conversation verbatim. One, she recalled, told his friend that the ravens were approaching, and that the pigeons were likely to be upset by that turn of events. Therefore, he solemnly concluded, all the chocolate bars and cotton candy should be removed from the kiosks, or else they'd be seized by the birds.

Overseeing this unruly cast of characters were the waiters, often large, dramatis personae themselves; they were usually older, always men, and on occasion well-educated and well-groomed immigrants who had fled the horrors of central and eastern Europe to find refuge in Palestine, trading in social status for safety. Therefore, they were the perfect conductors for Jerusalem's cloak-and-dagger foibles, capable of observant participation. They would, for example, wordlessly warn a certain gentleman who was wanted for questioning by the British authorities that a group of plainclothes officers was taking the table adjacent to his, giving him just enough time to pay the check and disappear without attracting attention. They would serve as go-betweens, passing notes and messages and packages back and forth between parties that preferred to remain discreet. They would also often serve as a Greek chorus of sorts, providing a newcomer to the scene with an exposition, yet careful not to betray the secrets entrusted to them by their clients.

Although Marlin frequented the cafés while off duty from the *Post,* his reportorial radar was never as alert as when sipping coffee and eating a slice of pie on the sidewalks along Ben Yehuda

Street. That day, his first as a journalist in Jerusalem, Marlin and Mike Eskolsky were sitting down and looking around, slowly unveiling countless little dramas. When the time came to go home, the two got up, paid the check, and began crossing the street. Suddenly, a series of explosions, and the whining ***whoosh*** of bullets flying a little too close. From its pace, a feverish barrage of rattling dins occurring in short intervals, Marlin could tell the fire was coming from a machine gun. It was not too difficult to guess the source: the British had posts in nearby Zion Square, right beneath the Generali Insurance building; they would be the only ones in several blocks' radius to have access to such heavy weaponry. The Generali building was, and still is, a major monument in Jerusalem. Built by Italian Fascists after the Ethiopian war, the building's facade sported a gargantuan stone lion, lean and regal and awe inspiring, meant to commemorate Mussolini's African conquests. The building also overlooked Zion Square, a major site of pedestrian traffic at the bottom of the Ben Yehuda Street mall, and was therefore chosen by the British as the location from which to supervise the bustling commercial zone that lay below. Not taking any chances, the British erected two posts in the area: one on the Generali building and one in Zion Square. It was from the direction of the latter that bullets were now flying.

Upon hearing the sound of the machine gun, Marlin and his colleague threw themselves on the ground. They paused for a minute, assessing the situation, agitated by the sounds of shouting and shooting and sirens, keeping their heads down. Then they scurried on all fours to the doorway of a nearby building, where they were sheltered and safe. Several more minutes passed, and the all-clear siren, the sweetest song for Jerusalemites at the time, was sounded. Standing up and shaking the dust off their suits, the two, journalists at heart, began questioning everyone in sight. It took them a little while to figure out what had happened: apparently, an elderly Armenian cab driver was approaching Ben Yehuda Street from Zion Square, taking a wide turn in his little car. A British soldier on top of the Generali building, agitated either by the angle at which the man turned or by the speed at which he drove, alerted his colleagues down in the street, and they in turn called on the driver to stop for inspection. The call, however, was never heard, stifled by the cab's shut windows, protecting the old driver from the bitter Jerusalem winter.

Interpreting the man's failure to comply with their orders to stop as a sign of clear and imminent danger, the policemen in the street did not hesitate before pulling out the Sten submachine guns slung across their shoulders and shooting. Recalling the account, Marlin remembered that the British bullets "made a sieve out of the taxi, killing its driver and sending showers of bullets over our heads. At that moment, the news editor and I happened to be crossing the street. Luck was with us." Still, one could not escape the thought that luck's grace is unlikely to be bestowed on the same person twice. The next time, Marlin knew, might not be so fortunate for him. Having scheduled their departure from Palestine for the late spring of 1948, the British were getting increasingly nervous, wishing, at all costs, to prevent the country from deteriorating into bloodshed before the last of the British soldiers had left Palestine. Under those circumstances, fingers leaped to the trigger too quickly, and paranoia often prevailed. As Marlin could tell by looking at the perforated corpse of the Armenian cabbie, it was enough for one old man to be in the wrong place at the wrong time.

Marlin was, of course, no stranger to blood and bullets. He had seen men die before, during the war. But these men were soldiers, virile and uniformed, fighting one another on true battlefields, prepared to accept the consequences. The Armenian, on the other hand, was wrinkled and plainly dressed, unsuspecting and unprepared, dying in Zion Square, the city's epicenter of dining, commerce, and entertainment. It was unforeshadowed, his death, a supremely dramatic event occurring at the least likely of places, making it, for a split second, unbelievable: Did this really happen, Marlin asked himself, did a man just lose his life right here, on Ben Yehuda Street, for failing to stop his car? The shell casings, however, and the smell of charred flesh and burned fuel and gunpowder, were all the proof one needed to know that the man's death was painfully real.

A few weeks later, Marlin, Betty, and some of their expatriate friends celebrated New Year's Eve in a friend's apartment, one of few such celebrations carried out mainly by American-Jewish immigrants and British soldiers in a city that marked its New Year's Eve in September, according to the Jewish calendar. Over a small supply of canned goods sent from home—grapefruit halves in heavy syrup were the pièce de résistance of the evening—the small group of friends, no more than eight or ten young men and women, talked and laughed and sang "Auld Lang Syne." Yet, in between the genial chatter were silences pregnant with wary anticipation. New Year's Eve marked the beginning of 1948, the year in which the Jewish state would finally be born. It was also certain to mark the beginning of the war for the state's survival, a war in which some of them were likely to perish. It was to be a year of momentous occasions and great trials. Everyone in the room had expected it; that was the reason they had come to Palestine, to witness and participate in the process of creating the nation. Still, the uncertainty was sometimes incapacitating. That night, no New Year's resolutions were made; all present figured out that they had better just take 1948 one day at a time.

The Arab leadership in Jerusalem, on the other hand, had made a plethora of resolutions. Under the leadership of Mufti Haj Amin el-Husseini, the city's Muslim spiritual leader, Palestine's Arabs prepared for the end of the mandate, adhering to a rather restrained military strategy and determined not to escalate the conflict prior to the British forces' departure and the official declaration of the Jewish state. Then, went the logic, the Arab forces in Palestine would summon the help of all surrounding Arab countries and, in one sheer and decisive blow, annihilate the nascent state. Therefore, Arab fighters, mostly villagers from the greater Jerusalem area, engaged in local, targeted activities, such as small-scale bombings and sporadic ambushes.

The date set for the final departure of British forces from Palestine was May 14, 1948. With several months to undo a tangled web of governance that had taken almost a decade to weave, the British authorities had no choice but to watch vestige after vestige of order collapse. The first casualty was the mail; previously run by British clerks proud of the immense responsibility entrusted to them, the few post offices scattered around town were now run by Arabs appointed by the British in the hope of establishing an instantaneous bureaucratic tradition by providing locals with titles and uniforms. More often than not, however, the Arab postmasters were vengeful, abusing their authority to curtail the influx of mail to Jewish Jerusalem and Jewish communities across Palestine. At first they would merely create pedestrian difficulties, sending, for example, a package to a remote post office so that its recipient would have no choice but to travel across inhospitable parts of town in order to retrieve it. Soon thereafter, however, the mail was mostly robbed or destroyed; the only safe method for Jewish Jerusalemites to transport letters to loved ones across the country and around the world was by personally delivering them to emissaries who were traveling out of the city. In many such letters an almost uniform disclaimer appeared, begging those to whom the letter was addressed to respond, yet warning them not to send money or valuables, as that would almost guarantee the untimely demise of the package.

The sight of British soldiers relinquishing control, whether over the postal service or over the policing of the city, carried with it great cathartic value. Yet, nobody was elated; the effects of the British departure became graver with each day that passed. Arab attacks grew more frequent and more devastating, as did Jewish retaliations, which, in turn, would invite further destruction. Although the Arabs were far more proactive, the Jewish underground movements executed the occasional raid as well. In January of 1948, for example, the Haganah blew up the Arab Hotel Semiramis in the Katamon neighborhood, and the more extreme, right-leaning Irgun planted bombs in both the Jaffa Gate and the Damascus Gate in the Old City. The Jewish combatants often dressed up as British officers or Arab merchants to ensure an easier approach to and escape from their chosen target. Adopting this tactic, Arab combatants began dressing up as British officers or as Jews. General disarray spread over the city.

Gradually, the Arabs began focusing most of their efforts on curtailing Jewish access to Jerusalem. This was no difficult task: at the time, the city had but one major road leading into it, a road enveloped by the looming, wooded Judean Mountains, all controlled by Arabs. All that needed to be done, then, was to open fire on each and every convoy approaching the city. The Haganah learned of this new tactic with dismay, and responded by diverting a major portion of its already dwindling human resources toward serving as security officers on the increasingly perilous rides to and from Jerusalem. One point in particular was favored by Arab snipers, a narrow spot leading into a curvy ascent that marked the last leg of the journey into the city; known as Bab el Wad, Arabic for the Door of the Valley, the short stretch of road gradually turned into a cemetery for men and machines alike, littered with the carcasses of burned armored vehicles destroyed while trying to reach Jerusalem with manpower, supplies, or communications. Supplies in the city, therefore, started to run low, the stores gradually emptying out. Soon after the supplies went missing, so did the people: of the approximately 120,000 Jews living in Jerusalem in the months prior to the UN declaration in November of 1947, as few as 70,000 were living there in mid-1948; some had been stationed elsewhere as soldiers, but others had fled, fearing an all-out catastrophe. The small community of approximately one hundred American Jews living in the city was particularly hard-hit, with frantic letters from home sending more and more people packing. The Levins, however, stayed.

As 1948 rolled in, el-Husseini grew more and more restless, eager to land several major blows on the Jewish community in Jerusalem and thereby cripple its preparation for the upcoming war. Particularly valuable in this respect was Abdul Kader, a local lieutenant based in the village of Bir Zeit, approximately twelve miles north of Jerusalem. A charismatic man, Kader had an uncanny talent for attracting mercenaries and misfits. In his hilly headquarters gathered deserters from the British army, Yugoslavian Muslims smitten by the idea of pan-Arabic brotherhood, Polish demolition experts, and random Nazi Germans who had deserted Germany in the early 1940s, preferring the disorganized and gritty Arab militias to the highly hierarchical and stifling demands of the Nazi army. Above them all, however, stood one young Palestinian Arab, a thin and wiry man named Fawzi el-Kutub.

Since the late 1920s, the days of the first organized and violent Arab uprising against Palestine's Jewish community, el-Kutub had shown a knack for explosives, preparing devastating devices out of even the most banal of items. Without training, however, it was clear to his commanders that his chances of being anything but a dilettante of destruction were slim. Using his personal relationship with Adolf Hitler, el-Husseini arranged for the young man to travel to Germany in the late 1930s to study demolitions. The relationship between the two of them came about after they met in the thirties and prevailed via letters and other communications until Hitler's death in 1945. At one point Hitler even considered teaming up with the mufti to annihilate the Jewish community in Palestine, but the war efforts prevented this from materializing. At first, el-Kutub was welcomed by the Germans, who were impressed with his inventiveness and dedication to the cause. After completing his studies of explosives, he was therefore granted the highest honor the Nazi military complex could offer, and was invited to join the elite SS commando course. There, in the strictest of disciplinarian environments, el-Kutub's hot-tempered Mediterranean nature proved anathema to his instructors' rigid demands. On several occasions he refused to follow orders; insubordination not being a matter taken lightly by the Nazis, el-Kutub was quickly arrested and sent to a concentration camp.

Realizing that his major strategic asset was behind bars, Abdul Kader asked the mufti himself to intervene. Drawing again on his friendship with Hitler, el-Husseini contacted the fuehrer with an emotional plea to let el-Kutub go. While the road to the concentration camp was never intended to be a two-way street, Hitler was nonetheless persuaded by el-Husseini, who explained that the major reason el-Kutub was urgently needed back in Palestine was to orchestrate the murder of mass quantities of Jews. Discreetly, el-Kutub was let go, traveling from Europe through Africa and eventually, in the late 1940s, arriving back in Jerusalem, where he became the chief engineer of terror, utilizing for his purposes Abdul Kader's renegade band. As 1948 rolled in, el-Kutub was ready to take his attacks to the next level.

Late at night on February 1, 1948, Marlin was at the *Post*'s city room, doing some rewrite work. With a sizable portion of the newspaper's staff having left the city, Marlin was often assigned multiple duties, from rewrites to editorials. That night he was in the midst of a rather mundane assignment: a stream of reports had come in describing the day's violent attacks on Jewish targets, and Marlin was charged with aggregating them all into a coherent and interesting news narrative. A little wary of being struck by a wayward bullet, Marlin left his usual desk by the window that night, choosing instead another desk at the far corner of the newsroom. For several days, the *Post* had been receiving threatening phone calls; that very afternoon, Marlin himself had answered one. No one at the paper, however, took the threats seriously; the *Post,* they were well aware, was hated by the British, the Arabs, and some factions of the Jewish community as well, yet they never suspected that they themselves would be targeted. Sitting at the safer spot, Marlin was mechanically pasting paragraphs together, flinching as he read line after line describing death and chaos. Rewriting the news of one particular attack that occurred near the *Post*'s office, he wrote, "They brought the casualties to the Hadassah clinic on Hasolel Street." As he wrote the last word of that paragraph, the lights in the room suddenly went out.

Then came a whooshing sound, like an evil wind.

He cannot, from the distance of years, remember hearing an

explosion, yet he realized instantly that the building was under attack. There was a tinkling of broken glass, then, for a brief moment, silence.

Then someone screamed.

Bright orange flames began consuming the corridor, making their way toward the newsroom. Marlin got up to leave and then, with the irrepressible newspaperman's instinct, reached back to his desk and grabbed the copy he was working on. With a quick stride he headed out the door, fearing the building would collapse. On his way out, he encountered Margarete Katzke, an elderly proofreader, blood trickling down her forehead, holding her face with one hand while staggering blindly down the corridor groping with the other. Marlin grabbed her hand and led her through the bilious smoke and out of the building.

Others at the *Post* were not so lucky. Hit hardest was the room containing the press; the force of the explosion had sent pieces of the type, bulbous chunks of lead, flying through the room, cutting half of one employee's ear off, blinding two others, wounding and lacerating and killing. Those not hit by the shrapnel of lead or glass were threatened by fire and smoke. As the building burned, *Post* editors, reporters, and typesetters stumbled out, shocked, their clothes shred, coughing and teary-eyed, confused. Outside, the scene was not more comforting; shattered glass was scattered everywhere, wooden beams hung from windows and doorways, and dark soot covered the entire neighborhood with a blanket of blackness.

Marlin was standing outside in silence, watching the flames, when a small army of rescue workers and journalists rushed to the scene. At that moment, however, the two were virtually indistinguishable: John Donovan, NBC's correspondent in Jerusalem, rushed into the building and carried out the last of the wounded survivors, while Fitzhugh Turner of the *New York Herald-Tribune* attempted to climb the stairs as well, focused more on finding survivors than stories. As the fire cut off all access to the building, Turner jumped out to safety from the first-story window. After all the injured were evacuated, the *Post*'s journalists took a moment to mourn another casualty of the attack: the newspaper's archive, containing clippings dating back to its inception in 1932, was lost forever.

Almost instantly, theories regarding the identity of the blast's perpetrators began circulating at high velocity. The first theory, suggested by the *Post*'s assistant editor, Ted Lurie, was that the British were behind the attack. He claimed passionately that he had seen a British army truck barreling up Hasolel Street shortly before the explosion, which was probably caused by a forceful car bomb, possibly emanating from a truck full of explosives parked in front of the *Post*'s building. The theory was quickly adopted by some, especially those adhering to the Irgun's staunch militaristic and anti-British line. Lurie himself, however, would years later play a part in expounding an entirely different theory. After the Six-Day War, he met in Ramallah with Abu Khalil Jahno, one of the attack's planners, who told him that the real target may have been the Zion Cinema at the nearby corner of Ben Yehuda Street and Jaffa Road. The perpetrators, Jahno claimed, arrived at the movie theater too late and, seeing that the audience had already dispersed, decided to attack the *Post* instead. Other theories offered shortly after the attack identified yet other alleged targets. Some claimed that the real target was the Himmelfarb Hotel, across the street from the *Post*'s offices, which was used as temporary housing for Haganah members serving as security officers on the convoys traveling to and from Jerusalem. Marlin, for his part, believed that the blast was intended for the building next door to the *Post* on Hasolel Street, used by the Haganah as a small-scale workshop for making and mending light weaponry. The wide array of theories suggested that all Jewish institutions in Jerusalem, great or small, were now potential targets.

Amid the uncertainty, however, one thing was clear: if the attack was indeed a deliberate attempt to annihilate the *Post,* then the bomb could not have been placed at random, as it was set off just inches directly below the office of the editor in chief, Gershon

Agron. Agron himself had spent the night in Tel Aviv; nothing in his office remained intact. When he returned to the *Post* the next day, he surveyed the ruins with a smile; nothing, he was determined to prove, would stop him from putting out his paper. Making a point, he removed several tiles off his floor, burned ocher and disfigured, and mounted them on his wall as a mural of sorts: atrocity had become art.

In Agron's absence, Ted Lurie was the most senior editor on the scene. Ten or so minutes before the blast he had left the *Post* with his wife, Tzila, for his nightly coffee break at Café Atara, a local institution run by an elderly Austrian-Jewish couple. Just as he was about to sit down at his usual table, he was thrown to the ground by the force of the blast. Dusty and disheveled, he ran to the café's back room and tried frantically to call the *Post* and inform his reporters that a huge blast had occurred and that someone needed to run out immediately and cover the story; not for a moment did he imagine that the *Post* itself was about to become the story. After several futile attempts to get through to the newsroom, Lurie ran back out to Ben Yehuda Street. Seeing the towering flames, he began to run toward his office. He was greeted there by the silent survivors of the blast.

Under such conditions as befell the *Post* that evening, the journalistic task becomes negligible, deferring to more acute matters of life and death. Under any other circumstances, common sense and reason call for precaution, for a time of healing, for calculated measures. That night, however, Lurie thought of nothing of the sort. He thought of Agron and his inspirational speeches, stressing that the *Post* was no mere for-profit newspaper but a mission, "the English-speaking world's only window into Palestine," as he would often repeat. He thought that what they all needed to focus on at that moment was making sure the newspaper was published on schedule.

Calmly, Lurie collected the remaining, unscathed staff members, giving each different editorial assignments. Back at the Café Atara, Ruth and Heinz Gruenspan, the proprietors, were overwhelmed by the influx of reporters crowding the tables, frantically writing their recollections of the blast. Lurie directed his staff to the café, persuading the Gruenspans to keep it open throughout the night. Simultaneously, someone was dispatched to the nearby Lipshitz Press, a small, privately owned operation that agreed immediately to stop whatever materials it was printing and let the *Post* use the presses instead. Darting between the presses and the café's tables, Lurie directed his staff; he wanted, he said, only two pages, focusing entirely on the attack.

Early the next morning, the newspaper was printed. As the small, unprofessional machinery employed by Lipshitz Press could not print the normal amount of copies, Lurie decided to staple a copy of the paper to the front door of the *Post*'s charred offices, defiantly, for all to see. On the front page he ran an article by the paper's top columnist, Roy Elston, who wrote under the pseudonym David Courtney. "Truth," the article read, "is stronger than TNT and burns brighter than the flames of arson." Like some of their counterparts in New York who, years later, in the aftermath of the terrorist attacks of September 11, 2001, saw it as their supreme duty to continue and report even in the face of disaster, the *Post*'s staff did not allow even a direct attack on their newspaper to faze them, and of that they were immensely proud.

After fulfilling his journalistic duties the night of the attack, Marlin was driven home by a colleague. Having run out of the building in his shirtsleeves, he was freezing in the biting Jerusalem winter. He was also still shaking from the shock of what had happened. He knocked hard on the iron door of his apartment, and Betty opened it. She had heard the explosion, but believed it came from the fighting in the nearby Katamon neighborhood. Seeing her quivering husband, she asked Marlin why he was in his shirtsleeves. His jaws rattling, he answered that the *Post* had been bombed. Betty rushed over and hugged her husband; at that moment, the Levins' friend and roommate, Jack Cohen, entered the apartment as well. Having returned from guard duty for the Haganah, he had already heard of the attack. He, too, rushed over to Marlin, hugging him firmly. Marlin told his wife and friend that he needed a shot to help him overcome the shock and get to sleep. Jack Cohen ran out, and returned several minutes later with a doctor. The doctor took a long needle and a vial out of his black bag, and began to read, with great attention, the instructions printed on the back of the vial. Marlin was terrified.

"Jack," he whispered to his friend, "what kind of a doctor did you bring me, a veterinarian?"

"The only one I could find," Jack replied. "He is a gynecologist."

As it turned out, the man, a famous German immigrant named Dr. Oppenheimer, administered the shot successfully, and Marlin soon fell asleep.

Early the next morning, Marlin took the bus back to the *Post*'s office on Hasolel Street. He stopped, as did most Jewish Jerusalemites that day, at the door, taking a moment to proudly observe the paper displayed for all to read. Then he climbed what remained of the stairs to the newsroom. Devastation was abundant. Above, on the ceiling, loose wires hung limply, torn from one another, now dysfunctional. Below, on the floor, the tiles had been baked by the heat and were misshapen and discolored in a lifeless mixture of red and black. Marlin approached his desk, his usual one next to the window, the one he had abandoned for the safety of the remote corner. A sizable piece of shrapnel protruded from the wall at approximately the place where his head would have been had he stayed at his desk when the bomb went off. Marlin's body shuddered. Inspecting the area further, he discovered something even more disturbing: shreds of glass and shrapnel had somehow materialized inside one of the shut drawers of his desk. It was one of the ominous mysteries of terror.

As the day progressed, most of the *Post*'s staffers were, quite naturally, preoccupied with the conditions of their wounded friends. Around noon, reports began to trickle in from the hospitals and clinics: more than fifty *Post* employees and neighbors were wounded in the attack. Four people, including three of the *Post*'s staff members—Haim Farber, Nathan Rabinowitz, and

Moshe Weinberg—and a neighbor, Deborah Daniel, had lost their lives.

These were facts that not even the most determined and devoted of journalists could ignore. Putting out the *Post,* it became clear, would prove increasingly difficult. Even after the presses returned to normal, the blast had incapacitated most of the newspaper's employees, leaving Agron and Lurie with a cadre of four or five reporters and editors, Marlin included. And everyone at the *Post* understood the message implied by the attack: the explosion was but the first act in a long series of violent attacks.

Like most of his colleagues, Marlin could no longer simply assume the guise of the disinterested and objective reporter. The principles of journalism instilled in him, while still strong, were confronted by another, even stronger emotion. He had come to Palestine to participate in the building of the Jewish nation, and for that he had to do more than report its chronicles. True, he wholeheartedly believed in Agron's dictum about the *Post* being a window to the world, and was proud to provide accurate reporting about events often neglected by the major international media organizations. Still, he was a reporter, his weapons the pen and the typewriter. He could never, he realized, be like the Haganah members, younger men, warriors from birth. He could never, with his bad back and new wife, ambush the Arabs or shoot at the British. But he could help in other ways.

By that point, Marlin had already had some contact with the Haganah. Shortly after settling down in Jerusalem, late in 1947, he and Betty were visited by a young man; the Haganah, he told them, had learned of their Hallicrafter radio receiver, and was in dire need of such equipment. The Hallicrafter SX-42, the radio Marlin had bought strictly out of whim and on the basis of its nifty futuristic design, turned out to be one of the only two-way radios in Jerusalem and a most valuable asset to the Haganah, eager for more means of communication between its different cells, which were gradually becoming isolated from one another because of Arab control of major roads. Also, the Hallicrafter had the capacity to monitor shortwave transmissions, which made it especially valuable for anyone wishing to listen in on the local communications of either the British or the Arabs. Word had gotten out—how, Marlin did not know—that he was in possession of the Hallicrafter, and the radio was now being asked to join the Jewish underground. Marlin gladly volunteered the device, suspecting that it was his Arab landlord, Dr. Jamal, a man with deep ties to the Haganah's leadership, who informed the Jewish underground movement of the radio's existence.

Several months later, early in 1948, Marlin was sitting one day at Ben Yehuda Street's Café Atara when he was approached by Shalhevet Freier, a high-ranking officer in the Haganah's intelligence corps. The future head of the Israel Atomic Energy Commission, Freier possessed, even then, the quiet intensity required of a man in his position; in a few words, he asked Marlin to do some undercover work for the organization. True to his vocation, Marlin politely refused, saying that he was a journalist and wanted nothing to do with spying.

The Haganah's attempts at recruiting Marlin, however, persisted. As 1948 unfolded, and as the situation in Jerusalem became less and less tolerable, the organization sent various emissaries to offer Marlin various positions. One Haganah officer, for example, promised him the rank of major if he agreed to don a uniform and move to Tel Aviv. There was, the man told Marlin, only one other person in Palestine who had Marlin's experience and knowledge of cryptography. Again, Marlin declined the offer. He had no desire, he told the officer, to wear a uniform again, and was not ready to leave Jerusalem or his job at the *Post*.

Dismayed, the man asked Marlin if he would at least help out by organizing the security system of the Haganah's communications headquarters. That, Marlin felt, was an offer he couldn't turn down; he would, after all, be helping the Haganah on a casual, noncommittal basis, in a way that would not impinge on his career and ethics as a journalist. While he still felt that by working at the *Post* he was serving the national interest, he was nonetheless happy to participate, in a slightly more proactive way, in the building of the Jewish nation.

The Haganah's headquarters were located in the now-evacuated British Camp Schneller. As his workdays at the *Post* didn't start until the afternoon, Marlin spent his mornings setting up the Haganah's cryptography system, making and breaking codes. One morning, the Haganah radio operator brought him a strange message, written in Latin letters yet still incomprehensible. Marlin immediately realized that it was in cipher, and a short while later, he broke the message's code. It had been sent by the Arab command in Jordan to the frontline troops, ordering them to attack a certain location in Jerusalem. The message was passed on to the Haganah's command, and Marlin was brought one encoded message after another until he was finally able to break the Jordanian key. With the key at hand, the Haganah radio operators were able to decode messages within minutes, thereby giving the organization a definite advantage over the Arab militias.

Marlin, however, was not the only one in the household working for the Haganah. Needing English speakers to monitor the British army's radio communications, the organization enlisted everyone who came forth professing any degree of command over the English language. As all the men left in the city were either occupied with careers or, more likely, already drafted as soldiers, the monitoring task was assigned largely to the women. At first the Haganah set up a post, consisting of a desk, chairs, and the Hallicrafter radio, in a shack located in the garden of a villa not far from Agron's house. For reasons that are not entirely clear—quite possibly because of the discomfort caused by the heat on the one hand and the chilling breezes on the other—the post was soon relocated. Knowing that the British were especially sensitive to illicit communications and well aware that their own transmissions were often being intercepted, the Haganah needed to move the monitoring post somewhere safe, somewhere no one would ever look; the Hallicrafter was therefore carried a few houses down and into a back room in Agron's home. Often, while senior British officials were being served fine brandy from Agron's private stock, lounging on his leather sofas, and listening to him deliver witticisms in impeccable English, a cadre of young women were busy at work down the hall, listening intently, taking notes, using Marlin's system to decode and deliver messages.

Betty was one of these women. Already working part-time as a typist for the *Post,* she made the perfect radio operator, not only being a native English speaker but also being acquainted, with varying degrees of intimacy, with both the man who hosted the clandestine monitoring post in his home and the man who, through his knowledge of cryptography, had helped set it up. Listening to hours of communications and taking extensive notes, she realized right away that an altogether different skill was required of her, a skill that had nothing to do with the acuteness of her ear or the swiftness of her hand; as she listened to the British soldiers talking over the radio, she was often forced to bear witness, in silence, to Arab attacks on Jewish targets. As if the searing sensation of helplessness wasn't enough, that terrible burden of hearing the lives of young men come to an end yet lacking the ability to do anything to help them, Betty was also incensed by the repeating pattern that unfolded every time anew. She would listen as British soldiers arrived on the scene while the Arab attack was in full throttle, listen as they would report of the attack, sparing no detail, to their superiors at headquarters, and then—this was the part that drove Betty mad—hear the superiors give the same reply time and again, instructing their subordinates on the scene to simply walk away. Still, even considering the mental and emotional toll, Betty was immensely proud of her position. Even though most of the women in the room were, like her, recent immigrants, working for the Haganah nonetheless made her feel as if she had been accepted, as if she was now, officially, the same as all the others.

Marlin, too, felt a sense of increasing satisfaction; his personal and professional lives were gradually fading into one another and into the prevalent situation of prewar Jerusalem, and he moved from Haganah headquarters in the morning to the *Post* in the afternoon, knowing that his wife was over at his editor's house spying on the British. With that, Marlin felt eerily complete. Just four months before, he had arrived on the *Marine Carp* from New York, enthusiastic and idealistic but uninitiated and misguided. He fondly remembered the time, not long ago, when the worst problem imaginable was the severe spells of diarrhea brought forth by the strange and unfamiliar Middle Eastern foods. Although the stakes were now much higher, with supplies running short and attacks growing more frequent and deadly, Marlin's heart was calm. He had come in search of history, and history had found him. Every day, he felt, was history in the making; every event, every attack, every occasion, belonged in a prominent place in the chronicles of the Jewish people. And he was the one writing it, composing history's first draft. He was witnessing it. He was participating in it. And he was not alone. Around him were other young men and women, some born in Palestine and others abroad, who could not afford despair, who went about their lives despite the terror and fear. He was inspired by them, moved by the minutest outbursts of ordinary life, touched to see routine regaining control where only the day before a bomb had taken its terrible toll. It was true, food was running out, and often Betty and he would go to bed with crackling, empty stomachs. It was true, every morning when he left for work he said good-bye and felt an involuntary flinch in his heart, unconsciously fearing that this good-bye might be the final one. It was true, it was impossible to live in isolation, to duck under one's desk with every loud crash, to calculate each step, every move. Yet, he didn't feel as if he had a choice. Furthermore, he felt like there was no other place on earth he would rather be at that time.

CHAPTER FOUR

One day shortly after the attack on the *Post,* Marlin and Agron were strolling down Ben Yehuda Street on their way to work. Marlin had spent the night at Agron's house, as he did every now and then when whispered rumors spoke of an imminent attack that would make the nightly commute from Jerusalem's city center to the more remote neighborhood of Talbieh, where Betty and Marlin were living at the time, a risk not worth taking. While such nights kept him away from his young wife, Marlin didn't mind spending time with Agron at all. For one, he was still very much in awe of his boss, who was worldly and funny and caustic and infinitely passionate about his newspaper. Sitting in Agron's sunken living room, surrounded by his immense library, Marlin would watch his boss closely, as one watches an actor on stage. First of all, Marlin didn't drink, never liked the taste of liquor, and watching Agron down glass after glass of his precious brandy was a reassuring sign, a morsel of normalcy. Second of all, the two were seldom alone, as Agron was the Jewish community's unofficial designated entertainer; every celebrity, intellectual, or dignitary who made his way to Palestine was ushered into Agron's living room. Marlin remembers meeting there singer and entertainer Eddie Cantor, author and journalist I. F. Stone, and movie star George Jessel. The favorite guest, however, was not a celebrity, but Meyer Weisgal; a statesman, theater producer, fund-raiser, and raconteur extraordinaire, Weisgal, a Polish-born American, had a knack for showmanship. When Leon Uris's book *Exodus* was made into a movie in 1960, Weisgal played the part of David Ben-Gurion, charging $1 million for his performance, every cent of which was donated to Weisgal's pet project, the Weizmann Institute of Science. He also had an absolute command of the English language; when he and the Ukrainian-born Agron, himself a man of many words, got together and got drunk, the conversation, Marlin remembers, would seem more like a Marx Brothers film than a somber meeting between two Jewish diplomats on the eve of war.

Even during those rowdy evenings of entertainment and drink, however, politics were unavoidable. While both Marlin and Agron belonged to the more centrist faction of Jewish political thought, favoring the mainstream Haganah over the militant, and often murderous, Irgun and Lehi, each day, each additional attack, each tinge of hunger, was enough to encourage one of the men to at least consider the merits of the fringe movements. The *Post* somehow managed to remain, more often than not, above the fray of the political discussion, careful to present a cohesive and unified Jewish narrative that would not dissolve into the dissonance that was frequently the local debate between the rival factions. Still, late at night, inebriated and exhausted, the men often allowed their speech a great amount of freedom; the next morning, together with the hangovers and the headaches and the perpetual pangs of hunger, a stronger sense of camaraderie remained nonetheless.

As Marlin and Agron walked to work, passing the familiar facades of now-empty stores, starving for supplies, they suddenly heard a whistling sound, followed by an explosion. The two, by now veterans of Jerusalem's battles, were able to tell one din from another, and could tell that the loud crash they were hearing emanated from a British artillery shell, no doubt launched in retaliation for an attack by Jewish militants earlier that day or, as was increasingly the case, out of sheer panic and growing disarray. Accustomed to such attacks, Marlin followed the often practiced three-step response of survival: duck, observe surroundings, crawl for cover. Only when cover was found, in the doorway of a nearby building, was Marlin able to notice that Agron was not following him. Lifting his head just high enough to observe the potholed street, he could see his editor sitting on a small chair in an utterly exposed part of the street, underneath the marquee of a local cinema, getting his shoes shined by an elderly man in raggedy clothes.

"What are you doing?" Marlin screamed at the stout Agron, who looked as composed as ever. "You'll get yourself killed! Come over here at once!" Agron didn't reply, staring down at his shoes for a few, long moments. When the bombing died down, Agron got up, paid the man, and calmly marched toward Marlin. Met by his employee's shocked, inquisitive look, Agron explained to Marlin that he had had no choice but to do what he did. "If that old man," he said, "was brave enough to sit out there while shells fell, then I could do nothing else."

Marlin didn't say anything, but Agron's words were loudly reverberating in his mind. What if it was all a matter of instinct? What if what set him, a Pennsylvania-born Jewish boy, apart from the brave Sabras, the native-born Palestinian Jews, was strictly inherent, some gene that they possessed and he didn't, some automaton in the brain that commanded them to jump into the line of fire and him away from it? True, Agron himself wasn't a Sabra, but he was an anomaly; in every other matter, he displayed the courage and the conviction that Marlin imagined were hereditary, not acquired, traits, the kind of courage that Marlin himself simply did not possess. Sure, to his friends back in the United States, he was the epitome of bravery, choosing to leave safety behind and settle in a war zone. Yet, he thought, his views on courage were more traditional; to him, Agron's bravado was not a sign of courage, but of foolishness. Having fought in World War II, Marlin had come to develop a simple yet compelling theory concerning danger: There was a bullet out there with his name on it, and until that bullet came, he was relatively safe from all the other bullets fired in his direction. Still, he valued caution, while Agron and the Sabras didn't even take it into consideration. He was practical; they seemed oblivious. What, he worried again, if he didn't have what it took?

As the days passed, however, Marlin was presented with hundreds of opportunities to prove himself wrong; the *Post*'s building was shelled almost every day, mostly a result of miscalculated bombings aimed at the Haganah weapons workshop next door. At first Marlin's heart would skip a beat, his eyes frantically looking for flames, his ears expecting the sounds of destruction that followed the explosion. Gradually, the shelling became routine: hit by a "twenty-fiver," vernacular for the popular British shell which carried twenty-five pounds of explosives, Marlin and his colleagues would simply get up, take cover underneath their desks, and continue their editing or rewriting assignments, unfazed by the occasional shattered window or broken window frame. Some of the *Post*'s employees joked that theirs was truly a desk job, as so much of their time at the office was spent crouching under their desks. The decor of the office changed as well: to protect themselves against shrapnel, the *Post*'s staff piled up all the unsold copies of the newspaper against the windows, creating a paper barricade. Then, to prevent sniper attacks, they hung thick black curtains on top of the newspaper piles, thereby blocking all visibility of the outside world, sunshine included. The *Post* was very much a newspaper under siege.

Eventually, Marlin stopped thinking about courage; courage now seemed like a foreign concept, a conscientious measure which propels one toward actively heroic deeds, and he was neither propelled nor heroic but simply present, going about his routine as thoughtlessly as he could and avoiding any true analysis of his situation.

But even this hermetically sealed resistance to introspection was occasionally penetrated by the force of external events, the most significant of which occurred no more than three weeks after the nocturnal bombing of the *Post:* on Sunday morning, February 22, 1948, Jewish Jerusalem was once again struck by terror.

It was a bright day, unseasonably warm for winter, and the sun motivated many to leave their homes and once again try their luck at the nearly empty stores of Ben Yehuda Street, in the vain hope that something, a rare article of clothing or a coveted canned good, might have found its way into the city despite the increasingly tight Arab grip on Jerusalem's main veins of transportation. At around 6:30 a.m., the streets around the city center were already busy with shoppers, each one anxious to be the first in line. Among the pedestrians along Ben Yehuda Street was Chaim Herzog, then an official in the Jewish leadership who would subsequently become president of Israel, and his wife. The two walked briskly, passing along the way a parked truck bearing the insignia of the British forces. Next to the truck stood a twelve-year-old boy, whom the Herzogs knew to be the only son of Holocaust survivors from Germany, and who was employed as a delivery boy for the *Post.* The couple moved on, and the boy lingered for a minute longer, taking in the crisp morning air. Then the truck exploded.

Later on, it would become evident that the explosion was caused not by one car bomb but by three, all placed in British army trucks. At the time, however, nothing was clear. Ben Yehuda Street was ravaged beyond recognition. Proprietors rushing to the scene could not even identify which of the burning, gutted stores were their own. The impact of the blast brought the neighboring buildings tumbling down, crushing to death many who were unharmed by the initial explosion. The city center was burning.

The rings of fire surrounding the stores and the hazard of imploding buildings made rescue efforts particularly perilous, yet hundreds of Jewish residents streamed to the scene, each frantically attempting to dig up survivors, none actually trained to lend any real help. Families, fearing the collapse of their homes, fled to the street, only to be greeted by chaos—by swarms of people running in different directions, a carpet of debris covering the road and the sidewalks, the swirling smoke and noxious odor of fire consuming wood, rubber, and flesh. In the buildings surrounding the epicenter of the explosion, a thousand tiny dramas unfolded.

Yardena Yehezkely Stern, for example, was seven years old and still at home when the blast occurred. Home was a tiny apartment several blocks away from Ben Yehuda Street, where her parents, aging immigrants from Czechoslovakia, had a photo studio and camera store. Despite being a family of meager means, the Yehezkelys took great pride in their store, bedecking it in marble and mahogany. Hearing the blast, Yardena's father ran out to Ben Yehuda Street, anxious to salvage whatever he could. He returned home several hours later, a blank stare on his face, dark soot staining his clothes, carrying nothing in his hands but a pile of wood. Everything, he said, was destroyed; not a single camera was left unharmed. The only thing remaining was the mahogany paneling, now reduced from splendiferous ornament to charred wood, useful only for burning in their stove. Still, he told his wife and daughter, the family had plenty to be thankful for; in an interview given years later to an Israeli newspaper, Yardena remembers the grim look on her father's face when he told them curtly that "the building opposite the shop had collapsed; everybody in it was killed."

Not far from the Yehezkelys' store lived Miriam Amdur, whose in-laws, Tova and Yerachmiel Amdursky, ran a small hotel located at 10 Ben Yehuda Street. Just several months before, Miriam; her husband, Joseph; and their four-month-old son, Eliezer, had emigrated from the United States to Jerusalem. On the morning of the attack, the family was at the hotel, waking up to their daily routines. At 6:00 a.m., the hotel's dining room manager brought Miriam a warmed bottle of milk for Eliezer, a privilege in a city so short on supplies. By 6:30 a.m., the baby was already fed and put back in his crib, with Miriam and Joe sleepily enjoying the last moments of slumber. Several moments later, the bombs exploded. Debris fell everywhere: bits of wiring, blocks of cement from the ceiling, shards of broken windows. Instinctively, Joseph stood up and straddled Miriam with his body to protect her from the falling rubble. Panicking, Miriam began to yell, "Where's the baby?

Where's the baby?" The two jumped out of bed and climbed over chunks of wall and ceiling now lying in the center of the room. Although the crib stood just several feet away, traversing the distance took time because of the clutter, smoke, and general disarray. When they finally reached the crib, Miriam and Joseph were struck by an awful sight: opposite the crib was an armoire, on top of which the two had stacked all of the books they had brought from the United States. The blast had knocked the armoire over, and the books were now scattered, covering the baby's crib completely.

A few long and torturous seconds later, the two heard a muffled sob coming from underneath the pile of books. Frantically they began throwing the books off, until they finally saw baby Eliezer, who had miraculously been saved by the sides of his crib folding under the pressure of the blast, protecting him in a tentlike fashion against the falling debris. The baby was alive, but his face was covered with blood. Miriam's first instinct was to run out of the building; she grabbed Eliezer and Joesph, and the three of them were relieved to find that the hotel's staircase remained intact. As they were making their quick descent into the street, they ran into Joseph's uncle Shmuel, who in Yiddish asked, *"Vas hat da paseert?"* What happened here? Joseph, as calmly as he could, said *"Gornit,"* nothing.

As they reached street level, the Amdurs saw that someone had already put down long wooden boards over the broken glass, allowing the hotel's residents and employees, most of whom were still barefoot and undressed at that early time of the morning, safe exit. Seeing the sobbing young woman with the bloody baby in her arms, scores of passersby surrounded Miriam, pleading with her to take Eliezer to the hospital. She, however, refused; the last thing she wanted to do was let go of her baby. It was only after she saw her brother-in-law, a doctor, standing nearby, his raincoat over his pajamas, that she agreed to allow the medics, who had already arrived on the scene, to take Eliezer away.

With Eliezer gone, Miriam had time to survey her surroundings. Years later, she wrote a personal, unpublished account of the day, the images still vivid in her mind's eye. "When I reached the street," she wrote, "I looked back at the building and saw flames shooting up the side of the hotel at the location of our room. I saw a piece of the building cut out like a slice of pie. Diagonally opposite our hotel where there had been another hotel, there was nothing but a pile of rubble in a huge hole in the ground." Scared by the sights of devastation surrounding her, Miriam wanted, again, to hold her baby tight. With the help of her adolescent sister-in-law, she traveled in a taxi from hospital to hospital, asking the overworked and impatient nurses if they had seen a young infant, brought in just an hour or so before. Finally, at the Bikur Holim hospital, one nurse replied that the description sounded familiar. She led the two women to a small bed containing a tiny body. Eliezer's head was entirely bandaged. His earlobe was cut, as was the bridge of his nose. A piece of glass was lodged in his forehead, near the hairline; the doctors told Miriam the glass would have to stay in her son's forehead until it fell out naturally, as removing it surgically was too much of a risk for such a young patient.

Back at the scene of the attack, chaos still reigned supreme. Zipporah Porath, a young American teenager who had arrived in Jerusalem several months before to study at the Hebrew University, had made her way to Ben Yehuda Street at around noon. She had just completed a rudimentary first aid course offered by the Haganah; she had several first aid supplies in her backpack, mainly a few bandages. A cordon had been set up by Mishmar Ha'am, volunteer Jewish home guard units, mainly to keep looters and curious bystanders from interfering with the rescue efforts. Porath waved her Haganah-issued first aid armband, and in a voice pretending to be older and more official-sounding than it actually was, said, "Let me in. I'm a first aid attendant." She was admitted through the perimeter, and immediately set out to find the first aid station. There was none. With debris still falling, a permanent post was too dangerous to uphold, and rescue efforts consisted of grabbing survivors outside of the immediate range of the blast and pulling them away to safety. Porath sought cover beneath a doorway, took out her bright red lipstick, and drew a large

Star of David, the local equivalent of the Red Cross, on the wall above her head. She was in business.

Her clients, however, were few and far between. Most of them were rescue workers who had injured their hands while frantically clawing through the rubble in a desperate attempt to find survivors. She also offered emotional help, previously unavailable on the scene. In an interview with the *Jerusalem Post* years later she said, "I only remember people being in such a stage of confusion and disorientation. I was trying to keep my cool, gather them around me and let them feel it would be okay. Children came and clung to me. They were petrified. They hadn't had word of their parents. Nobody knew who to turn to for information." So they turned to Porath, and she did her best to provide comfort where none was available. Later that afternoon, a middle-aged Romanian woman approached Porath's makeshift first aid station. She was panicky and distraught, although she had sustained only minor wounds. She told Porath that her whole family had perished in the Holocaust, and that she had come to Palestine by herself. Her house had been completely demolished. She had no family and no home. At nightfall, Porath sneaked the woman back to her student dormitories, where she stayed for a few days until Porath was able to find a Jewish Agency official who would attend to the poor, lonely immigrant.

As these dramas were taking place, as people were tending to themselves and others in an effort to survive, Marlin was taking pictures. He had arrived at the scene shortly after the attack, carrying with him his Kodak camera. His first instinct, of course, was to join the rescue efforts, but a minute or two at the site of the blast sufficed for Marlin to realize that there was nothing he could do that would not add to the general confusion. So he moved away, allowing the rescuers space to work, climbing on nearby walls, rooftops, or any other stable plateau from which he could take photographs of the scene.

The photographs he took bordered on the surreal: a woman in an evening dress, who was just returning from a night out when the blast occurred, all covered in blood and helped by two burly men whose simple clothes could not be further from her own nocturnal elegance. A hand protruding from the rubble, unheeded. People running around, their belongings wrapped in blankets and towels and sheets, eager to run away somewhere yet not sure where to go. Marlin could take only so much of such graphic misery. Shortly after noon, he went to his office at the *Post* to drown the horror with work.

At the newspaper, one question alone was on everyone's mind: Who had done it? Roy Elston, the *Post*'s front-page columnist and a British non-Jew, reflected the anger and eagerness for vengeance when he wrote the next morning, "Who did this thing? It is better to wait and make sure; but make sure . . ." The unfinished sentence hung between the lines, a promise that whoever was responsible would pay dearly.

For most of Jewish Jerusalem, there was little doubt as to the identity of the culprits. Witness after witness recalled that the trucks carrying the bombs had British army insignia on them. But in an environment where disguise was a commonplace tactic, no one could be certain about anything. Some were unperturbed: Lehi members, for example, saw the attack as an opportunity to escalate their campaign against the dwindling British Mandate, kidnapping and murdering ten British officers in the weeks that followed the explosion. Others, such as the Haganah, were more reserved, retaliating by merely marching down Jerusalem's streets, immediately after news of the attack began circulating, with their ramshackle weapons on display, a defiant and previously unthinkable act. The British, however, weren't around to take notice of the Haganah's parade; sitting in the back room of Agron's house and monitoring the radio, Betty heard, several hours after the explosion, British policemen nervously asking their superiors for instructions; they were ordered to "leave the scene at once."

It was not until years later that the real identity of the perpetrators became known; they were six British soldiers who had deserted from the British army and had been promised payment by the Arab forces of Abdul Kader in return for their assistance. Of the six, two—Peter Mersden and Eddie Brown—had also participated in the attack on the *Post;* the remaining four—George Anthony White, George Ross, Godfrey Alan Stevenson, and a man identified simply as Harrison—were newer recruits. They drove an armored vehicle from the British base in Latrun; because the driver was a blond, blue-eyed man and therefore not suspected of being a combatant on either side, they were waved through all roadblocks. They had also brought three trucks, each loaded with explosives, as well as potash, aluminum, and Molotov cocktails, aimed at intensifying the damage. With the armored vehicle leading the way and the three trucks following, the convoy looked every bit like an official British army convoy. The convoy arrived at the entrance to Jerusalem shortly before 6:00 a.m., passing through a roadblock there. Then it drove along King George Street, passing another roadblock next to the Tal Or building, before making a left on Ben Hillel Street and finally stopping at the corner of Ben Yehuda Street. One truck parked in front of a building known as the Vilentchik building, and the remaining two in front of the Atlantic Hotel, across the street from where Miriam Amdur and her family were sleeping at the time.

The men in the trucks got out, set the charge, shot and killed a suspicious guard stationed in front of the nearby Discount Bank, and then jumped into the armored vehicle waiting nearby and drove away. Again, seeing an armored vehicle, British soldiers at a nearby roadblock let them pass. Those same soldiers, in their own armored truck, then drove down Ben Yehuda Street, and saw three trucks, their doors open, with slim pillars of smoke coming out of each. They retreated just quickly enough to be out of range when the charges went off.

According to Dr. Uri Milstein, an Israeli historian who specializes in Israel's War of Independence, the six were paid by Abdul Kader, and were also motivated by the hope of becoming important generals in the event of an Arab victory. The attacks, the Arab leadership hoped, would reverse the United Nations' partition plan and establish a new reality in Palestine, one of Arab dominance. The British, on their part, were baffled by the attacks; Sir Alan Cunningham, high commissioner to Palestine and the most senior British official in the region, dispatched a secret document to the British foreign service two days after the attack, stressing that despite the common practice of disguise—on the very day of the attack on Ben Yehuda Street, Lehi members disguised as British soldiers robbed a Barclays Bank in Tel Aviv—the Jewish community in Palestine was still certain that the British were to blame. Disinclined to let anyone steal his thunder, Abdul Kader claimed responsibility for the attack, but was quickly silenced by Arab leaders claiming that admission of guilt would only provide an excuse for counterattacks and international condemnation. Abdul Kader's cousin, the mufti Haj Amin el-Husseini, went on to publicly deny any Arab involvement in the attack. The perpetrators themselves mostly fled Palestine, taking refuge in neighboring Arab countries. Brown and Mersden traveled to Cairo, where they met with the mufti and demanded their pay; breaking his promise, the mufti refused to pay the two, and made sure they were kicked out of Egypt; then they disappeared. Harrison and White were killed while dismantling a car bomb placed by a Lehi member in an Arab headquarters near Nablus. Stevenson and Ross participated in an Arab raid on the Jewish community of Neveh Ya'acov, not far from Jerusalem, and were captured by the Haganah. They were extradited to Great Britain, tried, and sentenced to ten years in prison, from which they escaped and fled to Egypt.

The attack claimed 54 victims and more than 180 wounded. As Jewish Jerusalem was burying its dead, terror deferred to a different, more harrowing problem: hunger. While terror struck unwarranted, inflicting great damage on a specific space and its inhabitants, and leaving in its wake rubble that could be rebuilt, hunger crept up on everyone, lingered in stomachs and minds, undefeatable and omnipresent. As the British governance of the city waned to nonexistence, the orderly supply of food was curtailed by the Arab siege of the Jewish parts of the city; convoys were ambushed, packages intercepted, supplies cut off. From a city with modest means of sustenance, Jerusalem slowly became impoverished. It was not uncommon for Marlin to see on his way to work older women shooing off stray cats lounging near garbage cans, attempting to retrieve a morsel of edible waste, any tiny scrap of leftovers that could be salvaged and eaten. The city's economy, subdued by the laws of demand, degenerated into a medieval economy of barter; money was now largely useless, whereas a loaf of bread was nearly priceless.

Luckily for the Levins, Betty proved to be a canny and creative cook. She learned how to create substitutes for almost anything, making, for example, "fried chicken" from the white pith of orange peels, or "chopped liver" from yeast. When neither oranges nor yeast was available any longer, Betty discovered *khubeizah,* a dandelionlike weed that grew in abundance in the fields surrounding their house. Marlin was dispatched to pick as much of the weed as he could carry, and Betty would chop it, fry it, sauté it, or serve it raw. The Levins, like all of Jewish Jerusalem, now lived on strict daily rations: one sardine, some noodles, two slices of bread, and some chocolate syrup that they had received in a package from relatives in the United States back when the postal service was still operational. As winter turned into spring, even those meager rations were often unavailable.

Trying to overcome the dizzying hunger, the *Post*'s staff developed a method of transmutation. They had found several American women's magazines that had been lying around the office, and scanned them for enticing advertisements featuring foodstuffs. Then they would cut the photographs and tack them to the wall. Every night, when someone or another complained about hunger, his colleagues would refer him to the glossy pictures, and a humorous discussion soon ensued: How, one reporter would ask his colleague, does your steak taste? Marvelous, his friend would answer, what about your apple pie? One night, as Marlin walked into the newsroom, he discovered that someone had adorned the bulletin board behind his chair with an appetizing picture of a ham roast.

"That's not kosher!" Marlin yelled, smiling, and the offensive photograph was replaced with that of a couple of frankfurters.

Hunger, however, was often not as daunting as thirst. With the Arabs in control of the city's water supplies, Jerusalem's Jews had to resort to the privately owned wells scattered around the city, or to water supplied, once a day, by armored vehicles dragging large oblong tanks behind them. Without exception, each household was supplied with one bucket of water each day, meant to suffice for drinking, cooking, washing, and laundry. Water-preservation techniques abounded; Betty and Marlin developed their own system, keeping the water in constant motion. First they would set aside a few cups of water for drinking and cooking. Then they would unscrew the pipe underneath the sink in the bathroom, placing a bucket where the pipe had been. After plugging the sink with a stopper, they would "bathe" with a washcloth, a process which Marlin referred to as the "dry bath." Done bathing, they would remove the stopper and collect the bathwater in the bucket, using it to hand-wash their clothes. The same water was then used to wash the floors. They would then re-collect the thrice-used water with a mop and use it to clean and flush the toilets.

Despite hunger, thirst, and terror, Betty and Marlin were determined not to succumb to despair. Constantly, and jovially, they would enumerate the positive qualities of their situation: their slimming figures, their swelling bank accounts, their newfound domestic skills. They were also enamored of the newly enforced romanticism: Jerusalem was now under a permanent blackout, with the scant energy dispersed, for a few hours each day, to hospitals, bakeries, and the *Palestine Post.* Marlin and Betty, then, along with countless other young Jerusalemites, were forced to conduct their lives by candlelight, which shed a warm, soft glow on even the most mundane of chores. No electricity also meant no radios, which left Marlin and Betty more time for candid conversations with each other. The hungrier and more exhausted they were, the more desperately they clung to their cheerful outlooks, constantly reassuring each other that the siege, the famine, the war, all those would end someday and better times would come. Deep in their hearts, however, neither was certain that the Jewish state would prevail.

The events of the spring of 1948 gave Marlin and Betty plenty of fresh reasons for concern. The Arabs refused to allow UN representatives, seeking to monitor the implementation of the partition plan, to enter Palestine; on February 16, 1948, the UN's Palestine Commission reported to the Security Council, stating that "powerful Arab interests, both inside and outside Palestine, are defying the resolution of the General Assembly and are engaged in a deliberate effort to alter by force the settlement envisaged therein." Arab attacks, once sporadic outbursts of violence, grew more systematic and more deadly. In mid-March, for example, a car bomb exploded next to the Jewish Agency building, the towering, fortresslike building in the city center housing the Jewish community's de facto leadership; thirteen people were killed, including the celebrated septuagenarian Dr. Leib Jaffe, one of the few men still alive who had participated in the First Zionist Congress in Basel in 1897.

Faced with the grim turn of events, the Haganah realized that it could no longer afford, as the original plan dictated, to wait for the official declaration of independence in May prior to launching an offensive against Arab forces. With each Arab blow, the Haganah leaders realized, the Jewish population's capability to persist, in terms of supplies, morale, and manpower, decreased dramatically. Identifying besieged Jerusalem as the predominant battlefield, and eager to bring relief to the city's seventy thousand Jews, the Haganah decided to strike first at Arab strongholds controlling the roads to the city.

Concurrently, the Irgun, previously focused on attacking British targets, decided to divert its efforts toward the Arab forces. On April 9, 1948, both the Irgun and the Haganah attempted to conquer two Arab villages on the outskirts of Jerusalem, Kastel and Deir Yassin, both of which were positioned on the hills directly above the only road to the besieged city, and both of which served as outposts for Arab snipers firing on the Jewish convoys traveling below.

About a hundred Jewish warriors, mainly from the Irgun and the Lehi, were dispatched to Deir Yassin. They were preceded by a truck equipped with loudspeakers, determined to allow the Arab villagers a peaceful alternative to fighting: leave now, said the message broadcast in Arabic over the loudspeakers, leave now, as we do not mean to hurt you. The message, however, was never well received; some historians claim that the truck carrying the loudspeakers fell into a ditch, while others say that the message was simply ignored by Deir Yassin's Arabs. The Jewish warriors, in any case, approached the village and were greeted by barrages of gunfire. They fired back, and a gun battle ensued, lasting several hours. Several hundred of the village's residents fled, using a narrow corridor purposefully left open by the Jewish forces for that reason. The remaining Arab forces in the village feigned their surrender, only to resume their attack once the unsuspecting Jewish forces entered the village. Another battle ensued, short and bitter, with some Jewish warriors, fearing further ruses, firing indiscriminately into the crowd. As the bodies fell to the ground, confusion reigned; some Arab warriors were dressed as women, making it nearly impossible to distinguish combatants from civilians. Finally, the Jewish forces captured Deir Yassin. The death toll, however, was staggering: more than two hundred Arabs, as well as four Irgun members, were killed in the attack.

Immediately after the battle, the Arabs began referring to the event as a massacre, claiming that Jewish forces, unprovoked, simply entered the village and indiscriminately shot at the unarmed, defenseless population. The strong, unequivocal Arab rhetoric spread like wildfire; ignoring the actual development of the battle, the deceit by Arab warriors, and the perils facing both sides, they insisted on fanning the instantaneous myth portraying one side as absolute evil and the other as absolute victims. The Jewish Agency, fearing a backlash, published a statement expressing its "horror and disgust" with the events at Deir Yassin, as well as a letter, sent to King Abdullah of Trans-Jordan, expressing shock and disapproval of the Jewish warriors' conduct.

The events at Deir Yassin were a watershed in the conflict between Palestine's two peoples. Wishing to avenge their defeat, in April 1948 Arab forces ambushed a convoy transporting doctors, nurses, and patients to the isolated Hadassah hospital, killing 77 Jews. A few weeks later, on May 4, the Arab Legion attacked the Jewish community of Kfar Etzion, a secluded mountaintop settlement on the fringes of Jerusalem's city limits. After a two-day battle, fatigued and unable to receive any assistance, the Jewish defenders of Kfar Etzion surrendered to the Arabs; still, most were massacred, leaving 148 men, women, and children dead and only 4 survivors.

Fearing Jewish retaliation, weary of battle, and ordered by Arab leaders to vacate Palestine until the great Arab invasion liberated the entire country, many Arabs left the country, heading toward Egypt, Trans-Jordan, or Syria. While the official reason for this exodus is still, more than five decades later, a hotly debated topic, Marlin himself was provided with a clear explanation; one day he and Betty heard a knock on their door, and opened it to discover their landlord, Dr. Jamal, and his petite wife standing there, suitcases in hand. "My dear Mr. and Mrs. Levin," Marlin remembers the landlord telling him, "we are Christian Arabs and we are leaving not because we are being thrown out by the Jews. The fanatics—the Muslims of the Arab Higher Committee—are threatening that if we do not leave they will kill us. If you leave this house, please rent it to Jews. Good-bye." And with that, the doctor and his wife left for Jericho. Soon, Betty and Marlin realized, they would have to leave as well; Talbieh was gradually becoming the front line of the battle for Jerusalem, and almost every night they were awoken by loud explosions or the unmistakable din of shattering glass. Walking around one day, they ran into a friendly and talkative British police officer, who told them, referring to a recent Arab attack on a Jewish community near Jerusalem that cost many lives, "You Americans would be wise to leave, because when we British pull out the

Arabs will do the same to you." The British were scheduled to leave Palestine on May 14, 1948. Marlin and Betty were determined to remain. As Talbieh was no longer safe, they accepted Agron's offer, and moved in with him.

In the days leading up to the end of the mandate, life in Jerusalem took on a hectic pace. Marlin and Betty were mainly busy running down Jerusalem's streets, each street now a battlefield, avoiding sniper fire and the occasional shelling, visiting friends whose houses were hit, sharing their meager rations and dispensing jokes, advice, and words of encouragement. The more dire things looked, the more important it became, for the beleaguered Jews of Jerusalem, to stand together. Marlin and Betty captured this sense of mutual responsibility in a group letter sent in late April to their friends and family in the United States. "There are few shirkers here," they wrote, "not because these people are any more courageous than any other, but because every problem is immediate and personal, and must be faced. Here everyone feels he is his brother's keeper. It is the psychology born of common troubles, common experiences, and common destiny."

Finally, on Friday, May 14, 1948, the British Mandate came to an end. Sir Cunningham, the last British high commissioner, sailed from Haifa's port, along with the final vestiges of British officialdom. Gathered at the Tel Aviv Museum, the members of the Jewish People's Council, now the provisional Jewish government, crowded in along with reporters, photographers, and laymen to listen to David Ben-Gurion read aloud the Proclamation of Independence of the new Jewish state, named Medinat Israel, the State of Israel. The declaration contained a concise summary of the struggle for Jewish nationhood, as well as a statement of intent for peaceful coexistence with Israel's Arab citizens and neighbors. It read:

> *Eretz Yisrael was the birthplace of the Jewish people. Here their spiritual, religious and political identity was shaped. Here they first attained to statehood, created cultural values of national and universal significance and gave to the world the eternal Book of Books.*

After being forcibly exiled from their land, the people kept faith with it throughout their Dispersion and never ceased to pray and hope for their return to it and for the restoration in it of their political freedom.

Impelled by this historic and traditional attachment, Jews strove in every successive generation to re-establish themselves in their ancient homeland. In recent decades they returned in their masses. Pioneers, ma'pilim [Hebrew for immigrants coming to Eretz Israel in defiance of restrictive legislation] and defenders, they made deserts bloom, revived the Hebrew language, built villages and towns, and created a thriving community controlling its own economy and culture, loving peace but knowing how to defend itself, bringing the blessings of progress to all the country's inhabitants, and aspiring towards independent nationhood.

In the year 5657 (1897), at the summons of the spiritual father of the Jewish State, Theodore Herzl, the First Zionist Congress convened and proclaimed the right of the Jewish people to national rebirth in its own country.

This right was recognized in the Balfour Declaration of the 2nd November, 1917, and re-affirmed in the Mandate of the League of Nations which, in particular, gave international sanction to the historic connection between the Jewish people and Eretz-Israel and to the right of the Jewish people to rebuild its National Home.

The catastrophe which recently befell the Jewish people—the massacre of millions of Jews in Europe—was another clear demonstration of the urgency of solving the problem of its homelessness by re-establishing in Eretz-Israel the Jewish State, which would open the gates of the homeland wide to every Jew and confer upon the Jewish people the status of a fully privileged member of the comity of nations.

Survivors of the Nazi holocaust in Europe, as well as Jews from other parts of the world, continued to migrate to Eretz-Israel, undaunted by difficulties, restrictions and dangers, and never ceased to assert their right to a life of dignity, freedom and honest toil in their national homeland.

In the Second World War, the Jewish community of this country contributed its full share to the struggle of the freedom- and peace-loving nations against the forces of Nazi wickedness and, by the blood of its soldiers and its war effort, gained the right to be reckoned among the peoples who founded the United Nations.

On the 29th November, 1947, the United Nations General Assembly passed a resolution calling for the establishment of a Jewish State in Eretz-Israel; the General Assembly required the inhabitants of Eretz-Israel to take such steps as were necessary on their part for the implementation of that resolution. This recognition by the United Nations of the right of the Jewish people to establish their State is irrevocable.

This right is the natural right of the Jewish people to be masters of their own fate, like all other nations, in their own sovereign State.

Accordingly we, members of the People's Council, representatives of the Jewish Community of Eretz-Israel and of the Zionist Movement, are here assembled in the day of the termination of the British Mandate over Eretz-Israel and, by virtue of our natural and historic right and on the strength of the resolution of the United Nations' General Assembly, hereby declare the establishment of a Jewish state in Eretz-Israel, to be known as the State of Israel.

We declare that, with effect from the moment of the termination of the Mandate being tonight, the eve of Sabbath, the 6th Iyar, 5708 (15th May, 1948), until the establishment of the elected, regular authorities of the State in accordance with the Constitution which shall be adopted by the Elected Constituent Assembly not later than the 1st October, 1948, the People's Council shall act as a Provisional Council of State, and its executive organ, the People's Administration, shall be the Provisional Government of the Jewish State, to be called "Israel."

The State of Israel will be open for Jewish immigration and for the Ingathering of the Exiles; it will foster the development of the country for the benefit of all its inhabitants; it will be based on freedom, justice and peace as envisaged by the prophets of Israel; it will ensure complete equality of social and political rights to all its inhabitants irrespective of religion, race or sex; it will guarantee freedom of religion, conscience, language, education and culture; it will safeguard the Holy Places of all religions; and it will be faithful to the principles of the Charter of the United Nations.

The State of Israel is prepared to cooperate with the agencies and representatives of the United Nations in implementing the resolution of the General Assembly of the 29th November, 1947, and will take steps to bring about the economic union of the whole of Eretz-Israel.

We appeal to the United Nations to assist the Jewish people in the building-up of its State and to receive the State of Israel into the comity of nations.

We appeal—in the very midst of the onslaught launched against us now for months—to the Arab inhabitants of the State of Israel to preserve peace and participate in the upbuilding of the State on the basis of full and equal citizenship and due representation in all its provisional and permanent institutions.

We extend our hand to all neighboring states and their peoples in an offer of peace and good neighborliness, and appeal to them to establish bonds of cooperation and mutual help with the sovereign Jewish people settled in its own land. The State of Israel is prepared to do its share in a common effort for the advancement of the entire Middle East.

We appeal to the Jewish people throughout the Diaspora to rally round the Jews of Eretz-Israel in the tasks of immigration and upbuilding and to stand by them in the great struggle for the realization of the age-old dream—the redemption of Israel.

Placing our trust in the Almighty, we affix our signatures to this proclamation at this provisional Council of State, on the soil of the homeland, in the city of Tel-Aviv, on this Sabbath eve, the 5th day of Iyar, 5708 (14th May, 1948).

While these historic words were read to a trembling nation, Marlin was sound asleep. Just as had happened during Kaf Tet Be'November, as the United Nations approved the partition plan, this historic moment found Marlin unprepared. Exhausted by the constant attacks, weakened by pangs of hunger, and far from the actual center of events, he simply collapsed on his bed, waking up on Saturday morning to discover that a state had been established overnight. His journalistic senses slowly taking hold, he grabbed his camera and ran out to the streets to document the spontaneous outbursts of joy. He took dozens of photographs, all of which look eerily similar; in all, large throngs of people, dressed in dirty and drab khaki outfits, crowd the streets of Jerusalem, climbing on cars and trucks and rooftops, waving makeshift Israeli flags. Their faces bear the same expression, that of an unmediated, blissful soul emanating from within a collapsed body, that of sheer joy unperturbed, for a second, by all the battles that had been and all those that were sure to come.

And come they did. The day after Ben-Gurion's declaration, five Arab countries—Trans-Jordan, Egypt, Syria, Lebanon, and Iraq—invaded Israel. Together with the vanguard of local Arab warriors, the Arab forces numbered approximately eighty thousand men. The Haganah, on the other end, now renamed the Israel Defense Forces, Israel's official army, had fewer than twenty thousand warriors, most of whom were overworked and undertrained. The IDF, as it came to be called, had no tanks, no cannons, and an air force comprising nine antiquated airplanes.

What happened next remained, from Marlin's point of view, largely unseen. For the Jewish population of Jerusalem, there were a few uplifting moments—such as the retreating British forces handing over Bevingrad, the symbol of the mandate's oppression, to Haganah officers—engulfed by days and days of dismay. On May 29, the tiny Jewish community in the Jewish Quarter of the Old City, approximately two thousand men, women, and children, surrendered to Jordanian legionnaires and were taken captive. This marked the end of two millennia of continual Jewish presence in that holiest part of Jerusalem. Also, hunger became a true epidemic, sending dozens to their beds, no longer able to go about their daily routines. With most of the Arabs having fled the city, Jerusalem was a Jewish enclave, dependent on the ability of IDF forces to break through the Arab siege. If they could not, Marlin and his fellow Jerusalemites knew, the city's Jews would be forced to choose between starvation and surrender to the Arab forces.

The breakthrough occurred the following month. Oddly enough, it was coordinated not, as Marlin might have imagined, by a virile young Sabra, but by an American Jew, Colonel Mickey Marcus. A graduate of West Point and a veteran of the battle of Normandy, Marcus later headed the War Crimes Division that gathered evidence and prosecuted the Nazis at Nuremberg. Although he was never an ardent Zionist, his experiences after the war nonetheless led him to believe that an independent Jewish state was indispensable for Jewish survival. He was approached by Ben-Gurion and asked to move to Israel and help fight the War of Independence; still a U.S. Army reservist, he applied to the U.S. Department of War for permission to do so, and his application was granted on condition that he did not make his own name or American military affiliation known. And so Colonel Michael Stone, Marcus's pseudonym of choice, was born, joining Ben-Gurion and IDF chief of staff Yigal Yadin in orchestrating the seemingly hopeless war.

Marcus's first, and most memorable, step was the one that brought relief to besieged Jerusalem. Imitating a tactic used by the Allied Forces during the Second World War to cross the mountainous region between Burma and China, Marcus devised a path, therefore nicknamed "the Burma Road," bypassing the main highway to Jerusalem. Stealthily, under the cover of dark, Marcus commanded IDF squads as they blasted away large chunks of the mountains surrounding Jerusalem, creating a makeshift passage. On June 9, just days before the United Nations negotiated a cease-fire, IDF forces were able to arrive at Jerusalem with desperately needed provisions. Ben-Gurion appointed Marcus lieutenant general, the first general in a Jewish army in nearly two thousand years. Tragically, he was killed shortly thereafter; six hours before the June cease-fire went into effect, a sleepless Marcus left his tent for a nocturnal walk. Upon his return, an IDF guard asked him, in Hebrew, to identify himself. Marcus had never learned Hebrew, and was unable to provide the proper response. He was shot and killed on the spot.

His efforts, however, along with the indefatigable fighting of IDF soldiers on all fronts, gave Israel the upper hand. By the time the cease-fire was signed, it was abundantly clear that the small state had been successful in fending off attacks from the south, east, and north. Local battles broke out, but quickly died down. Israel's War of Independence was over, and the Jewish state had stood its ground.

In Jerusalem, Marlin, Betty, and their friends allowed themselves several days of relaxation. They ate their first real meal in months. They had, once again, running water and electricity. They could send and receive packages. These small tokens of normalcy delighted them no end. It did not matter that Jerusalem was now a divided city, with everything from the Old City eastward controlled by the Jordanians. It did not matter that more battles were likely to erupt, that Arab belligerence, although temporarily subdued, was likely to continue to try and annihilate the Jewish state. It did not matter that their lives were still a great distance from what they would have been had they stayed in Manhattan, or even in Harrisburg. Having experienced the battle for independence, both Marlin and Betty knew that they would stay in Jerusalem for the rest of their lives.

Several years passed, each year with its share of tragedy and excitement. There were other attacks, and acquaintances who lost their lives. Marlin had the pleasure of documenting Jerusalem's first Independence Day parade, and the couple found a nice two-bedroom apartment not far from their original house in Talbieh. They had two children. One day, in 1958, Marlin received an offer to become *Time* magazine's correspondent in Jerusalem. Smiling, he thought of the day, a decade earlier, when he refused an offer from his university's president to go and work for the publication in New York. Back then, he was not ready to commit to such a job, unwilling to join the ranks of corporate America, seeking instead the adventure and ideological satisfaction of aliya, immigration to Palestine. Now, however, having moved to Palestine and having witnessed Palestine become Israel, having survived terror and hunger and war, and having worked for a newspaper under constant shelling, he was ready. He accepted the offer, and a circle was completed.

PART II

FROM HARTFORD TO KIBBUTZ MISGAV AM, 1969

CHAPTER FIVE

In the dry, prickly wind of a late June afternoon in kibbutz Misgav Am, a group of American-Jewish teenagers were sitting in an outdoor observation point and staring at Lebanon. The kibbutz was another stop in their monthlong tour of Israel, which included nature hikes, sightseeing, and the occasional lecture. This, they could sense, was going to be one of those lectures, another talk about Israel's geography or history or some other topic that doesn't mix well with the heat, the fatigue, and the average teenager's attention span. But the man standing in front of them looked intriguing enough: he was large, blending to the point of assimilation with the scenery around him, his limbs like lumber, his bushy mustache resisting the wind, his sandaled feet the color of dust. Pointing toward the horizon, he spoke of Israel's tumultuous history with its neighbor to the north: the terror attacks, the mortar rockets, twenty years of war. The one thing you must understand, he kept on telling the kids, is that size does matter: Lebanon is right here, not even a city block's distance away, and back there, a mile or so to the east, lies Syria. You can cross the whole thing, three countries, in less than a minute's flight. It takes, he told them, more than three hours just to fly over Texas.

A seasoned speaker, the man knew that adolescent attention is hard to get and harder to keep; in between facts and figures he wove in the occasional four-letter word, grinning at both the teenagers' delight and the embarrassment of their middle-aged tour guide. He hardly needed profanity, however; a large man carrying a gun, standing feet away from the border and talking about terrorism, he was captivating enough as he was, appearing like a figure from the Wild West replanted in the Middle East.

But there was one more reason the man commanded his audience's attention. He had been one of them once, born and raised in the United States, and even now, as he stood and spoke of Israel's security, he still wore a Brooklyn baseball cap and had a slight Brooklyn accent. His name, he told them, was Mike Ginsberg, and before he lived on the border, with guns and dust and constant mortar attacks fired by Hizbollah terrorists from the neighboring hills, he grew up like them, an American; as his cap and his accent suggested, Mike Ginsberg was born in Brooklyn.

Brooklyn of the 1950s has settled in collective American memory as a series of vignettes: Coney Island and Ebbets Field, Nathan's hot dogs and egg creams, Don Newcombe on the mound and Jackie Robinson on third, trolley cars careening by and chalky Spaldeen balls rolling about, all have transcended locality, traveled in time and space to become all-American emblems. Moments before race riots and antiwar protests, before the surge in crime and the rise of suburbia, Brooklyn was where childhood still meant innocent days spent on the stoop or the street corner, at the candy store or the malt shop, in the yard or at the beach.

Brooklyn of the 1950s was also home to a large, robust Jewish population: whereas Jews made up between 2 and 3 percent of the general national population, they accounted for over a third of Brooklyn's population in 1950, approximately 920,000 people out of the borough's total tally of 2,738,175 residents. Jewish life in mid-twentieth-century Brooklyn had such a ubiquitous presence that historian David Kaufmann referred to the borough as "the largest Jewish community in the history of the world." Even if slightly overstated, Kaufmann's dictum still captures the essence of a neighborhood where a plethora of kosher delis sold kishkes and knishes and even the gangsters had names like Abraham "Pretty" Levine, Albert "Tick Tock" Tannebaum, and Irving "Knadles" Nitzberg.

As Brooklyn's kingdom flourished, taking hold of the American imagination, strong subterranean trends were already at play, trends that, within a few short years, would put an end to the borough's golden age. The Jewish population, now sufficiently removed from the memory of immigration from Europe, became more affluent and sought a change in lifestyle, away from the crowded urban shtetl and toward the more spacious suburbs of New Jersey and Westchester. From nearly 1 million people in 1950, the Jewish population of Brooklyn rapidly dwindled: in 1963 there were 765,000 Jews living in the borough, and in 1976 only 514,000. Not only the Jews, however, were leaving. The shipping industry, once a staple of the Brooklyn economy, was largely lured away and migrated southward, where costs were significantly cheaper; as jobs left Brooklyn, many people followed. The population of Brooklyn began to change, and the neighborhood became home to large contingents of black and Hispanic residents; given the racially charged political climate of the times, Brooklyn started tearing at the seams. By 1968, Brooklyn was once more in the national forefront, this time as a symbol of racial divisiveness, as a predominantly black school board fired nineteen white educators, some of whom were Jewish, resulting in a three-month-long teachers' strike. The event, known as the Ocean Hill–Brownsville Crisis, was one of the most racially divisive moments in New York history, kindling angry confrontations and increased interracial animosity.

Looking at Brooklyn's history in retrospect, one year stands out as being both the pinnacle of the borough's glory and the beginning of its disintegration: 1955. That was the year the *Brooklyn*

Eagle, the influential local newspaper that had chronicled the life of the borough since 1841, closed down, depriving Brooklyn of one of its most idiosyncratic, brash, and beloved voices. It was also the year the Brooklyn Dodgers won the World Series for the first time in their history. And it was in Brooklyn, in 1955, that Mike Ginsberg was born.

Mike's timing was off by several years. The youngest of four children born to Lester and Harriet Ginsberg, he never saw the Dodgers play or paid a quarter for a crisp copy of the *Eagle*; the streets where his older brothers played stickball and catch were now dense with traffic; and in Lilly Santangelo's wax museum, a popular Coney Island attraction, figures of Clark Gable and Humphrey Bogart were replaced by those of Brooklyn Dodgers' stars Jackie Robinson and Roy Campanella, reflecting the shifting sensibilities of the museum's patrons.

Still, Mike's first years were relatively carefree. The family lived in a co-op in Sheepshead Bay that had seven entrances, each entrance leading to a four-story brownstone, each brownstone with eleven apartments. Most apartments were owned by people much like the Ginsbergs: the men had fought, like Lester Ginsberg, in the Second World War, then returned to Brooklyn and settled down into jobs they would probably keep for a lifetime. The women, like Harriet Ginsberg, mainly stayed at home, building up a tightly knit community around them; brownstones became small, autonomous units, with all of one's friends and family conveniently concentrated in one building, run by a council of mothers that seemed to know what everybody's child was doing at any given moment. The building being a minuscule urban collective, Mike didn't have to look beyond his own house to find close friends; he would run around with Randy, and embark with Robby on "dinosaur-bone" excavations on the Coney Island beach. Conveniently located across the street was a candy store, which Mike and his friends would frequent as often as they could, and when he got tired of running around he would come back up, plop himself on the couch in front of the family's new black-

and-white Zenith television, and watch *Car 54, Where Are You?* On Sunday evenings, the Ginsbergs would march down the street to the local Chinese restaurant, where everyone who lived within a five-block radius would congregate for chicken and conversation.

The cohesiveness of the local community was made stronger by the fact that not only did the Ginsbergs and their neighbors share a geographical space, a socioeconomic background, and common personal histories, they were also, for the most part, Jewish.

The Ginsbergs, like many Jews in Brooklyn at the time, had constructed their own Jewish identity: while high holidays were observed and the dinners served were mainly kosher, Saturday, the Jewish Sabbath, was less a time for prayer and reflection and more a time for *Howdy Doody* and *The Mickey Mouse Club*. Rather than the synagogue, the local Chinese restaurant served as the community's nerve center. Mike's brothers, who went to public schools, did attend Young Israel, a Jewish youth group, but rather than imbibe traditional values, the boys were boys: one year during Passover, at a Young Israel celebration, Mike's brother Jay drank the grape juice offered in paper cups, and pretended to be drunk. After he swirled and staggered about for a short while, his mother was called to collect her prodigal son. In a sense, the Ginsbergs lived up to a popular credo of the time: the synagogue they didn't go to was Orthodox. To them, egg creams were just as much a Jewish elixir as the wine served during Friday night's kiddush ceremony. And so the Ginsbergs lived, mostly indistinguishable from their friends and colleagues, a typical Jewish family in a typical Jewish neighborhood with a typical Jewish identity that was just too typical to bother to define.

Then, however, in 1960, the family's fortunes shifted when Mike's father, Lester, suffered a fatal heart attack. Suddenly, the typical Ginsbergs weren't typical anymore: single-parent families or working mothers were still uncommon phenomena, and Harriet, nearly forty years old, was left with four sons, no source of income, and a neighborhood that was slowly shedding its Jewish identity. Contemplating the best way to allow her sons a good education and quality of life, Harriet knew it was time to leave Brooklyn.

What happened next is still unclear, as each member of the Ginsberg family has a slightly different account. According to Mike, his mother had spent some time in Hawaii during the war, serving in an army auxiliary unit, and therefore contemplated moving her family there. Larry, Mike's older brother, tells a similar story, only instead of Hawaii he recalls his mother planning a move to Alaska. A third option, which none of the Ginsbergs dispute, was Israel.

Then only twelve years old, Israel was scarcely ever mentioned in the Ginsberg household. The only time it was mentioned was during the Passover Seder, the traditional Jewish celebration, which is concluded by saying *"Le'shang haba'ah be'Yerushalayim,"* Next year in Jerusalem. Next year, however, was—until that point—nothing more than a figure of speech for the Ginsbergs.

Yet for Harriet, Israel must have been appealing: a young country with a hot climate and a law that stated that each and every Jew who wished to immigrate to Israel was instantly entitled to citizenship and a handsome financial aid package. Furthermore, it was a country that supported a unique form of community, the kibbutz, which could be seen as an ideology-infused agrarian replica of the communal Brooklyn brownstone; in the kibbutzim of the time, a socialist spirit ruled supreme, barring individual property, stressing egalitarianism, and providing each member with all of her needs. In short, it was just the right place for Harriet Ginsberg and her sons.

The next summer, Harriet sent her sons to Camp Ma Na'im, an Orthodox camp in New York State, and sailed to Israel. There she volunteered in Sasa, a kibbutz in northern Israel. Sasa was the perfect choice: established in 1949 by a collective of immigrants from North America, it was, in 1961, still a place where English was spoken by all, and where many people still had strong memories of their previous lives in the United States. There, in the verdant upper Galilee, at the foot of Mount Meron, Harriet broke bread with the several dozen members of the kibbutz, experiencing a radically different lifestyle than any she had known in the past. There, one woke up before the crack of dawn, ate a humble breakfast in the communal dining hall, and proceeded straight to the chicken coop or the barn to collect the eggs or milk the cows, or down to the fields to pick apples or water the avocado trees. From her window, Harriet could see not brownstones but green valleys, not the corner store but the remains of the Arab village where the kibbutz now stood, that village itself having been built on top of the ruins of an Ottoman fortress, which in turn was built on top of a decrepit citadel constructed by the Crusaders, who themselves settled on the remains of a biblical Jewish village. And while the archeological pastiche served as a living memory that this was the land of the Bible, the communal facilities of the kibbutz served as a reminder that the Jews living there, with their uniquely impossible combination of Marxist ideology and Zionist convictions, were a different breed of Jews than their ancient ancestors.

Harriet's summer at Sasa was enough to convince her that neither Hawaii nor Alaska was right for her family. The next summer, in June of 1962, all five Ginsbergs boarded the *Olympia,* a Greek ocean liner, and headed for the port of Haifa, the largest city in northern Israel.

When told that they were about to travel across the world, away from everything that was familiar to them, and settle in an unknown, underdeveloped country, the Ginsberg kids were torn, each child's response influenced mainly by his age. For Marc and Jay, the two oldest sons who were then teenagers, adolescence was bad enough without having to face a dramatic move separating them from their friends, their television shows, and their baseball team. They protested loudly, swearing, with teen bravado, that they would never adjust to the new country. Larry, who was slightly younger, had other concerns: a tragic medical mishap as a newborn had burned his retinas, blinding him for life; if the United States had hardly any adequate facilities to help him overcome his disability, the family feared, then Israel, still in its infancy and suffering from crucial security problems and a perpetual lack of funds, would surely be much worse. Of the four brothers, Mike, then seven years old, was the only one truly giddy about the upcoming adventure. He was too young to have had the chance to make any real friends in Brooklyn; a new country meant more freedom, more excitement, more options.

During the two-week sail to Haifa, with stops all over southeastern Europe, Mike ran amok on the deck, exploring and befriending the crew. For a child whose world had been limited to a few blocks' range, the ship and the endless horizon of the ocean were thrilling. One time, while the ship was docked at Naples for a short while, Mike befriended a young sailor, who offered to take him to the bridge and introduce him to the captain. Thrilled, Mike agreed, and spent the next hour or so touring the ship's command center. Harriet, on the other hand, knew what her mischievous little boy was capable of, and was certain he had run off to shore. As the ship began sailing back to sea, Harriet ran around in a frenzy, yelling, "Stop the ship!" It was not until several minutes later, when Mike rushed back to his room to change his wet socks, that Harriet understood where her son had been. Another time, as the ship passed the Strait of Gibraltar, Mike woke up with the other brothers at 5:00 a.m. to watch the wonder. To him, the magnificent view seemed like the famous logo of the Prudential insurance company. Nevertheless, he insisted he wanted to take pictures. As he was focusing, the camera dropped to the ground and shattered.

With so much maritime merriment, the actual arrival at Haifa was entirely uneventful for Mike. Years later, he would remember the port as if it were a scene from the movie *Exodus;* at the time, however, Haifa's docks were plain, dirty, and noisy, with burly longshoremen who just all happened to be Jewish. Mike was not elated, not excited, not enthralled. After the initial joy of adventure slowly died, the Ginsbergs were left with the uneasy feeling that they had not made aliya to Israel as much as they had escaped New York.

One central component that contributed to this sense of malaise was the notorious Israeli bureaucracy. Governed by an omnipresent socialist party for the first three decades of its existence, Israel was largely run by a potent class of clerks, who oversaw most aspects of the country's public life. Even simple exchanges with public servants could drive civilians to despair, as they endured long lines, and confronted short attention spans on the other side of the desk. Harriet Ginsberg must have realized all that, yet she had high expectations; after all, here she was, a Jewish woman living up to the reasons for which Israel was established, leaving behind an affluent country to come and participate in the building of the Jewish state. Armed with confidence, she went to the Ministry of the Interior to settle her status as an immigrant. What she heard next, however, shocked her; the clerk, far from hospitable and appreciative of her personal exodus, told her that as a forty-two-year-old widow with four young boys and no independent source of wealth, she was far from welcome. While public records of the day are not available, an official who worked for the ministry at the time of the Ginsbergs' immigration, although unfamiliar with the case, expressed surprise that she was even allowed in the country. "We had ideology, of course," he said, wishing to remain anonymous even after four decades. "We wanted to accommodate every Jew, we wanted to be a national home for Jewish immigrants from across the world. But we were also living in a tiny country with hardly any budget, and taking in people like that [Harriet Ginsberg] simply didn't pay off. She would have been a burden. It's sad to admit, but it's true."

Myriad other factors contributed to creating a landscape that the Ginsbergs found far from welcoming. The first, most obvious, barrier was language. In Brooklyn, Mike had learned some Hebrew, but it was mainly the Hebrew used in daily prayers. In Israel, however, Hebrew was a living, spirited language, infused with Arabic slang, army abbreviations, and local vernacular. Arriving in Haifa during the summer, Mike was sent to a day camp; he spoke to the other children in English, and was livid when they couldn't understand a word he said. He would then slowly repeat the words in his mind, wondering why the others were stupid and incapable of understanding such simple, lucid sentences. The beginning of the school year was no better, and Mike doodled in class, transcribing Hebrew phrases into his notebook and understanding little.

But whereas Mike had the desire to learn, his older brothers—particularly Jay and Marc—didn't. They considered themselves Americans, attended the only American school in Israel, spoke in English, and yearned to return to the United States. Larry was more enthusiastic, having spent a short time in a Brooklyn yeshiva and therefore possessing a rudimentary knowledge of Hebrew and Israeli history. Still, he, too, often faced a culture shock: early on, his newfound friends demanded that he decide which one of the local soccer teams—Hapoel Haifa or Maccabi Haifa—he would root for, a critical decision for one's future social prospects. Larry considered this for a minute, and then said with confidence that his allegiance lay with none other than the Brooklyn Dodgers.

For the older brothers, Haifa was provincial and pathetic. The Ginsbergs lived on the western side of Mount Carmel, in a whitewashed three-story building. The building, one of many cheap, drab houses built to accommodate Israel's booming population in the early 1960s, possessed little of the urban majesty of the brownstone. Neither was the Ginsbergs' new street anything like a city block: there were five houses on their street, followed by woods, large lots of dirt, a valley, and the Mediterranean Sea, always visible in the distance. Not yet entirely formed, the city was a hodgepodge of sensibilities. Made famous by the prophet Elijah, who slaughtered more than 450 priests of Ba'al on the Carmel, modern-day Haifa emerged as a hub in 1905, when the Ottoman Empire chose it as the departure point for a railway leading all the way to Damascus, nowadays the capital of Syria. As the British replaced the Turks as caretakers of Palestine, they used the already existing infrastructure to construct a second, more ambitious line, this one connecting Haifa with Cairo in Egypt. Haifa's real ascension into national prominence, however, began in 1934, with the completion of its harbor, the first modern port in Palestine and one of few in the entire region. The harbor catapulted Haifa from a sleepy northern town with a train station to a national center of commerce, shipping, and industry, as well as a terminal point for oil pipelines. This influx of industry gave birth to a popular saying of the time: "While Tel Aviv plays and Jerusalem prays, Haifa is doing the work!" The maxim was further strengthened in the early 1950s by the fact that most of Israel's major enterprises, from the state-owned electric company to the Israeli navy, chose Haifa as their base of operations.

Yet the city that the Ginsbergs found in 1962 was no New York or Detroit, no bustling international harbor or megalopolis of production lines. Beneath the industrial facade was a loosely populated town, where neighborhoods were their own autonomous universes and everyone lived within walking distance of everyone else, where children in sandals and shorts played in the streets and cars were scarcely seen. In short, Haifa of the early 1960s was a lot like Brooklyn of the early 1950s. And now, finally, Mike was in the right place at the right time.

The largest barrier standing between Mike and his peers, language, was quickly removed. Mike's elementary school teacher, with typical Israeli machismo, believed that the best way to help Mike learn the language was simply to do nothing; that way, he was certain, Mike would have no choice but to learn it as fast as he possibly could. He was right: within six weeks, Mike was chatting freely in Hebrew, and was now largely indistinguishable from his Israeli-born peers.

Yet language was not the only cultural gear Mike had to shift. In Brooklyn, for example, no day was complete without a visit to the candy store, no morning the same without his beloved black-and-white cookies, so that the already tall and bulky Mike weighed over a hundred pounds. In Haifa, candy stores and delis were nowhere to be found, and the random kiosk sold nothing but soda and *metzupeh,* a mealy wafer covered with a thin layer of chocolate. Kids, therefore, ate oranges in the winter, grapes in the summer, and hummus and falafel year-round. Forced into a gastronomic shock, Mike lost nearly a third of his body weight within several weeks. His skin was scorched and tanned by the unremitting Middle Eastern sun. He joined the Israeli scouts, a co-ed youth movement dedicated to community service and the outdoor life. He spent his days in the streets or in the vast, open spaces surrounding the few houses in his neighborhood, playing games like *pif paf*, a local version of cops and robbers, catch, or duck duck goose.

Yet, despite his rapid acclimation in Haifa, tiny peninsulas of nostalgia for the United States remained firmly embedded in his heart. In Brooklyn, for example, television was an important part of life, and *Bonanza, Gunsmoke,* and *Rawhide* were as much an organic part of the daily schedule as were breakfast, lunch, and dinner. In Haifa, there was no television. There was a television set—the Ginsbergs brought their Zenith with them to Israel—but there was no broadcasting infrastructure, as Israel would not adopt the medium until 1968, believing it to be uneducational and detrimental to the fledgling country's moral well-being. For four hours each day, however, the few and privileged owners of television sets could intercept broadcasts from neighboring countries, particularly Lebanon. The picture was fuzzy, the sound was often indecipherable, and the content left much to be desired, but for the scores of friends and curious neighbors who gathered at the Ginsbergs' apartment it was nonetheless a miracle of technology. Among the few shows aired were the popular World War II drama *Combat!, The Mickey Mouse Club,* and similar contemporary American hits. With one channel to choose from, however, Mike and his friends often watched Arabic-language programming just as eagerly; especially popular was *Kan Ya Makan,* a children's program featuring Islamic fairy tales, not always amicable toward the much-hated Jewish neighbors to the south. Despite not understanding a word of Arabic, the children watched zealously: never mind the program's content or language, it was nevertheless on television, and was therefore treated with reverence. Another reminder of life in America was a bowling alley which opened in downtown Haifa around the time the Ginsbergs arrived, one of a handful of such institutions in Israel. As no Israeli native had any idea how to play the game, the Ginsbergs were sought-after guides to the rules of ball and pins. Jay, Mike's older brother, was immediately hired as an instructor, and Mike was permitted to clean shoes in return for free games.

While bowling and television were conduits for memories of what seemed a different life on a different planet, other, more immediate figures pushed Mike's shaping identity away from the streets of Brooklyn and toward the hills and the deserts of Israel. Even as a child, Mike could not ignore the omnipresence of the Israel Defense Forces, the country's nearly mythical army. Just a decade before, the army, outnumbered and ill-equipped, defeated the joint forces of seven Arab nations, took over vast territories, and secured the establishment of the state. A few years later, in 1956, the army, responding to the hostile takeover of the Suez Canal by Egyptian president Gamal Abdel Nasser, attacked the mammoth Egyptian army, capturing the Gaza Strip and the Sinai Peninsula before being forced to withdraw by international pressure. The army, then, was perceived as a miraculous and omnipotent force, a dedicated band of Jewish warriors that, with a little luck and a lot of providence, was defending the tiny, besieged Israel from malicious neighbors who were constantly contemplating its destruction. The army was also the largest national industry, as each and every eighteen-year-old, man and woman alike, faced several years of mandatory service, and most men continued to serve a month or two each year, for most of their lives, in the reserves. The army was everywhere, and the army's generals were Israel's equivalent of movie stars.

In 1964, Mike and his brothers went to see the annual Independence Day parade in downtown Haifa. As Israel's independence was solely attributed to the army, the parade mainly consisted of tanks, jeeps, soldiers, flags, ships, jets, marching bands, lines and lines of shiny uniforms and shinier shoes, drills, weapons on display, and any other conceivable kind of military fanfare. This was nothing like the Dodgers' ticker tape parade.

Standing on the sidelines, surrounded by every single person who lived in Haifa at the time, Mike felt many things. He was dehydrated, as the early summer sun beat down on his naked head. But that hardly mattered, as the queasy weakness made way for surges of joy, of might, of pride. Here were Jews who were nothing like his Brooklyn circle of friends and relatives. Here were Jews who could handle guns even better than Bugsy Siegel and were even braver than Sandy Koufax. Here were warriors. Of course, Mike had seen Jewish warriors before; his own father fought in the Battle of the Bulge. But these Jewish warriors were nothing like his shortsighted and affable dad: they were tall and tanned, driving their tanks and their jeeps down Main Street for the whole world to see the might of the Jewish state. At that moment, Mike had no doubt: he was an Israeli.

Three years later, Mike was feeling even more in his element. He had been in Israel for five years now, and although he did poorly at school, his schedule was always full of social activities, of games and get-togethers and rendezvous with girls. He was completely oblivious of the turmoil back in the United States, knew nothing of the Cuban missile crisis, the budding civil rights movement, or the first U.S. bombings of Vietnam. He was equally unconcerned with currents sweeping Israel's neighbors, such as the establishment in January 1964 of the Palestine Liberation Organization, or its foiled attack a year later on Israel's water systems. Unbeknownst to Mike, however, events on both a personal and global scale were set in motion that would tear him, for the second time in five years, from his home and transport him back across the globe. Those events culminated in the spring and early summer of one crucial year, 1967.

Eager to avenge his humiliating loss in 1956, Egypt's Nasser, in hopes of uniting and controlling the entire Arab world, plotted a second act in his ongoing battle with Israel. On May 15, 1967,

Nasser finally made his move, taking a series of steps that signaled a looming threat: Nasser concentrated large-scale Egyptian forces in Sinai, expelled the United Nations force that had served as a buffer between Egypt and Israel on the peninsula since 1957, and blocked the Strait of Tiran, located at the end of the Gulf of Eilat, preventing the passage of any Israeli vessels. Two weeks later, on May 30, Jordan joined Egypt and Syria in a military alliance against Israel, placing its army on both sides of the Jordan River under Egyptian command. Iraq, too, soon followed suit, and other Arab nations, including Algeria and Kuwait, also sent contingents of soldiers. In a matter of weeks, Israel was confronted by an Arab force consisting of 465,000 troops, 2,880 tanks, and 810 aircraft. For the third time in less than twenty years, Israel's existence was gravely in danger.

For those living in Israel at the time, the question was not whether there would be a war, but rather when the war would start. The country entered what became known as "the waiting period"; the most popular song on the radio at the time was titled "Nasser Awaits Rabin." A direct reference to the Egyptian president's threats to destroy Israel, threats broadcast in Hebrew directly from Cairo, the song captures the sense of tension as it rhymes that Nasser's "waiting sure as hell / for Rabin to ring the bell." Yitzhak Rabin, then the army's chief of staff, embodied the way Israel loved imagining itself; the man who several years later would become Israel's first native-born prime minister was tall, handsome, and courageous, a man who combined two thousand years of memory with a promise for a triumphant, secure future. Many decades later, Rabin would be assassinated by a militant Jew for initiating a peace process with the Palestinians; in 1967, however, he was still everybody's hero.

Days of waiting turned into weeks. As Israel futilely tried to solve the crisis by diplomatic means, Harriet Ginsberg was rethinking her own future. Unlike her neighbors, most of whom had experienced wars in the past and for whom there was no other place to go, Harriet suddenly yearned for the relative peacefulness of the United States, where at least the apocalypse did not seem imminent. Apart from the crawling fear of war and annihilation, Harriet had other, more mundane concerns to worry about: Jay was about to go to college, Marc and Larry to high school, and Israel—lacking funds and policies—didn't offer any free education after elementary school. The military threats and monetary woes eroded five years of life in Israel, and Harriet decided to move back to the United States, to Hartford, Connecticut.

This time around, it was Mike who was most affected by the move. Already an Israeli, he was sent to summer school to relearn his English, but there seemed to be much more he needed to relearn. During recess, for example, he would join the others in playing football, a game well suited to his physique. He did not, however, know any of the rules, as the game was, and still is, largely unknown in Israel. Every time he intercepted the ball he would stand on the field, baffled, convinced that he was interrupting the normal flow of the game and that the others were about to beat him for it. How great was his confusion, then, when his teammates gleefully hugged him, congratulating him on his move.

It was not only the rules of football that were foreign to Mike, but the rules of conduct in general. The Ginsbergs moved to Hartford at a crucial time in the city's history. Like countless other American towns of the period, Hartford experienced galvanizing trends: white residents moved out to suburbs, and were replaced by blacks and Hispanics. Hartford's black population more than doubled within ten years, from 53,000 in 1950 to 107,000 in 1960. The rapid shift in population caused tensions that sometimes resulted in race riots. In July 1967, just a few months after the Ginsbergs' arrival, a black man named William Tullis was arrested for his use of "vulgar language" while ordering a hot dog at Hartford's Battle Luncheonette; race riots ensued. On September 18, 1967, just a few days after Mike started his first academic year at Rawson Junior High School, a man named John Barber, a member of the New Haven Black Caucus, led a nonviolent march into the predominantly Italian-American neighborhood of South End.

He and his fellow marchers never got there, however, as they were stopped by the police, granting the city a moment in the national spotlight, which was turned toward the civil rights movement. The worst, however, was yet to come, and Mike was unfortunate enough to experience it in the flesh.

At school, Mike attracted attention, a horrible fate in any ecosystem composed of adolescents. First of all, he was the new guy, and as such subject to scrutiny. Second of all, he was tall and square-jawed, hard to miss in a crowd. Third of all, he was Jewish, by then an anomaly at the school. Finally, he had the wrong attitude. Having spent his formative years in Israel, Mike had none of that gene of victimhood, prevalent in the American-Jewish mind-set, and was therefore unlikely to shy away from confrontation. On the contrary: in Israel he had been taught the myth of the Jewish warrior, and it was as such that he perceived himself. Therefore, when he was called by some of his classmates a "dirty Jew," he was quick to react with his fists. Once, after a band of black students broke his ruler, he beat them up, ignoring their promises for retribution. That same afternoon, as he was leaving school, a small crowd approached him, punched him to the ground, then proceeded to kick him for several long minutes.

The frequent racially motivated incidents, the ethnic slurs, the anti-Semitism, all triggered an important awakening in Mike. For the first time he was beginning to realize that being Jewish was not to be taken for granted, that being Jewish sometimes resulted in being attacked, that being Jewish had its price. Wishing to extract her son from the tension and violence, Harriet moved the family to the nearby suburb of West Hartford. That might have been enough to achieve some stability in Mike's turbulent life; but then Martin Luther King Jr. was assassinated.

On Thursday, April 4, 1968, King, the leader of the civil rights movement, was shot down by a single bullet at the Lorraine Motel in Memphis, Tennessee. As in many inner-city neighborhoods across the United States, the assassination sparked great rage among black youth in Connecticut, which led to violent riots. At

Rawson Junior High, the next morning, an unidentified man ran into the school grounds, screaming that King had been shot dead. The shout was instantly repeated, passing from mouth to mouth, each time morphed to suit the sensibilities of the shouter and damn his target of choice. While some shouted, "King was killed by the police!" others shouted, "The white people killed Martin Luther King!" A small crowd of black students gathered in the school's football field, then dispersed across campus, committing random acts of violence on their way. By the time the hoodlums reached Mike's classroom, the shout took on a different shape; this time, someone shouted that King was killed by the Jews.

Mike's teacher, well aware of what was about to happen, tried to block the door, but to no avail. Within several seconds, several raging youths found their way inside the classroom and surrounded Mike. Someone threw a chair out of the window; then, five or six bullies grabbed Mike by his arms and legs and tossed him out the second-story window, a seventeen-foot fall. The bullies were still throwing furniture out the window, including a desk and two more chairs, and Mike, badly bruised, got up and tried to remove himself from the trajectory of flying objects. As he tried to run, however, he was again circled, again jumped, again beaten. Returning home that day, Mike told Harriet that he was never going back to that school again. Harriet made an urgent phone call to the school's principal, who shrugged and said there was nothing she could do. Harriet immediately pulled Mike out of school, enrolling him instead in a nearby Orthodox yeshiva.

While freeing him from anti-Semitic slurs, the yeshiva presented Mike with an entirely different set of challenges. Every morning at the crack of dawn, a representative of the yeshiva would knock on his door to make sure he attended *Shachris,* the morning prayer. Then the school day would consist mainly of prayer and religious studies, most of which were conducted in biblical Hebrew, so different in intonation from the vibrant language Mike was accustomed to in Israel. Most of all, the yeshiva had only one permissible definition of what it meant to be Jewish: a Jew was only such when he followed the Halacha, the traditional Jewish codex of rules governing everyday life, to the letter. For Mike, however, Judaism was not prayers and dietary restrictions but combat, bravery, Israel. He translated the lessons learned at the yeshiva into his own private logic: whereas biblical stories were taught as a testament to the glory of God, Mike interpreted them solely as proof of Jewish connectedness to the land of Israel.

The yeshiva proved to be but another station on Mike's odyssey. Fed up with an education so unbefitting his sensibilities, Mike transferred to another local junior high. Unlike Haifa, where he could walk everywhere, suburbia—and West Hartford was no different—required being driven around in a car. No longer able to roam about in the streets, weary of trying to befriend new people, Mike kept to himself. Watching copious amounts of television, he was struck by the ferocity of the war in Southeast Asia. What baffled him most wasn't the war, its horrors or consequences, but the fact that so many Americans seemed to denigrate their soldiers; the memories of the 1964 Israeli military parade still fresh in his mind, Mike couldn't fathom a reality in which soldiers, even if fighting an unjust war, were held in anything but the utmost respect and admiration.

Now politicized, Mike would drag his mother and brothers into endless discussions on anything from the ascent of Students for a Democratic Society to the reign of acid rock music. Sometimes, debate would lead to action; after Robert Kennedy's assassination by Sirhan Sirhan, Mike was incensed by the assassin's claims that he had shot Kennedy because of the latter's outspoken support of Israel. Afraid that the general public would perceive Sirhan's missive as a warning to disassociate from Israel lest more assassinations follow, Mike felt the urge for public action, yet did not know how to proceed. He consulted with Harriet, who directed him to the only person who came to her mind, the local rabbi. Excited, Mike telephoned the rabbi, carefully and respectfully presenting his point. The rabbi paused for a second, and suggested that the best option was to do nothing. "We can't rock the boat," he told a frustrated Mike. "Leave it alone. It will pass."

The incident strengthened a growing realization triggered by Mike's analysis of the political events around him. Israel and American Jews, he now thought, had two different platforms; while the rabbi's passivity may have been wise from an American-Jewish perspective, inaction was certainly not the desired course from an Israeli point of view. The United States and Israel appeared to be two different planets, and Mike had no doubt in which one he belonged.

It would take a blue-eyed Israeli paratrooper, however, to motivate Mike to move back there.

CHAPTER SIX

The most memorable thing about the Israeli paratrooper is that no one who came into contact with him remembers his name. The outlines of his story are broad: the paratrooper, young and virile, fought in the Golan Heights in the Six-Day War and was sent, late in 1967, to serve as an instructor in the Jewish Community Center in Hartford, Connecticut. Those who met him then and there all remember his sandy blond hair and blue eyes. The consensus ends there: some recall a tall, strapping figure, while others swear he was a stout, bulky man. Some remember the strong, silent type, while others tell of a loud, cocky, macho man, teeming with quintessentially Israeli bravado. Some recall the yarmulke on his head, others his penchant for cheeseburgers. No one, however, remembers his name.

Neither has anyone forgotten him: the anonymous Israeli soldier was, in the words of one of the JCC's members circa 1968, a "New Jew." He was the manifestation of the generation of Israelis who had just emerged triumphant from a gloriously short war that transformed the first Jewish state in two millennia from a perpetually threatened and besieged country surrounded by malicious neighbors to a secure nation capable of defending itself. The effect of the war on the American-Jewish community was immense; it has become almost clichéd to speak of the sudden sense of pride, of peoplehood, of potential. All these feelings are expressed in a letter a young Jewish woman wrote to the *Village Voice* immediately after the war, on June 15, 1967:

> *Two weeks ago, Israel was they; now Israel is we. I will never again be able to talk about how Judaism is only a religion, and isn't it too bad that there has to be such a thing as a Jewish state. . . . I was walking along the street listening to a transistor radio when I first heard that the Israelis, the Jews, had reached the Wailing Wall and with guns slung over their shoulders were praying there. No one was watching me, but I wept anyway. Sometimes even the tear glands know more than the mind.*

The blond paratrooper was a masterful masseur of American-Jewish tear glands. His stories fell right into that ephemeral realm of "We," into that emotional range that made Jews in Hartford feel as if they, too, were sinking their feet in the muddy soil of the Golan. Those who can't remember his name never forgot his stories. They remember his tales of how the Syrian officers chained grunts to outposts and fences to prevent them from running away. Or how the tanks would drive down the narrow roads, their rusting chains tearing the asphalt like the lashing of a whip tears the human flesh. Or of the Syrians surrendering, and what death smelled like, and how it felt to be back home.

For Mike, the Israeli paratrooper was an angel with dirty boots. Each one of his stories registered with Mike as a secret text which, once decoded, carried one simple message: Go back to Israel. Part father figure, part big brother, part throwback to that unforgettable military parade in Haifa in 1964, the paratrooper was a perfect antidote to Mike's malaise. He was so decidedly not suburban, so unlike the boys at the yeshiva, so different from Mike's own college-bound brothers. Instantaneously, Mike's mind was made up.

From that moment on, Mike became monomaniacal. With adolescent energy and dogged persistence, he made it known to everyone around him that he wanted to make aliya. He called the Jewish Agency in New York City. He frequented the JCC. He questioned anyone whom he thought might be of any assistance. Finally, not long after he started his crusade, he received a phone call. The man on the other end of the line presented himself as an aliya official working for the Jewish Agency. He asked Mike a couple of questions, and Mike, his voice shaking with excitement, did his best to answer eloquently. The man then invited him to a meeting in Manhattan early on Sunday morning. Mike, ecstatic, promised that he would come.

Feeling as if he were almost in Israel, Mike still had one major barrier to cross: his mother, Harriet, strongly objected to her son's newfound hope of emigration. She wanted him to follow his brothers and get a college education, not follow some unknown Israeli paratrooper into battle. She also thought her son's timing couldn't have been more unfortunate: Mike had just transferred from the yeshiva to a public junior high school, and was finally showing signs of adjusting to an educational environment. Fearing that his dream would implode, Mike mounted a feverish campaign to gain his mother's approval. He begged. He reasoned. He displayed every emotion on the scale, sometimes within alarming proximity to one another. Finally, Harriet could no longer resist; while still not enthusiastic about the idea of her son moving to Israel, she instructed Mike's brother Marc to drive him to Manhattan the following Sunday morning to meet the aliya official. She wasn't, she said, promising anything; but the meeting could be a trial balloon.

That Sunday, Mike and Marc left for Manhattan. They arrived at the Fifth Avenue address the man had given Mike several minutes before the ten o'clock appointment. Mike tried the door; it was locked. The brothers circled the block again; Mike tried the door once more. Still, no one was there. "Let me off," Mike said. "Leave me here. I'll wait." The older brother refused, and several rides around the block later, the two left the city and headed back home.

Mike felt angry. Betrayed. Foolish. Even worse, he felt lost. He wanted to make aliya, join the army, become Israeli. Yet, no one seemed to take him seriously. A few days after his futile trip to the city, Mike started a new school year.

I suggest, the principal told him shortly after the year started, that you try and adjust, settle in, calm down.

"I," Mike replied, "am moving to Israel before the year ends."

Angrier, more desperate, he tried to find someone to talk to. All the Jewish Agency officials he would call heard his prepubescent voice on the other end of the line and assumed the caller was just a kid fooling around. Call again when you're eighteen, they often told him. The few Israelis he met at the JCC proved to be of little help; more often than not, they would placate him with empty promises and then fail to return his calls. The one last alternative he had was Aliyat Ha'Noar, Hebrew for Youth Immigration, a project established in 1934 by Zionist leader and Hadassah founder Henrietta Szold. Still, Mike was skeptical; in his mind, Aliyat Ha'Noar was there to rescue Jewish youth from places like Nazi Germany or Iraq, places where one's demise was certain if one did not immigrate to Israel immediately. West Hartford, Connecticut, despite the occasional ethnic slur, was hardly such a place. Out of options and out of patience, Mike gave it a try.

Despite his initial doubts, several weeks and dozens of forms later Aliyat Ha'Noar arranged for Mike to move to Israel. His enthusiasm now fortified by official encouragement from the Israeli establishment, Mike was indefatigable. He began packing, first placing his collection of LPs in two brown cardboard boxes, and then tossing some less important items, such as clothes and shoes, in a small suitcase. He said his good-byes swiftly and was ready for departure several months later, in October.

Watching her son collapse the American chapter of his life into carry-on luggage, Harriet had to face a decision of her own. Of her four sons, she knew that two—Jay and Marc—would remain in the United States. Both were already in college, and both showed no signs of missing their melancholy youth in underdeveloped Haifa. Another son, Larry, was ambivalent about the future. And the youngest one, Mike, was determined to make his life in Israel. Staying in Connecticut, she was bound to be alone, with her sons either in college or several thousand miles away in Israel. If she moved to Israel, however, she would at least be near Mike, and maybe Larry as well. The choice seemed unavoidable.

And so on Wednesday, October 22, 1969, not one Ginsberg boarded the airplane to Israel but three—four counting Sir, the family's dog, a white mutt with a black spot which looked like a monocle around one eye, giving the dog his imperious name. Before boarding the plane, however, the Ginsbergs needed one last supper of Chinese food, the one type of food that was absolutely impossible to get in Israel at the time. With their luggage in tow, they asked the cabdriver to let them off in the vicinity of the Port Authority Bus Terminal in Manhattan, from which they would later take a bus to the airport. Hurrying through the narrow alleys of the Hell's Kitchen neighborhood, awash with rain and dust and omnipresent unctuousness slithering from every street, the family looked for a Chinese restaurant. Coming across a policeman, Mike asked for directions to the nearest place. The policeman pointed toward an alley across the street, even darker and more ominous than the rest. Wet, reluctant, but hungry, the Ginsbergs followed the officer's directions, with Harriet mumbling to Mike that they were bound to be assaulted at any minute. After several hesitant steps, the family faced a redbrick building at the dead end of the alley. With no other entrance into the building in sight, Mike tried the fire escape. Slowly he climbed up, followed by his family, until he reached a door. And opened it. And saw waterfalls and bamboo shoots and smiling Chinese waiters inviting him in.

The Ginsbergs gorged themselves with delights, savoring the taste, storing it for all the long years of pita bread and hummus lying ahead. Mike nibbled on crispy jumbo shrimp, the best he ever had in his life. By the time the check arrived, the Ginsbergs were officially ready to leave it all behind.

The flight itself was mostly uneventful. Unlike his first exodus, the Boeing 707 was no ship, had no decks to explore, and offered nothing to do but sit and wait for landing. Eleven hours later, Mike peeked out the window. In the distance, he saw the twinkling orange lights of the Tel Aviv coast. To himself he muttered, "I'm here."

The Ginsbergs were greeted at the airport by friends of Harriet, a young American-born woman who had been Harriet's protégée in Haifa and her husband, an Australian-born veterinarian who had recently made aliya. The couple lived in the southern town of Be'er Sheva, and suggested that the Ginsbergs might benefit from a short stay in the dry desert climate before they continued on their way. Larry, who had already enrolled in the Hebrew University in Jerusalem, declined, but Harriet and Mike found themselves in a battered blue Willis pickup truck en route to the Negev Desert. Mike sat in the truck's bed; soon, the chattering voices of his mother and her friends dissipated, and his mind was consumed by the vast, uninhabited spaces of the desert, by the dusty one-lane roads, the golden dunes that turned aquamarine in the nighttime, the thin, crisp air, the occasional howl of a jackal or a fox, the twitching lights of Bedouin encampments, the fierce glare of an army base's searchlight. The Negev, spreading over half of Israel's territory, was home to less than 8 percent of the country's population. Even compared to the underpopulated Haifa, the Negev seemed like a vast den of nothingness, the perfect setting for a rebellious teenager seeking reinvention.

Despite enjoying his stay in Be'er Sheva, Mike was anxious to get to Jerusalem. It was there that the Aliyat Ha'Noar offices were located, and Mike had done enough research to draft a plan of action: he would walk in, have a few interviews, and then ask to be assigned to Hadasim, a famous liberal boarding school in the center of Israel. The legend of Hadasim was contagious; the institution boasted a healthy mix of delinquent dropouts who couldn't make it in urban high schools and elitist idealists who chose its rustic setting as a preparation for a lifetime of serving the country as farmers or soldiers. The school was the alma mater of several of Israel's leading musicians, as well as businessmen and decorated officers. In short, it was a microcosm of all the good qualities Israel circa 1969 had to offer.

Three days into his stay in Be'er Sheva, Mike ran out of patience. He convinced his host to drive him to Jerusalem, and the two, together with a friend, hopped into the Willis, with Mike resettling into his seat in the back. Instead of retracing the same route they had taken from the airport, the two men took Mike on a scenic tour, driving through the newly conquered West Bank. Just outside of Hebron, one of the men up front reached into his bag and pulled out an Uzi submachine gun. Mike shrank in his seat; it was one thing to see guns in a parade or on television, but seeing his acquaintance casually fiddle with his Uzi made Mike shiver even more than the mild winter wind merited. Guns, he thought. Only bad guys just draw out their guns. Or maybe we are headed for a dangerous place?

Keeping his thoughts to himself, Mike held tight to the railing until the truck reached Jerusalem, then said an abrupt good-bye and jumped off. Walking around Jerusalem on his way to the Aliyat Ha'Noar's offices, Mike was struck, for the second time that day, with a sense of unease. The gun-toting driver was not the Israel he had expected to encounter, but neither was Jerusalem: seeing the fervently Orthodox men walk around in their traditional black garb reminded Mike of his yeshiva days, and of Hartford, and of the stereotypical Jew he was trying to leave behind. Was there anything, he wondered, between waving a weapon and wearing a black hat?

Needing to regain his bearing on reality, Mike bought a newspaper. The vendor was fresh out of *Ma'ariv* or *Yediot Aharonot,* the country's two competing and rambunctious tabloids, so Mike bought *Ha'aretz,* the Israeli equivalent of the *New York Times,* large, cerebral, and sometimes verbose. And so, with his ponytail tousled by Jerusalem's penetrating wind and the large sheet of newspaper folded under his arm, the burly Mike walked into the office to meet the man who would decide his future for the next several years.

The man, Aliyat Ha'Noar's program director, looked at the oafish youth coming through the doorway, tall, long-haired, and holding an improbable newspaper for a newly arrived immigrant to read. The man tried to convince Mike to consider Jerusalem as an option; Mike refused and said that he was set on Hadasim. Jerusalem, he said, was for the Orthodox, and he needed to go somewhere that was, quite simply, cool. The man promised to arrange an interview at Hadasim, and shortly thereafter informed Mike that an interview was set.

"One thing," the program director said. "Cut your hair."

Cut your hair? Mike was livid. Wasn't Israel supposed to be a haven of personal freedoms, inspired by the free spirit of the kibbutz movement, removed from the stark stigmas of the United States, where every long-haired man was a hippie? Once again that day, Mike was confronted by aspects of Israeli life he hadn't expected. All that, however, was diminished by the bottom line: he had an interview at Hadasim. Hair or no hair, he was going to make an impression.

Walking into Hadasim a few days later, Mike was relieved. All around him on the green lawns were young men who let their hair grow long. Dressed in his best outfit, black cotton pants and a white button-down shirt, Mike sat in a small grove, took in the bucolic beauty surrounding him, and waited to be called upon. Even an inconsiderate pigeon doing its business on his head could not spoil Mike's enthusiasm. He walked into the principal's office, politely answered a few questions, and returned to Be'er Sheva, to stay with Harriet and her friends until the positive response from Hadasim arrived. Three days later, no response had yet arrived. Mike returned to Jerusalem and marched into the office of Aliyat Ha'Noar's program director.

"Weren't you told?" the director asked Mike. "They rejected you."

Mike remained silent.

"They rejected you because of your long hair," the director said.

"But"—Mike was furious—"everybody else there had long hair as well."

"Yes," the director replied, unknowingly uttering the great truth about the immigrant's difficulty in breaking the tightly knit circle of Sabras, or native Israelis. "But everybody else there was already accepted."

The best option, the director told the melancholy Mike, was Havat Ha'Noar, Hebrew for Youth Farm, a boarding school in Jerusalem. Again, Mike conjured images of Orthodox Jews walking around in the streets of the holy city with their black garb and sidelocks. He had come to be a hero, a soldier—a paratrooper, to be exact—and now they were sending him back into the shtetl. In his mind, he had a mocking image of Havat Ha'Noar as a place where the Orthodox loomed, jumping out of their hideouts and forcing the unsuspecting Mike to lay tefillin. Sensing Mike's resistance, the director suggested that maybe, if only he could see the place, he would take a liking to it. Lacking other options, Mike agreed.

Founded in 1949 to accommodate several dozen young Holocaust survivors, Havat Ha'Noar had grown to become one of the primary institutions offering room, board, and education to Jewish youth who had immigrated to Israel without their families. The facilities hadn't changed much since the 1950s: the main hall was a long, narrow one-story building, built entirely out of Jerusalem stone, in the neighborhood of Katamon, then a hilly nowhere surrounded by open fields, olive trees, and oleander, with the nearest sign of urban life being a bus stop a third of a mile away. The building itself was surrounded by cedar trees, creating the atmosphere of a little Swiss town transported to warm weather and allowed to collect soot and dust for a few millennia.

Mike was scheduled to meet the principal. Wary of his experience in Hadasim, and still ambivalent about Jerusalem, he walked into the principal's office hesitatingly. There stood a large man, his red curls unkempt, a fiery goatee on his chin, and a ragged sweater hanging just above his enormous potbelly. As Mike entered the room, the man was unceremoniously scratching his behind. Mike was infatuated: this, finally, seemed like the real thing, the kind of uninhibitd Israeli he hoped to become himself one day. The two shook hands, and Mike enrolled at Havat Ha'Noar.

At the time of Mike's arrival, the school had approximately fifty students, originating from almost as many countries. Some, like Mimi from Morocco, were scions of generations of immigrants, carrying with them layer upon layer of cultures and languages. Mike's roommates were the redheaded Avraham Naji, who had emigrated alone from Iran; Yossi, who came from Lebanon; Israeli-born David Pe'er; and, the leader of the pack, Al Goldstein from Korea. Next door lived Yigal from Peru and his friend from Mexico, and at the other end of the corridor were Mimi and Odette from Morocco, who between the two of them spoke seven different languages. The urgency of absorbing Holocaust survivors and Jewish refugees from Arab countries having abated, Havat Ha'Noar was then ready to welcome a new species of youth, individuals who came from across the globe, some by force and some by choice, some eager to blend in and others still holding on to their roots. As is often the case, the eclectic nature of the group was soon overpowered by a sense of necessity, transformed into camaraderie, and finally forged into friendship; the young immigrants, most of them alone in Israel or with families facing rough acclimation processes, clung together, a live and rare manifestation of the melting-pot theory which had guided Israel's immigration policy for decades and which claimed that all immigrants from all cultures should just be thrown into the steaming cauldron of Israeliness, rub a little of their own culture off on the rest, and emerge cleansed, uniform, and with a shiny new identity. The group's melting pot blended socialism with Al Goldstein's demonstrations of aikido and karate.

Some differences, however, were harder to bridge. Meandering through school on one of his first days, Mike noticed a young lady trying to climb onto a window's ledge. Eager to appear gentlemanly, Mike rushed over to help her, gently putting his hand on the girl's shoulder. As soon as his hand touched her shirt, the girl turned around and smacked Mike in the face, screaming at him, "Don't touch me, I'm not your whore!"

Most puzzling, however, were the challenges posed by the school itself. Being a part of a larger bureaucratic mechanism of immigration and absorption, most of the equipment on the premises in Havat Ha'Noar was standard issue, and came directly from a central supply center. Entering his room on the first night, Mike found a bed, a simple metal frame with angular legs and a crisscross of serpentine springs; the bed has since entered the Israeli lexicon, dubbed "Agency bed," because it was issued by the Jewish Agency, the term serving as shorthand for uncomfortable furniture in general. Mike could perhaps have overlooked the comfort, or lack thereof, but the length was a different problem: all Agency beds were five feet long, and Mike was slightly over six feet tall. The makers of the bed had not taken into consideration that someone might not fit their configuration, so Mike was left sleeping with his feet suspended in midair. Only after the principal intervened was he allotted a chair, which served as an improvised extension of his standard-sized bed. To equally distribute the pain between head and feet, Mike alternated, laying his head on the chair one night and his feet the other.

The bed was just an introduction into a weird new world. Waking up sore each morning, Mike would face an even bigger hurdle: breakfast. Coming from the American tradition of pancakes, pastries, and cereal, Mike's intestines were assaulted by the Israeli concept of breakfast, which usually included much cheese, a thinly cut salad spiced with black pepper and dressed in viscous olive oil, often hard-boiled eggs, mashed and mixed with cottage cheese, and almost always chocolate milk. For a few months, Mike often ran from the dining hall to the doctor's office, his stomach in tatters from the onslaught of dairy early in the day.

The rest of the schedule, while anathema to some of Mike's peers, was titillating, as it was greatly inspired by army lore: wakeup call at 6:30 a.m., plenty of exercise, and, the highlight of the week, military-style training once every few days, courtesy of Gadna. The organization, the Hebrew acronym for Youth Battalions, was formed to train and prepare teenagers for the looming army service, a sort of military preschool for youth. More than actually teaching its trainees anything of real military value, the organization's expertise lay in instilling the spirit required to convince teens to forsake whatever notion of mortality they might have and proudly volunteer for the army's elite, most dangerous units. The actual physical preparation the organization provided was scant, and revolved mostly around athletics, running in particular. To provide the military air, Gadna provided training in *sada'ut,* Hebrew for proficiency in the field. Trainees were taken to a remote field, where they were taught how to build tents using nothing but a sheet, some twine, and two large rocks, ate kosher combat rations, and learned a little about camouflage, and then returned to their school. The main attraction, however, was the weapons instruction, taught using an antiquated carbine rifle, the last of which was produced in 1945 for the U.S. Army. Even though the rifle was, as many joked, more useful as a club than as a firearm, the feeling of holding a weapon was still plenty to make Mike infatuated with the gun, Gadna, and the Gadna instructor's uniform.

But whereas the make-believe army routine made him shine, the rest of Havat Ha'Noar's curriculum, especially the academic part, made him shiver. He owned but two notebooks, both of which he used for every subject, from math to biology. What mattered now, he realized, was not education, but fun. Unlike suburban Connecticut, where each kid was ensconced in his or her own house, dependent on parents for transportation, watched over by adults, fearful of urban unrest and race riots and violence, Havat Ha'Noar was an amalgam of loose supervision, free spirit, and choice circumstances: fifty young men and women, living in one house, outnumbering their teachers and counselors, isolated in a leafy valley surrounded by hills. Furthermore, Mike's friend Yigal had inherited an apartment in Jerusalem, not even a mile's distance from the school, where the eight o'clock curfew could be conveniently avoided. But the most important factor making Mike's experience optimal was the fact that the times were a-changing.

Just as he had missed the bliss of Brooklyn in the fifties only to experience a similar sensation a decade later in Haifa, so he had missed the sixties in the United States only to relive them in Jerusalem. The sixties took a while to travel across the ocean, but in 1969 they were finally arriving in Israel, albeit filtered through local sensibilities and tolerance. The soldiers of the Six-Day War, heroic and triumphant liberators of Jerusalem as they were perceived to be, had completed their army service. Israel, having defeated three Arab armies in such a short period of time, was collectively euphoric. After being besieged for so many years, the country now opened up in all directions. One obvious direction was the east, and many traveled to the now Israeli-controlled West Bank not only to buy cheap tobacco and fruit but also to learn of life on the planet that had always existed less than a mile away, but was now opening up for the first time. Gradually, the customs and clothes of the West Bank Palestinians became the bon ton, and young Israelis, just a year or two after shedding their uniforms, wrapped kaffiyehs around their necks as scarves, donned *sharawals,* the loose, baggy pants sometimes favored by Arab men, and spent a growing amount of time in east Jerusalem's tea or smoke shops.

But with the siege mentality exploded by the impact of military victory, young Israelis also began looking to the west. One reason, undoubtedly, was the influx of American Jews coming after the war, nearly three thousand people a year for the three years between 1967 and 1970, approximately twice the usual average, most of them young, single, and intoxicated with the victorious Jewish state. Young Israelis often reciprocated by clamoring for the cultural tokens the Americans brought with them, such as rock 'n' roll music, drug culture, promiscuity, and other instant values of the sixties. Having lived all their lives preparing for the next war, young Israelis now felt free from the burden of reality. Suddenly, the folk songs they'd grown up on—mostly inspired by old Russian tunes that were given Hebrew words praising bravery, collective life, or the beauty of the land—seemed grotesquely inappropriate for the new reality, and the "yeah yeah yeah" of the Beatles played like an anthem of liberation. Helping to further liberate the minds were ample amounts of hashish, mostly flowing in from Lebanon, sold at the time in east Jerusalem smoke shops for three to five liras, a few dollars in today's terms, and smoked in pastel-colored ceramic narghile pipes.

The epicenter of this cross-cultural fusion was Jerusalem, where native Israelis, wide-eyed Americans, and "newly liberated" Arabs all adopted each other's cultures, pastimes, and elixirs. And one key place for such blending was the Yellow Tea House. Located in a tiny cellar on Jerusalem's King George Street, just off city center, the coffee shop got its name from the bright, glaring yellow paint on its walls. Often crowded, the coffee shop was a marriage between a nineteenth-century European café, a traditional teahouse, and a hippie commune, and as such managed to attract a variety of people, including Mike, who frequented the place in 1970. The unfiltered cellar air was suffused with scents, saturated with swirls of smoke emanating from cheap cigarettes manufactured in the West Bank and sold piecemeal, together with the sweet smell of the occasional joint, freely lit, and drenched in strong undertones of steaming mint tea, served in small, simple glasses. It was the place where Jerusalem's drug dealers both started and ended each day. The manager of the place was Avi Bardugo, a young Israeli of Moroccan descent, who was mostly accompanied by his friends Sa'adia Marchiano and Charlie Biton, who, like Bardugo, hailed from the poorer neighborhoods of Jerusalem and felt oppressed by the Israeli elite, consisting mostly of Ashkenazi Jews of European descent.

Over tea and smokes, Marchiano and Biton struck up conversations with the Americans. Most boisterous among the latter was Steve, a tall young man with long frizzy hair who came from Borough Park, Brooklyn. He would walk around Jerusalem wearing a sheepskin jacket, and, with his quizzical phrases and hip talk, was the closest thing the city had to a Bob Dylan or an Abbie Hoffman. Steve and his friends listened for hours as Marchiano and Biton told them of the discrimination they felt was their fate as Moroccan Jews. The Ashkenazim, they said, were treating them as second-class citizens, relegating them to dead-end jobs and dooming them to live forever in the decrepit slums in which they were originally housed when they immigrated to Israel in the 1950s. Israel's politicians were mostly Ashkenazi Jews, as were the country's generals, artists, and businesspeople. This, Marchiano and Biton said, was outrageous. Commiserating with their newfound acquaintances, Steve and his friends replied that similar conditions existed in the United States. There, they said, black Americans, oppressed for years by racism and discrimination, were acting up against the white man, most militantly in a movement called the Black Panthers. They told the Israelis about Students for a Democratic Society, and about Hoffman's Yippie movement, with its antics and street theatrics. Fascinated, Mike listened to the stories. For him, both worlds were foreign; he was not old enough to fully grasp the social turmoil in the United States at the time, and not enough of a veteran Israeli to have been exposed to Marchiano and Biton's world.

The Yellow Tea House has its own minor place in Israel's history; it was there that Marchiano, Biton, and several others, inspired by the stories Steve and his American friends told them, stated a social movement to right what they believed were the Ashkenazi elite's wrongs. They called the movement the Black

Panthers. For three years, between 1970 and 1973, the Panthers held mass demonstrations, demanding racial and social equality, often violently confronting the police. They internalized many of the stories they imbibed along with tea at the Yellow Tea House. One of their best-known protests, for example, seems right out of the Abbie Hoffman–Jerry Rubin playbook: In March of 1972, the Panthers awoke at the break of dawn and stole all of the milk intended for the residents of Rehavia, Jerusalem's wealthiest neighborhood. Shortly thereafter, they distributed the bottles in the poor suburb of Kiryat Yovel. Taped to each bottle was a short note saying that poor children needed milk more than rich people's cats. Although their protest died down, curtailed by the Yom Kippur War of 1973, lack of a coherent ideology, and rifts within the movement itself, it was, nonetheless, the first of its kind, the first time social and racial issues were brought to the forefront in the security-obsessed Israel, the first time citizens challenged the Israeli establishment's right to govern. The Panthers' impact reverberated for years to come; they helped raise awareness of racial tensions in a society that had previously perceived itself as homogeneous, and began an era of increased sensitivity. Even more than their American counterparts, many of the Israeli Panthers went on to become respected politicians, artists, or businessmen.

But Mike's Jerusalem was still far away from the bohemian tea shop or the tumultuous race riots. Spending most of their time in Yigal's apartment, Mike and his friends concocted their own version of the sixties. Using watercolors or cellophane paper, they colored the lightbulbs red or blue. In a smoke shop in east Jerusalem they would buy, piecemeal, cheap, locally made cigarettes with regal names such as Ascot or Royal, then place them in a big bowl in the middle of the room. To feel a bit more rebellious, they would often coat their cigarettes with Vicks, inhale the fumes, and pretend to get high. Tea or Mitz Petel, a sweet, syrupy raspberry-flavored drink, replaced alcohol. Mike played the LPs he had carried from home, and the boys would slouch on the couch under the tinted lights, listening to Steve Winwood and

Traffic plead "Dear Mr. Fantasy, play us a tune, something to make us all happy," or to "Green Tambourine" by the Lemon Pipers, or to any other psychedelic rock track that lasted too long and made Hapalmach Street in Jerusalem seem a little more like Haight-Ashbury in San Francisco. Often, some of their female classmates joined Mike and his friends in partying; the sexual revolution among Havat Ha'Noar's youth, however, was as close to the real thing as the Vicks-coated cigarettes were to marijuana. Still, the apartment served as a small-scale den of iniquity, and the boys reveled in having a base of operations. One time, they smuggled the entire class, all fifty students, away from Havat Ha'Noar after curfew, into Yigal's apartment for a party. Tuvia, the school's counselor, went up for a chance routine check a short while later. Knocking on doors, he found nothing but eerie silence. Luckily for him, the reputation Mike and his friends had built for themselves was enough to guide him to the apartment, only to find fifty ninth graders fleeing in panic at his sight; the spirit of the sixties died down as soon as the counselor knocked on the door.

It was this kind of behavior, twinned with poor attendance in class and poorer success in tests, that eventually got Mike kicked out of school. Less than a year after finding a home, a group of friends, and very possibly himself, Mike was requested to leave Havat Ha'Noar. With his mother now living in Jerusalem, Mike moved into Harriet's small apartment in Kiryat Yovel. He enrolled at Ort Haneviyim, a technical-oriented school not far from the ultra-Orthodox neighborhood of Mea Sha'arim. There he was told that because of his poor performance, he had to begin the ninth grade for the third time, after having gone through it in Connecticut and at Havat Ha'Noar. Mike had no choice. Thinking himself a worldly man, a guy who could curse in several different languages, he balked at the thought of hanging out with boys two years younger than he; as most of his Havat Ha'Noar friends suffered a fate similar to his, some being shipped back to families abroad, Mike was again alone and confused. He passed his days sitting in the apartment and playing poker against himself, using matches instead of money and reveling in every clever move he would make, or going out to pick oranges in a nearby grove. On his rare appearances in school, he would talk back to teachers and talk down to classmates, building a reputation as a crazy Anglo-Saxon bully who feared no one. Soon he dropped out of school altogether, completing his high school requirements in a night school of sorts designed for misfits like himself, and working in road construction for meager pay.

When the time came to take his matriculation exams, required for a high school diploma, Mike decided not to go. The year was 1972, he was seventeen years old, and he didn't want to waste any more time. He wanted to become a soldier.

CHAPTER SEVEN

Despite his enthusiasm, the mechanisms of the Israel Defense Forces were a mystery to Mike. He knew, still bearing in mind the soldier he had met at the JCC in Hartford, that he wanted to become a paratrooper. But the paratroopers, or *tzanchanim*, as they are called in Hebrew, were something of an elite unit of the army, open, at that point, mostly to what Israelis would call, with no irony, the salt of the earth, Israel's finest, be they idealistic members of kibbutzim or dedicated urbanites who hailed from prominent families. The paratroopers were the ones who, five years prior, had liberated the Western Wall, making the picture of the three gruff men, with their red berets and maroon-tinted combat boots, standing next to Judaism's holiest place and weeping, an instant icon. Mostly unaware of the hierarchical nature of the army or of the unspoken requirements necessary to secure a place at the top of the pyramid, Mike clamored to wear the coveted wing-shaped pin on his chest, indicating that a soldier had gone through parachute training, the sole privilege of *tzanhanim*.

Yet, with few connections and little time to go before his pending recruitment, Mike was lost. His main support came from Avi, a friend from Havat Ha'Noar, who, like Mike, was anxious to don a uniform as soon as possible. Avi, however, fantasized about the heavy machinery of the armored divisions, dreaming about becoming a tank commander. With teenage bravado, innocent and ignorant, Mike would tease his friend, mockingly telling him that the paratroopers did all the real work while the armor guys just sat in their tanks; Avi replied that while paratroopers had to walk everywhere, armor guys drove around in cool, massive vehicles that boasted awesome firepower. Both wanted to become warriors; neither knew what war really meant. As they had but each other to count on for support, however, a compromise was made: they would join the Nahal.

A Hebrew acronym for Pioneer Fighting Youth, the Nahal was established by Israel's first prime minister, David Ben-Gurion, in 1948, in order to address the period's two most pressing problems, security and settlement. The Nahal thereby became a hybrid of sorts between youth movement, combat unit, and construction crew, with inductees alternating between military service and long periods spent working the land in kibbutzim. The unit's symbol, a sword crossed with a plowshare, was an homage of sorts to the Soviet crossed hammer and sickle, a fact which was not lost on many young, socialist Israelis who flocked to the unit because of its emphasis on communal living; many more young Israelis, however, flocked to the unit because it allowed one the opportunity of lacing one's army service with lengthy periods spent in lush surroundings together with female fellow Nahal soldiers. But, most important to Mike, Nahal soldiers got to wear the maroon-tinted boots, just like the paratroopers, and not the common, dreary, dusty black the rest of the army wore.

Armed with that knowledge, Avi convinced Mike that the Nahal was some variation on the *tzanchanim,* refuting all of Mike's doubts with the unquestionable proof provided by the color of their boots. Finally, Mike consented. The Nahal was good enough.

As a first step toward joining the Nahal, Mike and Avi had to become members of a youth movement. Part of the Nahal's complex split personality, as both a branch of the army and a civilian enterprise, involved a premilitary preparation period, usually carried out under the auspices of a youth movement, in which all those wishing to lead double lives as soldiers and settlers would meet, form a cohesive group, and experience all facets of their military service together. So adamant were the Nahal's creators about the idea of group unity that they called these groups *garinim,* Hebrew for nuclei.

The nucleus Mike and Avi joined was operated by a youth movement called Machanot Ha'Olim, literally meaning the camps of the immigrants, a more than accommodating title for Mike. Mike deduced from his experience that the movement must be something similar to the scouts or to the quasi-militaristic training of Gadna he had so enjoyed at Havat Ha'Noar. Looking forward to clutching a carbine rifle once again, he enthusiastically followed Avi to meet some friends he knew at the Bet Hinuch high school in Jerusalem who were members of Machanot Ha'Olim.

It took one afternoon for Mike to discover the youth movement was all talk: talk of socialism, talk of Zionism, talk of bearded men whose names sounded as foreign to Mike as did the movement's insistence that all members share all personal property with one another. Dumbfounded, Mike would look on as some of his colleagues made passionate speeches about the utmost importance of communality, urging their peers to contribute whatever they could for the common good; often, these speeches turned into ironic spectacles as a searing socialist, sweating with zeal, would finish a plea for sharing, just to observe that he himself had just received a package from home, bursting with candy or delicacies, and then, as an afterthought, conclude by saying that the sharing he had just advocated applied only to the next package, not his.

Despite the strong emphasis on equality, the movement's dynamic had an alienating effect on Mike, who, lacking a common past to share with his newfound friends, winced at their insistence on making him an equal. In a way, all of the institutions to which he had belonged during his three years as an Israeli accepted his foreignness as their focal point: at Havat Ha'Noar he was foreign, and therefore had to be taught the ways of the land, while at Ort Haneviyim he was foreign and therefore had to be avoided altogether. While both institutions, clearly, were not successful in completing Mike's transition into a bona fide Israeli, they provided him with a safety net of sorts, a voice whispering that it was all right, he was still different from the others, still allowed to make mistakes and fail to laugh at some references and get upset over customs that made no sense to him, as he was, after all, an outsider. In Machanot Ha'Olim, however, Mike's outsider status was lost in the quicksand of fraternity, dulled by the blind ideological insistence that all men are alike, even if one was born and raised in Israel and the other grew up in Brooklyn, watching television and frequenting the candy store. Often, Mike would sit silently as debates swirled around him.

Nevertheless, he was attracted to the socialist ideal for several reasons. First of all, for someone who had the opportunity to experience just a little of the counterculture turmoil before leaving the United States, any talk of a brotherhood of men fit right into the ideological matrix. But, and more important, socialism made sense because capitalism didn't; Mike was never one to pursue possessions, always more interested in doing than buying, poor and unfazed by it. His general agreement with the movement's social ideology, despite thinking it somewhat naive, helped Mike overcome his sense of uprootedness, assuaged his frustration every time the name of a socialist thinker was mentioned to the group's collective nod and to Mike's utter befuddlement. Slowly, he simplified matters in his mind: overall, he liked the group because it allowed him entry into the Israeli army and a pair of maroon boots, provided him with a sense of purpose, and welcomed him, for the first time since Havat Ha'Noar, into a circle of friends.

It was these social, rather than socialist, qualities that Mike craved. After every heated discussion about communality or kibbutz life, he would join the others to eat at Hassan's; Hassan, an elderly Palestinian, ran a hole-in-the-wall establishment near the Nablus Gate, one of the gates separating Jerusalem's Old City from its more modern quarters. Hassan's pride was his pizza, then an uncommon culinary occurrence in Israel, which he subjected to his own, eastern sensibilities: taking a flat pita bread, Hassan would fold its edges slightly to give it a somewhat octagonal shape. Then he would brush the bread with raw egg and garnish it with chunks of soft cheese and hard salami. Then he would put the whole thing in a *tabun,* a round-shaped brick oven which is a staple of Arab cooking. The result—steamy, sticky, and delicious—tasted nothing like American pizza, but instead conveyed a sense of gastronomic liberation, as it was not kosher, baked by an Arab, and served in a cavernous locale amid swarming alleyways in a part of Jerusalem that more resembled Tangiers.

Several months and many pizzas later, the time came for Mike, Avi, and their friends to join the army. The plan for their nucleus was to spend the first five months of their service on a kibbutz in northern Israel called Misgav Am. In August of 1972, not long after his seventeenth birthday, Mike and his friends boarded a bus headed north.

They had all been in Misgav Am before, spending one weekend every month on the kibbutz, working in the fields and sleeping in bomb shelters, the only location which could accommodate them at the time. But this ride was different, much like boarding a plane with a one-way ticket. Mike's nucleus, numbering slightly fewer than a hundred hormonal youths, got on a tattered bus one muggy morning. Soon they left Jerusalem's hilly surrounds for the plush greenery of the Jordan Valley, finally entering the Galilee, cool and leafy.

Even in the isolated, remote confines of the upper Galilee, Misgav Am stands apart, being in the northwesternmost corner of Israel. To arrive at the kibbutz, one must first traverse a chain of towns, slowly abandoning the safety of inhabited places as the houses, the lights, the storefronts one passes along the way grow scarcer and farther apart. The last such bastion of civilization is

Kiryat Shmona, an edgy little town arranged along a spine which is the main road that crosses it. The town's reputation as a habitual target for Lebanese terrorists firing Katyusha rockets has endowed it with a certain lore, as it has become, in the minds of most Israelis, the frontier where hostilities never cease. To get to Misgav Am, however, one passes Kiryat Shmona and continues even farther north. Several kilometers down the road is Tel Hai, where Jewish defenders led by Yosef Trumpeldor fought Arab militiamen to the death in 1920. Trumpeldor, a mythical figure in Israeli history, a one-armed warrior, was beatified for his alleged famous last words; as legend has it, the dying man cleared his bloody throat, looked up at his comrades, and said, "Never mind. It's good to die for our country." Tel Hai itself, not more than a tiny gated community, lies at the feet of the Naftali Mountains, on top of which Misgav Am is located. That hot summer day, taking the left turn at Tel Hai to start the climb up to his new home, Mike was excited, less by the appeal of what would become his final, fixed dwelling in Israel than by the allure of settling on the border, in a remote community surrounded by hostile neighbors.

If Mike was touched by even a smidgen of frontier romanticism, what happened next provided an additional boost to his already aroused inner frontiersman: at the Margalyot junction, about halfway up the mountain, the bus stopped at a roadblock, framed by a tin can with a burning candle on each side. Mike and his friends waited for several minutes, and then a noise was heard from above, and the bulky outline of a rumbling armored personnel carrier appeared at the end of the road, circling the bus and then escorting it for the remaining leg of the trip, all the way up to the kibbutz. As the APC left that day, Mike and a hundred of his friends, none older than nineteen, joined the hundred permanent members of Misgav Am to make the kibbutz their home, to cultivate its lands, to defend its borders.

As Mike's group now consisted of roughly half of the kibbutz's population, a sense of entitlement was hardly avoidable. With characteristic teenage bravura, oblivious of context and blind to subtleties, the young soldiers-to-be darted around as if each one was individually and solely responsible for the fact that the kibbutz was still standing; together, however, they were a formidable force, motivating each other, holding friendly competitions to see who could work the hardest for the longest period of time, who could endure on as little as possible—who, in other words, was the true, worthy manifestation of the spirit of Zionism, the spirit they had spent so much time debating. Their timing, too, was impeccable, as they arrived at the very beginning of the busy season. The rest of the kibbutz's members, pioneers from a different generation, mostly shrugged their shoulders at the new cadre and their convictions: on one level, the veterans were pining for working hands, even if those hands came with brash mouths; on another level, deeper still, the veterans smiled softly, recognizing in the eyes of the new volunteers the same glint that had once sparkled in theirs, guiding them to this remote corner of the earth all those years ago.

The young men and women raced from picking apricots and plums on the kibbutz, to picking apples in the orchards up the mountain, and grapefruit in the fields in the valley below, and the industrious schedule, following months of idling, filled Mike with enough joy to overlook some of the kibbutz's major inconveniences. He now shared a small, barely furnished shack with four other men, with the only available faucet located a good three-minute walk away. To make things worse, Mike was reacquainted with his old nemesis, the one-foot-too-short Agency bed, with this time not even a chair available to alleviate his discomfort. But, even more than the physical hardships, Mike had to learn to adjust to kibbutz life.

First, there was communality; the kibbutz, as its Hebrew name, meaning "gathering," implies, was conceived as an egalitarian community in which all is shared and nothing is private. While talks of such communality were odd enough to him prior to joining the kibbutz, Mike found the daily machinations of life on a kibbutz even odder. Every day, the entire hundred-member nucleus would convene and discuss every issue imaginable, from allocations of funds to members' personal needs and requests. "They could even decide," Mike said years later, "who would get what size shirt and why." Again, as was the case during the Jerusalem meetings, some members inevitably deployed the communal structure as a shield, while others brandished it as a sword. It was not uncommon for members to deny other members such petty requests as an additional item of clothing or a day off. One of the kibbutz's members, who had come to Misgav Am in the same group as Mike, recalls a perfect example. It was December, and his cousin had just given birth in Tel Aviv. As a member of the kibbutz could not just pick up and go, the man brought the matter up at the next communal meeting. He explained the situation and, politely, requested a day off, as well as one of the kibbutz's cars so that he could make the two-hour drive and visit his newborn relative. While some of his peers nodded their heads in silent accord, one vociferously objected. The kibbutz, too, is family, the man recalls his peer sneering at him, and driving down to Tel Aviv demonstrates preference of one's biological family over one's family of comrades, a bourgeois idea that must not be supported. Slowly, the objector convinced a small majority of those present; the man didn't get to see his cousin and her baby until months later. Even if the man's tale was made more gruesome by the failings of memory and the residual anger collected with time, his anecdote is still a telling tale of one dark undercurrent of kibbutz life. Even more telling is the fact that both the man and his antagonist still live in kibbutzim until this day, albeit in different ones.

Once again, Mike found himself in an ideological dead zone. While socialism appealed to his humility and sense of humanity, some of the kibbutz's affairs were an affront to his American sensibilities, as values such as individuality, freedom of choice, and other pillars of the American ethos were suddenly deemed undesirable by a strange and coercive system.

Mike's second problem, however, proved to be a more difficult one. While he did, eventually, learn to navigate the petty politics of the commune, Mike had another disadvantage, this one stemming from his almost complete lack of shared background and upbringing with his newfound friends. The seminal idea that dominated the hearts of his peers at the time was a romanticized notion of the Palmach, the predecessor to the army. As any child who grew up in Israel knows, the Palmach was a unique and heroic band of brothers, better known, perhaps, for its antics than for its tactics. Stories abound about dashing young men stealing chickens from farmers for barbecuing, then rolling in the hay with starry-eyed and uniform-clad young women. The Palmach lore came complete with an entire set of symbols and signifiers, such as bonfires, folk songs, and *chizbats,* popular stories rife with exaggeration and bravado. Furthermore, the Palmach chroniclers provided future generations with a ready-made set of heroes to worship, brave military leaders as well as colorful fools and poets. Mike, however, knew none of these people, nothing of their songs or their exploits. Every reference, triggering immediate nods and smiles from his friends, he met with a blank stare; often he would ask a close friend for an explanation, but reconstructing years and years of informal education seemed too demanding a task for anyone to accomplish overnight.

Somehow, however, that which he didn't like, the totality of communal life, and that which he didn't know, the folklore of Israel's heroic age, were both eclipsed by the magnificence of the scenery surrounding him, and by the expectation that one's life must revolve around constant cultivation of the land. Unlike the faux forests of Havat Ha'Noar, so green yet located moments away from Jerusalem, Misgav Am was a genuinely engaging wilderness. Engulfing the few shacks that were home to the kibbutz's few members were vast patches of rolling meadows, some shadowed by a canopy of trees, others demarcated by small clusters of rocks. The wind, particularly the eastern *Sharkeeya* wind, the most howling and capricious of all, blew through Misgav Am on its way down to breeze through the valley, and the sun beat hard on this exposed swath of civilization on top of a wild mountain. There, the air smelled of soil, and the soil of the hands which cultivated it, and one always had dirt under one's fingernails.

Together with dirt and ideals, kibbutz members reveled in the one great, unspoken joy suddenly allotted them in generous quantities: freedom. While Mike was a rather rambling youth, without father and new to the land, most of his peers belonged to the upper strata of Israeli society, and had spent their youth in tightly knit families. Now, despite the kibbutz's often-demanding communal obligations, they were unwatched, undisturbed, free. And for young Israeli men, freedom often translated into two elements: army and alcohol.

The latter was a great discovery. Tiptoeing into the kibbutz's tiny general store, an inconspicuous little shack stocking rudimentary food items, the men—and it was mostly men who excited themselves with such activities—stood up and, in the deepest voice they could muster, requested liquor. The selection available to them consisted of three brands of locally produced, mediocre brandy: Stock 84 was the king of local elixirs, the trusted 777 was a close second, and then, trailing behind in both price and, it was generally agreed, quality, was a brandy bearing the somewhat ironic name Extra Fine. On rare occasions, the store would stock a bottle or two of vodka.

Armed with their loot, the men would do their best to incorporate some bohemia into the spartan, ideological kibbutz life. Every day after dinner, the communal mess hall would be converted, with the aid of an eight-track tape, into an impromptu dance hall; and every day, members would dance traditional folk dances for hours, holding hands and spinning in circles to old Russian tunes with new Israeli lyrics, usually describing pioneers at work or praising the motherland, Hebrew names substituting in the original paeans to the productivity of Boris, Natasha, or Ivan. As the folk dancing died down, Mike and a few like-minded others placed some rock 'n' roll LPs on the battered stereo system, maybe some blue cellophane paper over the lightbulb, pulled out the booze, and pretended, if only for a moment, that they were somewhere else, somewhere not quite so close to the border.

Some of Mike's more purist peers, however, shunned what they considered the remnants of his past life as a fledgling member of the American bourgeoisie. For one, he was a foreigner, and then a drinker, and a dancer who preferred "Hey Jude" to the hora. Obviously not one of the kibbutz's leading ideologues, Mike had to find other ways to excel. One such avenue consisted of doing an incredibly foolish thing.

It is rather hard to believe today, considering the long and bloody history of skirmishes alongside the border between Israel and Lebanon, but in 1972 there was no physical border to speak of. Because Lebanon, then a rather tranquil country with intercontinental aspirations, was considered a minor threat next to the actively belligerent Syria, Egypt, and Jordan, Israeli leaders did not see fit to spend the money required to erect a fence and demarcate the two countries. The site of the border, adjacent to Misgav Am's old cemetery, consisted of a narrow stretch of barbed wire with a small sign that read, "Halt, Border Ahead."

The men of Misgav Am were the first to appreciate the thin irony of the border, existing and invisible at once, and they devised a small game designed to amuse themselves, prove their courage, and, one would suspect, defy what seemed like a rather artificial barrier tearing their environs apart. The challenge was simple: cross the border and go over to the other side. Actually attempting that, however, was more difficult. As soon as one passed through the small gate in the fence, past the cemetery, one was on a slope leading down to the valley below, which was Lebanese territory. There, a small village named El Adeysa lies, and the challenger had to enter the village, have coffee with one of the Lebanese men, and return to Misgav Am. On either side of the hill, disaster loomed: on the Lebanese side, the twin eyes of Sujud and Nabi el Awadi, two villages with a reputation of hostility toward Israel, were watching in anticipation for an Israeli infiltrator to try and cross the border. On the Israeli side, tense and jittery soldiers were lying on the hill next to Misgav Am, awaiting unwelcome Lebanese guests. Whoever entered the valley, therefore, was entering a spectacular shooting range, a green death trap surrounded by ruddy, sunburned hills, with two groups of combatants anxious to shoot first and ask questions later.

While the original challenge called for an actual, prolonged stay in the village, most of those brave and foolish enough to attempt it, Mike included, practiced somewhat more of a dash rather than a stroll. Breathless, back in the kibbutz, the men would bask in the approving grunts of their comrades, the slaps on the back, the silent comity of friends in transition from careless kids to soldiers.

And soldiers they soon were. Plucked out of the largely protected life of fanciful debates about socialism and apple picking at dawn, Mike and his friends were swallowed, several months after their arrival, by the army, expected to begin their military service. What followed were months of training, not in the least resembling the pleasantries of the make-believe Gadna that Mike had come to love while at Havat Ha'Noar. The army, once stripped of its heroic glow, was a series of exhaustions, a perpetual string of mind-droning drills devised to teach one both how to extract one's fullest physical and mental potential and how to become part of a larger team. Coming from a kibbutz, Mike was used to both: he was hardened by hours spent climbing on trees or raking in the field, he was programmed to replace the I with the We, and he was, therefore, relatively immune to the great shock most young Israelis experience when required to leave their juvenile existence behind and reinvent themselves as peons.

More than anything, Mike was looking for one seminal moment, one glimpse of himself in the mirror, in uniform, gun slung across his shoulders, one glimpse to help him close the circle which had started when he met the blond officer all those years ago. But such a moment never came; in the mirror was a tired, dusty young man, a common soldier, and the day was too full with sit-ups and target practice to allow any sentimentality to creep in. Routine, Mike soon discovered, governed the soldier's life.

On the morning of October 6, 1973, Mike and his friends, like the rest of Israel, were observing Yom Kippur, the holiest day for Judaism. Just before dawn that day, word of a joint attack by Syria and Egypt began circulating. By noon, Prime Minister Golda Meir had convened the cabinet for an emergency meeting, the impending threat obviously justifying the desecration of the religious ritual. By the time the meeting was adjourned, both Syria and Egypt had invaded. Several hours later, Meir read the following address on the radio:

Citizens of Israel,

Shortly before two p.m. today, the armies of Egypt and Syria opened an offensive against Israel, launching a series of air, armored and artillery attacks in Sinai and on the Golan Heights. The Israel Defense Forces have entered the fight, and are beating back the assault. The enemy has suffered grave losses.

Our enemies had hoped to surprise the citizens of Israel on Yom Kippur, when so many of our people are fasting and worshipping in the synagogues. . . .

We are in no doubt that we shall prevail. . . . This is not the first time that we have been compelled to endure ordeal by battle. I am confident that none among us will fall prey to panic. The mobilization will no doubt cause hardships and interference in the normal course of life and work but we must try to accept these difficulties as we have done in the past, with full understanding. We are called upon to demonstrate responsibility and discipline in our conduct. We must be ready for every burden and sacrifice needed for the defense of our survival, our freedom and our independence. Let us, then, conduct ourselves so as to be worthy of our soldiers of Israel who are valiantly doing their duty in the air, in the armored forces, on the ships, in the artillery, in all units and services in the outposts, in the villages and settlements, along the lines of fire in all sectors.

We have full confidence in the spirit and the strength of the IDF to overcome the enemy. The victory of the IDF is our certain assurance of life and peace.

Despite Meir's assurances, the enemy, at that stage, was not suffering grave losses of any kind. Attacking Israel with the equivalent of NATO's forces in Europe, the two Arab armies moved in twin pillars, meeting a mostly unprepared Israeli army, understaffed, overwhelmed, and unorganized. In the Golan Heights, for example, approximately 180 Israeli tanks were attacked by nearly 1,400 Syrian tanks, and along the Suez Canal down south, 500 baffled Israeli soldiers were mobbed by over 80,000 raging Egyptian troops.

It took the Israeli army two seemingly endless days to mobilize its reserves and begin the recovery process. Blocking the advance of the Syrians—and their Iraqi, Saudi, Jordanian, and Moroccan allies—was the army's top priority, as the Syrian army was in a dangerous position in a corridor leading from the Golan Heights to northern Israel. After days of bitter battle, aided by recurrent air raids, the Israel Defense Forces were able not only to halt the Syrian onslaught, but to pursue the Syrians back into their own territory, positioning, at one time, thirty-two kilometers (approximately twenty miles) from Damascus. Then, all attention was focused on the less-threatening Egyptians down south; while the Egyptian army had begun the invasion in full force and with great numbers, the largely inexperienced, often confused Egyptian soldiers were held at bay by a desperate band of Israeli soldiers, who were able to keep the neighbors from the south from crossing over the Sinai Desert and into Israel proper.

At this point, with Israel enjoying a modicum of breathing room, a celebrated general by the name of Ariel Sharon proposed a plan to decimate the Egyptians altogether. The Egyptian forces, he noted, were divided into two main parts: the Second Army, sitting to the north of the Great Bitter Lake, one of the three saltwater lakes connecting with the Suez Canal; and the Third Army, located to the south of the lake. Sharon identified a narrow gap between the twin pillars of Egyptian belligerence, and drove his tank column through the gap to victory, dividing the Egyptian force into two parts and then destroying both.

It was to the Great Bitter Lake that Mike was sent. As a recently trained noncommissioned officer in charge of explosives, Mike's job was placing explosives on the openings carved by the invading Egyptians in the Suez Canal, in order to prevent additional Egyptian backups from using the same channels.

In Sinai, Mike saw war. It included the death of some of his friends, from explosions or from accidents or from the biting bullets of Egyptian snipers. It included the exhilarating feeling, that which Elias Canetti has defined as the rawest form of survival, upon seeing the enemy defeated after a long, violent struggle. It included shell shock and shame and piles of shoes, left behind by the fleeing Egyptian soldiers. What struck Mike most about the war is how chaotic it was. The combat he had seen on television or in the movies was always structured, always planned, the battlefield resembling a chessboard manipulated by masterful artists. Sinai, however, was no such chessboard; it was a desert run by young men, dirty and scared, who would curse to hide their despair and shoot to assuage their fears. More than once, Mike was almost killed by a fellow soldier, who, seeing a figure moving on a moonless night, squeezed the trigger indiscriminately. The dust and the heat caked on his body like a second skin. Mike treated each day like an eternity, too tired to try and see the big picture of the war unfolding around him. For him, the war was a series of endless sweltering days, of hours spent idly talking to his comrades, of moments of fear and boredom and excitement often collapsing into each other in a whirlwind of emotions.

Golda Meir, perhaps, didn't get it quite right when she stated, the day the war started, that this was not the first time in which Israelis were compelled to endure the ordeal of battle. For Mike, it was the very first time. And, as much as that could be said about war, it felt good. Before he was even nineteen years old, Mike had not only worked the Jewish land, but also participated in defending its borders. No image in the mirror leaped at him, no circle closed, but neither was there any need. Mike Ginsberg was now an Israeli, able to share with his friends the seminal experience of having fought a war together, a war that would replace the Palmach and its lore as the defining moment of their generation, no heroic fiction but true experience, the culmination of all of their fights and all of their losses.

As the war ended, Mike served the remainder of his time in an elite reconnaissance unit with the armored corps, and, after his discharge, returned to Misgav Am. There he met Haya Halperin. Scion of a celebrated family of pioneers who came to Palestine in the early 1880s and helped establish Zikhron Ya'akov, one of the first Jewish settlements in the land, Haya's father passed away when she was a young girl, and her family eventually moved to Misgav Am. After a brief courtship, Mike and Haya got married. He assumed a series of positions in the kibbutz, working mainly in agriculture, stationed wherever he was needed by the greater will of the group.

When the war ended, Mike was happy to return to the tranquillity of Misgav Am, relatively remote from the unquiet borders with Syria and Egypt, overlooking the mostly peaceful Lebanon. The war, however, was about to follow Mike home, as the Lebanese border, once scarcely an issue for concern, flared up almost instantaneously.

The history of the border's descent toward chaos began in the 1970s, shortly before Mike and his friends first set foot in Misgav Am. Based in Jordan, several Palestinian terrorist organizations, such as the Palestine Liberation Organization and George Habash's pseudo-Marxist Popular Front for the Liberation of Palestine, began using Jordan and its large Palestinian population as a base for strikes against Israeli targets. Jordan's King Hussein, a member of the Hashemite royal dynasty, feared that the Palestinian upheaval would eventually be turned against his own regime, and therefore moved to quash it. On September 6, 1970, after two skyjackings by the PFLP on the same day, Hussein ordered his army to move against the Palestinian guerrillas, some of whom were by now actively inciting the Jordanian population to strike against the government. A brief civil war ensued, during which thousands of Palestinians were killed. Martial law was imposed, and both the PLO and the PFLP were ordered to leave Jordan immediately.

They left for Lebanon, where tensions between various ethnic factions were already simmering, and from Lebanon concocted further attacks against Israel. Slowly, the Israelis began erecting a bigger fence, sending more troops to patrol the border. The Palestinians sent more terrorist squads. The Israelis grew more and more nervous. Finally, in March of 1978, a small group of Palestinian terrorists managed to infiltrate into Israel, shooting an American tourist to death and then hijacking a bus, eventually killing thirty-four of the hostages before they were overtaken by Israeli commandos. In response, approximately twenty thousand Israeli troops entered the south of Lebanon shortly thereafter, with the purpose of establishing a "security zone" to protect the communities of northern Israel from the growing danger of violence.

All this was more than just geopolitics to Mike. As one of his many positions in the kibbutz, he was also the *ma'ez,* Hebrew acronym for *mefaked ezor,* or regional commander. The regional commander is a civilian, appointed by the army, who in case of emergency works with and for the army to provide an immediate response to any threat on a local level. In other words, the regional commander is the first line of defense, often required to be the first on the scene and the only one present until significant army forces are notified and mobilized. Each infiltration attempt sent Mike, very often in the wee hours of the morning, into the kibbutz's cemetery, the most vulnerable point of entry, gun in hand, scanning for terrorists.

Early in the morning of April 7, 1980, however, Mike was fast asleep. Around half past midnight, he was awoken by what, to his trained ear, sounded like gunfire. Haya, his wife, pleaded with him to come back to bed, arguing that the noise must have come from a distance; but Mike refused. He thought the gunshots sounded too close for comfort. He ran to the bathroom window in an attempt to ascertain what was happening, and when that failed, he simply ran outside, in the direction of the noise. As he was approaching the kibbutz's nursery, he was nearly hit by a hail of bullets, which sent him crouching on the ground. Lifting his head some, he could see other kibbutz members sharing his predicament, lying on the ground in a semicircle around the nursery, horrified, paralyzed by the ongoing fire.

A small eternity later, details began trickling out. A squad of five terrorists, belonging to the PFLP, had left the nearby Lebanese village of Rab al-Talatyin earlier on that night. Guided by a man from El Adeysa, the village into which Mike and his friends would foray to prove their courage, the terrorists cut the fence at the topmost northwestern point of Misgav Am. Armed with weapons, ammunition, explosives, and a prior knowledge of the kibbutz's topography, they crept through the narrow path leading to the nursery, or, as it's called in kibbutz vernacular, *beit yeladim,* the children's house. Most kibbutzim at the time, true to their calling, shunned the traditional nuclear family structure, placing children instead in communal housing units where they spent most of their time. The five men approaching Misgav Am's nursery knew that well, and assumed that the nursery was the only building in which hostages—unarmed ones to boot—were readily available.

Misgav Am's nursery was a gray, cubic, unassuming duplex, with the upper level and the lower level connected by an external flight of stairs. The upper level housed the older children, aged one to two and a half years, while the lower level housed the nursery, home to infants aged six weeks to a year. The nursery was surrounded by a vast patch of grass, leading directly to the upper level. The upper level, then, was the terrorists' first stop that night.

According to kibbutz regulations, each level of the building had to be constantly manned in case of emergency. The person on duty that night, kibbutz member Meir Peretz, was dozing when the terrorists stormed into the building, and he was soon bound, gagged, and moved to a corner of the room. The terrorists conducted a quick scan of the building, and were disappointed by what they discovered: only four children, hardly enough hostages for serious negotiations and spectacular suicide threats. With Peretz tied up, the terrorists decided to scan the lower level for additional bodies. At the same time, Sami and Esty Shani, the kibbutz's secretary and his wife, were in the lower level visiting their newborn son, Omer. Also in the lower level were two young female kibbutz members on nursery duty, the boyfriend of one of the women, and four babies.

As Sami was leaving the lower level to return to his home, the terrorists were going down the staircase. Upon spotting Sami, they opened immediate fire. Sami, in a frantic attempt to stop the men from entering the house, engaged them in hand-to-hand combat, striking with his fists, trying to disarm the terrorists. One of the terrorists, however, managed a clear shot. Sami collapsed and died on the spot. At the sound of gunfire, one of the women inside, along with her boyfriend, escaped through the porch and ran to call for help. The other woman, together with Esty, Sami's wife, hid in the bathroom. Having killed Sami, the terrorists entered the lower level. In one room, they found Omer, Sami and Esty's son, an eight-month-old infant, and another baby, two months old. They grabbed both babies by their arms and dragged them back to the upper-level building.

Meanwhile, Misgav Am was fast asleep. The Sharkeeya, the powerful gust of eastern wind, muffled the sounds of gunfire, carrying them west, toward Lebanon. No one, therefore, learned of the attack until the two escapees, the young woman and her male friend, frantically alerted the army and the kibbutz's security officials. The main such official at the time was Ze'ev Peled, the kibbutz's chief security officer. Groggy with sleep, and unable to ascertain from the young escapees' histrionics what exactly had transpired, he assumed that the commotion must have been caused by drunken volunteers, not an entirely unprecedented possibility at the time. He approached the nursery and yelled into the darkness, "Who are you?"

The response from inside the nursery was quick to follow, in the form of a hand grenade and a round of gunfire. This time, with the wind somewhat subsided, the shots were clearly audible throughout the kibbutz, and they were the ones which awoke Mike. Several kibbutz members, Mike included, approached the house, but were kept close to the ground by repeating rounds of semiautomatic fire.

Shortly thereafter, a small band of kibbutz members, alerted by the escapees, arrived at the scene. They entered the lower level and removed Esty and the other woman from their hideout. Sayeret Golani, an elite IDF unit trained for such scenarios, was also on the scene. Their battalion leader, acting without any intelligence pertaining to the terrorists barricaded in the upper level, wanted a quick, clear resolution; he ordered the elite unit to storm the house immediately. One of the kibbutz's members was a reservist of the unit, and he was given a machine gun and instructed to provide constant backup fire. The rest of the squad, approximately twenty soldiers, stormed the upper level.

With a clear line of fire on the storming Israeli soldiers, the terrorists fired all their weapons at once. Eldad Tzafrir, the unit's medic, was killed instantly, his body perforated by bullets. Seven or eight additional soldiers, including the unit's commander, fell to the ground wounded.

Inside the house, the terrorists were now more agitated, more desperate. They began a shouting negotiation with the IDF brass, which was meanwhile rushed to the patch of grass outside the nursery. The terrorists wanted three things, they yelled: they wanted to meet with a representative of the Red Cross; they asked for the Romanian ambassador to Israel, believed to be sympathetic to the Palestinian cause, to be brought to the scene; and they demanded the immediate release of three hundred of their friends who were locked up in Israeli prisons. The army brass stood there, debating, strategizing, stunned. The members of the kibbutz lingered on too, terrified. At 5:40 in the morning, a sobbing woman came up to Mike. Grabbing his shirt lapels, she looked him in the eye and, in between sobs, begged, "Mike, get my baby girl out of that house." Mike, angry, vengeful, frustrated, mumbled a few inane words. The crisis showed no sign of resolution.

A little while later, the terrorists shouted out their list of demands one more time. This time, however, they were more concrete: either the demands would be met by 10:00 a.m., they said, or they would blow up the house and everyone in it.

Several minutes before the deadline, a helicopter appeared in the kibbutz's airspace. The army brass outside on the grassy patch yelled out, their voices hardly overcoming the din of the spinning rotors, that the helicopter carried the Romanian ambassador, just as the terrorists had wanted. The helicopter lowered down, preparing to land on the grass. Suddenly, it did an about-face and took off again, this time in the opposite direction. Using that moment of distraction, IDF special forces, concealed outside the nursery, stormed the house. Exactly twenty seconds later, it was all over.

Among the bodies of the five terrorists, however, the soldiers found one more. Stunned Meir Peretz, now untied, trembled as he told of how the two-month-old baby wouldn't stop crying, and of how the terrorists refused to untie him so he could calm the baby down, and of how, finally, to stop the incessant sobbing, one of the terrorists crushed the baby's skull with the butt of his rifle.

The attack on Misgav Am sent shock waves throughout Israel. The next morning, the newspapers provided a detailed account of what had happened. "Like lambs to the slaughter," one newspaper reported, and another lamented the "once-again reoccurring helplessness of Jewish toddlers in the face of the human beasts seeking to murder them." Almost every paper paraphrased a poem by Chaim Nachman Bialik, Israel's poet laureate, who, after witnessing the pogroms in Russia in the late 1890s, wrote, "not even the devil can conceive of revenge / for the spilt blood of a little child."

Calls were made for retaliation, and several military operations in Lebanon were executed. The border, once an innocuous barbed-wire fence with a small sign, became Israel's most threatening perimeter. Two years and two months later, following an assassination attempt by Palestinian militants on Israel's ambassador to England, the IDF attacked mostly Palestinian targets in Lebanon. The PLO, in return, fired mortar rockets on civilian targets in northern Israel. Then Minister of Defense Ariel Sharon ordered the army into Lebanon on June 6,1982. For three years, the war raged on, comprised of an endless series of attacks and counterattacks. The national consensus for the war rapidly waned, and Sharon was fingered by some as having used the assassination attempt as his Gulf of Tonkin moment in order to drag the country into an irresponsible and deadly military escapade. Doubts were cast upon whether Sharon was honest in his reports to his superiors, which led to the resignation of Prime Minister Menachem Begin and to a statement by an investigatory committee headed by a former chief justice of Israel's supreme court that Sharon was "not fit to serve, now or in the future, as the State of Israel's Minister of Defense." A national unity government assembled after Begin's resignation ordered the army's withdrawal from Lebanon in 1985, setting up a narrow swath of land as a security zone. The zone was to be protected by the newly assembled South Lebanese Army, a collection of mostly Christian local villagers motivated to protect their land by the twin reasons of rejecting the Islamic militant terrorists on the one hand and craving the financial benefits offered by Israel on the other. Rotating units of Israeli soldiers also patrolled the zone, with constant battles causing hundreds of deaths. Violence had become routine for Mike and his friends.

CHAPTER EIGHT

Every other night since 1985, with alarming regularity, Mike's sleep was interrupted for security reasons. At times, the interruption would arrive in the form of a phone call from worried army brass, suspecting terrorist movement not far from the kibbutz's perimeter; at others, a sound far in the distance would make Mike bolt from bed. And then there were the rare, eerie nights, with no phone calls or suspicious sounds, but rather a hunch, haunting and ghostly, that the fence was being breached, that men with guns were practically at his doorstep. In all three cases, Mike's routine was similar: grab the shoes and the gun, alert the men, a small band of soldiers and fellow kibbutz members, and run into the darkness, a dash that almost always led first to the cemetery, the kibbutz's soft spot and the most convenient venue for potential infiltrations. Physically, Mike's midnight ritual remained the same, silently crouching beneath the tombstones of the kibbutz's long-dead members, straining to spot a suspicious silhouette in the dark. Mentally, however, each phone call, each suspicious noise, each ominous hunch, further forced Mike to come to terms with an emotion foreign to him: fear. Now a husband and a father, each nocturnal showdown brought thoughts to his mind, thoughts of mortality and its consequences. Any tombstone, he knew, might conceal a man with a gun and an ax to grind, and any shot would probably be directed at him, the largest figure around, a towering presence even when engulfed in shadows. I can't be killed, he would often think in vain attempts to calm himself. I can't be killed because I can't be replaced; I'm too essential to the kibbutz's security. Then, a moment later, Who am I kidding? Look around you, Mike. This place is filled with people who couldn't be replaced. Then fear would drip back in. Yet every other night since 1985, Mike rushed out in the dead of night and faced whatever was there to be reckoned with.

Despite the occasional nightly forays into the darkness, however, Mike finally had time to concern himself with the one task his life's reality had kept postponing since he first landed in Israel all those years ago: settling in. kibbutz life, for all its flaws, allowed Mike plenty of time to build a home and a family, something he was only delighted to do. Haya and he had settled into a marriage, amorous whispers and lovers' quarrels conducted entirely in Hebrew. They gave birth to three sons, who were now growing rapidly. Mike watched the boys become men, Israeli men, army-bound, tall and bronzed and bereft of any traces of their father's origin in the Diaspora. In their mouths, English sounded foreign, convoluted, alien. With each conversation he had with his sons or wife, Mike seemed to shed another ounce of his former identity; finally, by the time the new millennium rolled in, no passerby could have picked Mike Ginsberg as the odd man out in a lineup of Israeli men. By then he had given up a string of random jobs in the kibbutz, including one as a member of the kibbutz movement's national committee on the absorption of immigration, for a permanent one as an ambulance driver, serving several remote northern communities which had sprung up adjacent to Misgav Am. Like so many Israeli men, he would spend his days in a tiny office, consuming copious amounts of Turkish coffee, slowly boiled, with more sugar added than any doctor would recommend. His accent betrayed no sign of Brooklyn, the way he carried himself no clue of Connecticut. He would speak in that quintessentially Israeli way: a bit brash, one tone louder than necessary, with a face that brightens up whenever an acquaintance happens to pass by and a voice that, happy and jovial even to strangers, almost always sounds one degree more familiar than any non-Israeli might feel comfortable with.

Sitting on his porch in the summer of 2003, Mike Ginsberg is an Israeli, his metamorphosis complete. His large frame slouched in a plastic chair, his house cluttered with memorabilia collected over the years, from his children's artwork to the empty shell of a Lebanese missile that landed nearby several years before, he is at home and at peace. Even though it is late in the afternoon, he is still wearing his work clothes: an oversize short-sleeved white button-down shirt with a red Star of David on the chest, the symbol of Israel's emergency medical association, and, clipped to his belt, a holster containing a handgun. He drinks more coffee, his umpteenth cup of the day, and nibbles on an old-fashioned bundt cake he bought the day before in the kibbutz's general store.

A colleague walks by Mike's porch, a short, stout man with a rapidly receding hairline and a heartwarming smile. "Ah," he says, nodding. Mike nods back, his motion more accentuated.

"Nu?" the man asks, the Israeli word connoting impatience, hurry, and anticipation. Mike shrugs his shoulders in return. Both men look toward a tall gray building looming to their left.

"What do you think?" the man asks, all the muscles in his face contracted, his eyebrows furrowed and his lips tight. "Walla, don't know," Mike replies, letting his head jerk back and forth as he takes a deep breath to emphasize the sincerity of his reply.

"Accchhh," the man says, a guttural sound, his face now calm, his head shaking gently from side to side, his fingers drumming softly against his thighs. *"Ma la'asot?"* Mike replies with half a smile, Hebrew for What can we do about it? The man says, "Yalla, see you later," and walks away without further gesticulation. Mike waves him away. "Later," he says.

When the man is no longer in sight, Mike explains the meaning of the minuscule kibbutz kabuki he and his colleague have just enacted. The kibbutz movement, he says in a tone difficult to decipher, has been, for most of its existence, revered by Israel's Labor Party, the party in power for the first twenty-nine years of the state's existence. The kibbutzim symbolized all that was promising about the new enterprise, all the potential of the nascent Jewish state. They were socially just, they were cultivating the land, they were defenders of the borders, and for such exquisite services rendered the government paid generously, never concerning itself with questions of economic value, supply and demand. Then, in the late 1970s, the Labor Party's hegemony ended, and the kibbutzim woke up with a bad headache and a stratospheric deficit. As is sometimes the case with stock markets, oil companies, or telecommunications conglomerates, they realized, almost overnight, that years of hype and endless budgets based on speculation rather than on sound financial practices weren't the healthiest path an institution could pursue. And with that began the descent of one of the more idealistic social experiments ever undertaken.

The first practices to vanish were exactly those that had determined the unique spirit of communal living. Canceled were the daily meetings, gone were most of the social events, vanished were the agricultural endeavors. Instead, kibbutzim across Israel were now searching for means to get rich quick; many opened their gates to industry, offering factories a lucrative deal, complete with government tax breaks and a ready-made workforce not entirely accustomed to the principles of a free-market economy. While some kibbutzim tried to lure industries, the high-tech industry in particular, to take the place of tomatoes and oranges and apples, others tried to get by based on location alone, converting several houses into guesthouses called *tzimmerim,* and offering price-sensitive Israelis a rustic local alternative to traveling abroad.

The last remnant, however, was the gray building Mike and his friend were eyeing: the communal dining hall. Beyond merely providing members with their meals, the dining hall was a symbol of social cohesiveness; a kibbutz member was obliged to congregate with the others thrice daily, maintaining, or so it was believed, a modicum of social unity. Gradually, the dining hall lost its shine because of financial cutbacks: first to go were the dinners, then the breakfasts; then lunch—the last vestige—was outsourced, in many kibbutzim including Misgav Am, to external catering services for a cheaper price.

Now, Misgav Am had decided to discontinue lunch as well, doing away with the dining hall altogether. That was the subject of the conversation between Mike and his friend, and in their facial expressions thirty years of hope and disappointment unfolded.

The state of the kibbutz's dining hall, however, seemed almost irrelevant on that afternoon in June 2003: three years before, the Israeli army withdrew from Lebanon, leaving Misgav Am with no buffer zone between its members and the Hizbollah terrorists in the villages of the valley below.

The withdrawal had been the result of a stirring political debate in Israel, catalyzed by a group of bereaved mothers who had lost their sons in the decade of fighting in Lebanon. The army's presence in the so-called security zone, the mothers and their political allies claimed, was strategically senseless. To make their case, they cited the repetitive rocket attacks on northern Israeli communities and the swarming Hizbollah presence around the border. The security zone, went their claim, gave Hizbollah a cause célèbre, arming them with ideology and sufficient reason to galvanize the villagers against Israel. The mothers cited the growing number of Israeli soldiers killed in action in the security zone, approximately 150 on average every year for fifteen years, as the final reason to immediately disengage and unilaterally withdraw from Lebanon.

Sensing popular support for the withdrawal, former IDF chief of staff Ehud Barak made it the focal point of his election campaign for prime minister in 1999. After Barak was elected in a landslide, Mike and his colleagues understood that the withdrawal was imminent.

Still, they fought. They protested. They petitioned politicians and army brass. If the zone was gone, they said, so would be their security, their safety, their peace.

To no avail. The army, following the political zeitgeist, concocted a plan that called for a gradual shifting of responsibilities from the IDF to the South Lebanese Army, followed by the eventual dismantling of the SLA and the transfer of authority over the beleaguered swath of land to the Lebanese government. The process, Mike was informed by the army, was scheduled to start on May 20, 2000, and slated to last approximately six months.

It lasted forty-eight hours.

On May 20, the IDF transferred control over the Teiba outpost, located on a strategic hill not far from Misgav Am, to the Seventieth Battalion of the SLA. Baffled by being transformed, overnight, from cohorts to commanders, and threatened by the massive pressure exerted by Hizbollah, the Seventieth Battalion imploded within one day, its soldiers and officers either returning to their villages or seeking refuge in Israel, fearing the retribution of Hizbollah. By May 22, the remaining South Lebanese Army followed the example of the doomed battalion, retreating into hiding or self-imposed exile. On the morning of May 23, 2000, the SLA was no more.

That night, chaos reigned over south Lebanon. Anybody who had a gun fired it. Mike couldn't sleep that night, not on account of the gunshot din, to which he had already become accustomed, but on account of one inevitable thought, on the minds of so many in the kibbutz that night: the withdrawal had, in effect, already begun.

Unable to sleep, Mike jumped into his jeep with a friend, and the two drove in silence across the *gizra,* army vernacular for operational region. Together, they stopped at Mitzpeh Adi, Parag, and the other outposts trusted with defending their well-being, trying desperately to gather information, trying to ascertain what the three batteries of cannons deployed by the IDF were firing at.

No one seemed to know anything. So on they drove, all the way to Har Dov, the white plateau to the east marking the official point of entry into Lebanon, and farther into the security zone to the Narkis outpost. There they found the army brass confused and overwhelmed.

Slowly, Mike realized what had happened. Dumbfounded by the unexpected, premature disintegration of the SLA, the IDF had a potential bloodbath on its hands. The worst-case scenario depicted Israeli soldiers trapped in Lebanon, trying to escape, running to the border without the strategic backup of the SLA, being slaughtered like sitting ducks by well-positioned Hizbollah gunmen on the surrounding hills. The army's objectives shifted overnight: on May 20, it was disengage according to plan; on May 23, it was get the hell out, any which way necessary, without attracting fire on Israeli civilian communities on the other side of the border. The artillery, therefore, was serving very much as a safety blanket does for a child, in the hope that order could be extracted out of chaos.

Almost miraculously, the plan worked. While the government's detractors on the right called the withdrawal a disgrace, pointed out that for the first time ever, IDF soldiers had fled the enemy instead of engaging, and lamented the great quantities of equipment and firepower left behind, army officials, with black rings around their eyes after days with no sleep, went on television and repeated, ad nauseam, their bottom line: withdrawal complete, no casualties.

At 5:00 a.m. on the morning of May 24, a small band of weary soldiers came running into Misgav Am. They had come, they told the guard at the gate, from the nearby outpost of Galgalit, and had left everything behind and fled as firefights raged around them. Now, they said, they didn't know what to do. No one had told them anything. No orders had been given. Where, they asked the guard, did he suggest they go? The guard told them that he didn't know, but that he knew someone who would. When, an hour later, Mike and his friend approached the kibbutz's gate in their jeep, still somewhat shocked by the pace of events and their consequences, they were greeted by the sight of tired soldiers sitting on the sidewalk, baffled, waiting.

Mike greeted the soldiers and introduced himself. They were, he noticed, members of the *hesder yeshivas,* a program combining religious studies with military service. He also noticed how young they looked, how frightened. God, he thought to himself, they aren't much older than my sons. He asked the soldiers to accompany him, and walked toward the observatory, the highest place in the kibbutz. There, he pointed at south Lebanon.

"*Hevreh,*" he told the soldiers, using the informal Hebrew word meaning guys, "I won't lie to you. We have no means. We have no light. But we also have no choice: we are the last line of defense. It's you and me, and if they can get past us, they're inside the kibbutz." Then Mike quickly drew a picture of the new reality: The IDF was still at the nearby Olesh outpost, but would very soon evacuate it, he said. Other than that, there was no fence, no means of demarcation, no barrier between us and them. Mike put on a bulletproof vest, grabbed some rifle magazines, and, in his deepest voice, said: "*Hevreh,* I won't leave you." It was the one thing, the one fatherly, reassuring sentence the young soldiers had needed to hear all night, yet the one thing that no one had told them until then.

Deep down, however, Mike wasn't as reassured as he sounded. He was intimately acquainted with the perimeters of the border, and in his mind dozens of ominous scenarios kept unfolding; a multitude of spots along the fence seemed to call tauntingly out to the terrorists, inviting them into the kibbutz. Mike felt betrayed, left alone, abandoned by the army he had served for so long. For one week he did little but patrol the fence and stare into the valley below. He was tired, yet too afraid to shut his eyes. He was scared, yet too much of a father figure for the young soldiers to show it. His day job at the time, as head of the kibbutz's tourism venture, came to a grinding halt, as no one of a sound mind would choose to spend a vacation on the cusp of a borderless border, engulfed by terrorists who may or may not strike at any minute. Thus free from his job obligations, Mike had the time to become consumed by anger.

Other members of Misgav Am reacted in much the same way. Two families left the kibbutz, citing the new uncertainty, the first time in Misgav Am's turbulent history that any member had left because of the security situation. The remaining forty-three families found themselves in a unique situation: For years, they had lived on the mouth of this geopolitical volcano, always braving the dangers, always certain that even if they were at the forefront, the army would always be there to back them up. In May of 2000, it seemed, this was no longer true; the people of Misgav Am felt as if all their efforts, their endeavors, their sacrifices, had been in vain. They had now been discarded for the sake of political expediency, left to fend for themselves, with not even a fence between them and Hizbollah.

This, at least, was the general sentiment in the many impromptu meetings that members held in the days following the withdrawal. Far from their antecedents of previous decades, these meetings contained none of the ennui and mental bookkeeping of yore; instead, they were raw, painful, and, in a sense, cathartic. What years of sheer ideology couldn't do for the members of Misgav Am, three days of harsh reality accomplished instantaneously: they had become a true, cohesive community.

And as such, their responsibilities abided. Frequently, several members, including Esty, the survivor of the 1980s terrorist attack whose husband, Sami, had died trying to overtake the terrorists, would drive around from outpost to outpost, giving soldiers there a kind word and a quick snack from the kibbutz's kitchen. Mike, in turn, would take kibbutz members for elaborate rides in his jeep, showing them the outline where the new border was scheduled for construction. After some negotiation, a permanent IDF base was set up inside the kibbutz; Mike objected, fearful of turning the civilian community into a full-time army encampment, but most of the other members welcomed the soldiers and the safety they provided. Slowly, life returned to normal in Misgav Am.

Or nearly so. Three years after the withdrawal, Mike is sitting on his porch, looking to the east, at Har Dov. The mountainous region is the last point of contention between Hizbollah and Israel, with the terrorists claiming, against official UN cartography, that the region, which Israel took from Syria in the 1967 war, is in fact Lebanese territory. Almost daily, Hizbollah attacks the IDF outpost in Har Dov with gunfire and rockets. In 2001, they managed to kidnap and kill three Israeli soldiers on patrol in the area. Mike, several miles away, notes all this well.

"This is my plasma TV screen," he says jokingly as he points away to the distance. "A million inches wide. And every night, there's something to watch: rockets, shootings, you name it." Recently, he recalls, friends from Ohio called him as he was having a Shabbat dinner on his porch, when suddenly the sky flared up with the red, fiery traces of rockets. "Can't talk now," Mike told his stunned friends on the other end of the line, in between mouthfuls of salad. "I'm being shot at."

In the dry, prickly wind of a late June afternoon in kibbutz Misgav Am, a group of American-Jewish teenagers were sitting in an outdoor observation point and staring at Lebanon. The man standing in front of them looked intriguing: large, mustachioed, dusty. He was Mike Ginsberg, born in Brooklyn and raised in Connecticut. He had come to Israel when he was fourteen, wanting to become a soldier. That he had accomplished, remaining in some kind of uniform for most of his life. He had married an Israeli woman, and fathered three Israeli children: the oldest is an officer in one of the army's most prestigious units, and the younger ones are likely to follow suit when the time comes.

He has never regretted the decision he made. Once, in the 1980s, he took his family for a yearlong sabbatical in a small town in Massachusetts, working as a delegate for a Jewish organization, promoting Israel and encouraging aliya. A member of the community took to him, to his ambition and leadership and skill, and offered him a job as the manager of a large chain of grocery stores. The pay was much greater than the meager salary of the kibbutz, and life much more comfortable than what it was in the tiny two-bedroom apartment in Misgav Am. Yet, Mike and Haya politely refused; they had no interest, they said, in ever leaving Israel.

Shortly after their return to Israel from their sabbatical, Mike's mother, Harriet, moved into the kibbutz, where she remains today. Every day, at around noon, Mike visits her with a plate of warm food.

Mike's brother, Marc, on the other hand, the one who, all those years before, drove him to that hapless first meeting with the Jewish Agency's aliya representative in New York, stayed in the United States. He joined the foreign service, and served at one time as the U.S. ambassador to Morocco. He also served as a special adviser on Middle Eastern affairs under President Jimmy Carter. On several occasions, U.S. congressmen and senators would be briefed by one Ginsberg in the State Department prior to visiting Israel, only to be briefed by another, in Misgav Am, several days later. The first Ginsberg, Marc, spoke of America's interests; the second, Mike, of Israel's. Both brothers often smiled when some dignitary told them, "But I just spoke with your brother and he thinks the opposite."

Talking to his brother or his American friends, Mike is often told that he would have been better off had he stayed in Connecticut. No shootings, they tell him, no one infiltrating the town and killing children in the dead of night. Mike won't hear any of it, though. He has done, he says, the only thing he should have. He came to Israel to help build it, he boasts, and he still is.

Sitting on his porch, sipping coffee, he refuses to discuss any what-ifs. “There are no question marks in my life,” he says, smiling, his mustache brushing against the tip of the steamy cup. “I can’t go back to the United States. I don’t want to go back to the United States. I’m perfectly happy where I am right now.”

PART III

FROM QUEENS, NEW YORK, TO HASHMONAIM, 2001

CHAPTER NINE

The house stood empty. Everything that it once contained, all the furniture and knickknacks and small souvenirs that make a house into a home, were packed long ago, crated and shipped to the new destination. Even the beds were gone, and so the members of the Kalker family—Danny, Sharon, and their two younger children, Rachel and Michael—found themselves on the floor, cocooned inside sleeping bags, sweating in the stifling heat of summer in Queens, New York. For the first time, after months of preparations and packing and long-winded debates and domestic dramas, it was clear to all the members of the family that there was no turning back. It was the summer of 2001, and the Kalker family was about to make aliya, about to join their two older children, nineteen-year-old Shoshana and seventeen-year-old Ari, who were already living in Israel.

Alone in her room, thirteen-year-old Rachel couldn't sleep. She stared at the empty walls, where posters of athletes and puppies and her favorite television stars once hung, and was overwhelmed by the dim blankness surrounding her. Trying to avoid being alone with her thoughts, she marched down the hall, toward the room of her ten-year-old brother, Michael. She knocked on his door. He seemed genuinely happy to see her, to have someone to talk to, someone to share his thoughts with.

The two placed their sleeping bags side by side on the floor. Although it was past 2:00 a.m., sleep was not an option for either sibling. In muffled voices, they joked, and reminisced, often pausing to exchange befuddled looks and say, "Can you believe we're moving to another country?" Then the two would burst out in laughter, born more of anxiety than of amusement. They played cards, engaging in some more mindless chatter. Finally, however, there was nothing left to say. After a few moments of uneasy silence, the two told each other that they were tired, although both knew perfectly well that sleep would not be likely that night. Then they bid each other good night, turned over in their sleeping bags several times until they struck a comfortable position, and pretended to be asleep.

With nothing else to take solace in, nothing to distract the mind from the inevitable issue of the impending flight, now just a few hours away, a one-way flight to a new country with new people and a new language, Rachel was slowly seized by dread. The first thoughts seeping into her mind were common enough for young women her age. Will, she wondered, the kids in the new place accept me? Or will I be left out? Will I be able to find new friends? And what will happen to my old friends, the ones staying behind, in Queens? And who will take care of my grandparents now that we're gone? Slowly, however, her concerns drifted in another direction. She wasn't, she realized, simply moving away, to another suburb in another city, to another place where the people would be different but the stores in the malls and the shows on television similar. She was moving to Israel, thousands of miles away. She had often heard about it, growing up in an Orthodox household with two parents who had often discussed making aliya, but she had never been able to conjure up a vivid image of the country, of what it was really like. The one thing that scared her was the explosions she kept hearing about in the news. What were explosions like? She closed her eyes and tried to imagine.

She pictured popcorn on top of a stove, popping loudly. She smiled, realizing that even her imagination was inadequate to grasp the experience awaiting her the next day. And with that thought, she fell asleep.

The next day the empty house was full of people. Friends and neighbors all poured in, popping their heads through the perpetually open door to wish the Kalkers luck and bid them farewell. Too busy to think, the family members shook hands and exchanged hugs and promises to keep in touch, trying to convince their friends, as well as themselves, that distance really was negligible in the face of such strong bonds, that their relationships would continue to be the same, that it would be as if they were just down the block instead of across the ocean. The stream of people gradually became a trickle, and when the last of the well-wishers said his final good-bye there was no longer any excuse to delay their departure. A friend would drive them to the airport, and a taxi would follow with their belongings. And so the Kalkers left their house, the home in which they had lived all of their lives as a family. They waved to their neighbors and were driven away.

Before going to the airport, however, they had one last stop: Sharon's parents who lived several blocks away. As Rachel entered her grandparents' house, she was struck by an incoherent feeling of discomfort. She loved her grandparents, and would miss them very much, she knew, but at that moment, she didn't want to have to be there, couldn't face the inevitable teary good-bye. Not knowing what else to do, she chose, as most teenagers probably would, to retreat into her own shell; she sat beside her grandparents' computer and checked her e-mail.

Out of the corner of her eye, however, she could see her mother, Sharon, was crying. Sharon was hugging her elderly parents, already beset by the plagues of old age. She was terrified at the thought that she was about to leave them behind, especially now that they needed her the most. But looking at Rachel and Michael, and thinking of her two older children living in Israel, she was overwhelmed by the equally potent feeling that the move would be wonderful for all of them. She felt as if she had to choose between her parents and her children. She couldn't stop crying.

Watching her mother cry, Rachel became petulant. She got up and curtly reminded everyone it was time to leave. She couldn't handle any more extreme emotions. She resolved to be practical. Another round of teary farewells, and the Kalkers were once again in a car, this time headed for John F. Kennedy International Airport. As the car drove through the sleepy noon traffic, Rachel was glued to the window. Each street now seemed like a monument: here was the 7-Eleven where she had spent so much time with her classmates over Slurpees and candy, and there the house where a good friend lived, and in the distance 164th Street. . . . For the first time in her life, the familiar geography came alive, and streets, no longer a lifeless grid, turned into rivers of sentimentality upon which memories floated, crowding her, choking her, whispering that this would be the last time she saw all of this, that there would be no more afternoons spent riding bikes or hanging out with friends, that this was, whether she liked it or not, forever. Rachel looked away. She would not cry.

Arriving at the airport, the Kalkers were confronted by the sight of their twelve pieces of luggage; their possessions had been packed gradually, throughout the course of days and weeks, items slowly disappearing from view. But now they were all reunited, not as organic elements in a natural surrounding but as lifeless objects, shaved of their emotional value, crammed on top of one another and stuffed into boxes. Danny seemed amused. "Look at this," he said to the others. "We're moving away, but we're taking the whole country with us." And then the luggage was taken away, headed for the plane's underbelly, and the Kalkers checked in and awaited their flight. Sitting on the terminal's plastic chairs, kicking her feet, anxious and antsy and overcome by sudden crests of emotion, Rachel asked her mother for a few quarters. Then she found a pay phone and called her best friend. She tried to sound calm, tried to be funny, to talk as she would always talk, with an adolescent bravado full of charming confidence that no one older than thirteen, no one who had lived life long enough to know of its despairs and disappointments, could ever muster. But when her friend's voice came on the other end of the line, her throat caved in. She kept the conversation very short, swearing that everything was all right, that the call was just her way to check on her friend, as if the friend was the one in need of consoling.

By the time the Kalkers finally boarded the plane, they had each settled down with a single emotion. The whirlwind of feelings in Rachel's stomach finally phrased itself into one coherent sentence: *It isn't fair.* She refused to accept the injustice of her parents tearing her away from friends and school and home. Michael, enthusiastic, was finally witnessing the culmination of a process he had spent months getting excited about; being the youngest, he realized he could partake of either his sister's rage or his parents' zeal, and he had chosen the latter, more out of convenience than out of sheer anticipation.

Danny, elated, was pondering the new life awaiting them in Israel, the new job as a computer programmer, the new house in Hashmonaim, a small community just outside the bounds of the Green Line, what some would call a settlement. He thought about his parents, who had always spoken favorably of Israel, had traveled there several times, and were supportive of Danny's brother, Joe, when he made aliya two decades before. He was also flooded with memories of the time he himself spent in Israel years ago, in 1970, when, as a seventeen-year-old high school graduate, he went on *Hachshara,* one intense year of travel and study in the Jewish state. During that trip, Danny spent some time in kibbutz Tirat Tzvi, on Israel's border with Jordan. As Gideon, the man responsible for assigning work duties, did not speak a word of English, Danny had to negotiate his way in Hebrew, the first time he had had to do so for practical, not religious, reasons.

He'd arrived on the heels of the War of Attrition, a long campaign waged by terrorists who conducted a never-ending series of guerrilla attacks, infiltrations, and so on. He had met children who had not, until the year prior, slept anywhere but in a bomb shelter. Once, on Yom Kippur, as he was praying at the kibbutz's synagogue, a loud boom was heard; everyone in the synagogue froze, looking around in horror. Then, a second boom sounded and sighs of relief—it was nothing but the sonic boom of a fighter jet. Danny was frightened but also relieved to survey his surroundings and see a band of Jews, all sharing in a sense of camaraderie. This communal warmth and caring became even clearer to him one night as he took the bus from the town of Bet Sha'an back to the kibbutz. An elderly woman got on the bus, sat up front, and appeared to doze off. As the bus passed all stops except for Danny's, which was the last one, the woman suddenly realized that she had missed her stop, and told the driver so. Nonchalantly, the driver turned around and asked Danny if he was in a rush. "If you don't mind," he said, "let's turn back." They did, dropping the old woman at the correct stop. Danny was overwhelmed. For him, the driver represented Israeli society, a society like no other Danny had ever seen. He knew, then and there, that it was a society, a country, he wanted to be a part of. And here he was, on a plane with a one-way ticket, making aliya.

Sharon, uneasy, was doing her best to avoid thinking. She shared a little bit of each family member's sentiments: Like her husband, she was elated to finally be moving to Eretz HaKodesh, the Holy Land. Like her son, she was certainly enthusiastic. She also, however, empathized with her daughter; they had always had a close relationship, and the girl's sulky and petulant behavior, she understood, was much more than a youthful misgiving. She identified in her daughter's tirades a sense of true urgency, of uprootedness, of confusion, that was not entirely unfamiliar to her. Then she closed her eyes and immersed herself in thought.

One fact in particular kept resurfacing in her mind; she remembered her mother telling her of the two boats that she, a Holocaust survivor, had registered to board, one headed for the United States and the other for Palestine. The year was 1945, and the few German Jews who had survived the atrocities of genocide were eager to leave Europe behind and seek a new beginning. Only two options were available, and Sharon's mother did not care which; the first boat to arrive, she decided, would be the one that would carry her to her new home. The boat headed for the United States arrived a few days earlier than the other one, so Sharon's mother found herself en route to New York City instead of on her way to Haifa. A year later, Sharon's father would make the same journey. Could it be that by moving to Israel, Sharon thought, she was, nearly six decades later, choosing the right boat, completing the circle? In a sense, she realized, she was a second-generation immigrant, leaving behind, just as her parents had, a life and a culture and a circle of companions, only to be thrust into the unknown.

The comparison was fascinating. There were, of course, so many differences between her decision, a voluntary act motivated by personal and spiritual considerations, and her parents', fleeing the smoldering ashes of a murderous state and seeking solace in another. Still, she couldn't help but think back on their experiences, retell the stories she had heard so often in the hope of excavating a small fragment of universal truth, a tiny morsel that would better prepare her for what was about to happen when the plane landed and her life in the new country would begin.

First in line was the question of identity. Both Sharon's parents hailed from fervently Orthodox families, yet both parents, especially Sharon's mother, were raised in reasonably affluent European petit bourgeois homes, in which as much attention was paid to operas and concerts as to prayers and religion. The Nazis, who failed to rob Sharon's parents of their breath, succeeded in destroying this delicate balance between their Jewish and European identities. And they took this sensibility with them to the new country, now viewing life solely through a Jewish prism. They still managed to find a balance between the requirements of Orthodoxy and everyday American life, often smoking or riding the subway on the Sabbath, never rejecting the merits of secular culture. But their thoughts and actions were informed by a new sensitivity; those who nearly lost their lives for being Jewish were now unable to see themselves as anything but. Accordingly, the newly arrived immigrants befriended mostly other Jewish immigrants, and moved, after a brief period of transition spent in seedy hotel rooms, to Washington Heights, a neighborhood on Manhattan's northern tip, which in the late 1940s was home to a largely Jewish population. Having settled in, the couple now had to adapt to the more mundane yet equally trying aspects of life in a new country. Sharon smiled, remembering her mother's stories about having to adjust to conducting her affairs in English, a language that she, a well-educated member of the German middle class, had been sure she knew well. Shortly after her arrival, however, she realized how wanting her vocabulary was, how obvious her accent. Sharon knew Hebrew, had studied it for most of her life; was she, she wondered, about to face a similar reckoning as her mother had a generation ago, about to realize that her Hebrew was not nearly as good as she imagined it to be? Still, her parents got along, her mother acquiring the language by reading such novels as *Gone with the Wind* out loud, listening with amusement to her own heavy German accent describing the distinctly American events of the Civil War.

As accustomed as her parents were becoming to their new country, however, as joyous about the freedoms they enjoyed and overwhelmed by the opportunities now available to them, Israel always remained in the background, an unspoken yet imminent force shaping the boundaries of their mental lives. In 1947, as the United Nations General Assembly voted on Proposition 181, better known as the partition plan, which guaranteed the birth of a Jewish state, Sharon's parents were glued to the radio. When the United Nations approved the plan, both screamed. It was a senseless and visceral reaction, an uncommon sound for two reserved people with a European upbringing. But it was the only reaction they could summon, the only one that could appropriately describe the significance of the moment. They screamed until they could scream no more, then they laughed, and then cried. Then, exhausted, they vowed to move there. Reality, however, intervened: Sharon's father, a successful restaurateur in Germany, had opened a small luncheonette on downtown Manhattan's Vesey Street, and was not anxious to emigrate once again, especially when business was picking up as the city's financial district, where the luncheonette was located, grew exponentially. Also, the two had already established a tightly knit community, mostly with other Holocaust survivors in their neighborhood, had joined a synagogue, already had one daughter, Sharon's older sister. Moving to a state struggling for its independence was a precarious and unlikely thing to do; still, the two conceived of Israel as a mystical place, a land in which Jews would always be able to find refuge. And they brought up their two daughters believing the same thing, cherishing the liberties of the United States while yearning, as generations of Jews had done, for Zion and its well-being.

Growing up, Sharon's life fully embodied that split identity. Her school, Yeshiva Soloveichik, had a tradition of teaching *Ivrit Be'Ivrit,* meaning Hebrew in Hebrew, a practice, rather radical for the time, of forgoing the old-fashioned and biblical-focused method of teaching Hebrew in favor of a modem, conversational one, which required students to speak the language constantly. And so, over the course of several years, for five days each week and four hours each day, Sharon spoke Hebrew. And because modern Hebrew was somewhat restricted, having been reborn and practiced mainly in Israel, the texts she learned were primarily borrowed from Israeli culture. She learned Israeli folk songs, themselves adaptations of Russian classics; she chatted in class of Israel's wars, of the Negev Desert, of the massive Jewish migrations to the nascent state. The majority of her teachers were Israeli, and the school celebrated distinctly Israeli holidays such as Yarn Ha'atzmaut, Israel's Independence Day, and Yom Yerushalayim, a celebration of Jerusalem's reunification in 1967 under Jewish rule.

By eighth grade, Sharon was the school's Hebrew valedictorian, but her knowledge was not limited merely to the language;

through the stories and the songs and conversations, she had imbibed a decent dose of Israeli culture, and she was thirsty for more. Arguably, her continual exposure to Israeli culture—so fundamentally different from the reserved quietude of Germany or the reverential respect of the United States—a culture created and defended by youth, where hierarchy was nonexistent and deference rare, enhanced Sharon's already robustly independent personality. Since she came from a background clouded by stories of persecution and annihilation and anti-Semitism, the yeshiva's blend of Zionism with religiosity was particularly potent. It seemed to provide an answer, an antidote, to the ailments that plagued older generations of Jews; it offered a good balance of faith and fact, of belief in God on the one hand and in oneself on the other.

Tall and slim, with light auburn hair and deep blue eyes, young Sharon warmly embraced this empowering message. The leading student in her yeshiva, she took great pleasure in her studies, fascinated by her heritage. A curious and confident girl, she shunned the concept, so common in her surroundings, of befriending only Jews, and instead took her bike and roamed the neighborhood, joining ball games uninvited, playing with the Puerto Rican kids on the next block or with the Indians another one over. She enjoyed their company, felt enriched by their presence. Important as tradition was to her, she could see no merit in isolationism, did not understand her parents and their generation, the way they regarded all gentiles with suspicion, the choice they had made to live in small communities, to avoid assimilating into the grand, cosmopolitan city surrounding them, to limit their social circles to Jews and Jews only. Lacking any personal experience of persecution, empowered by immersing herself in a culture of triumphant Judaism as embodied by Israel, and unaware, as most adolescents are, of her own limitations and those of the world surrounding her, Sharon was certain that she could, with ease, be an observant Jew on the one hand and a citizen of the world on the other. This thought was boosted by the zeitgeist of the late 1960s, transmitted to Sharon by television and radio; everywhere she looked there were young people, only several years older than herself, who defied their parents' logic and restructured their ideologies.

Those were happy days for Sharon; in the summers, the family would move to a bungalow in Rockaway, and Sharon spent long, idle days with her older sister, Hedy, almost nine years her senior, charming the young adults with her winsome smile and her conversation skills. At night, she and Hedy would huddle together in some remote corner outside on the porch, under a clear sky, and talk about the older sister's love interests. Barely a teenager, Sharon felt privileged; she was being allowed into adulthood as a respected member, her advice sought by someone older and more accomplished. She couldn't wait to be older herself, to fall in love, to be truly independent and free to explore the world around her.

As Sharon grew older, however, she realized that growing up also meant accepting responsibility. She graduated from the yeshiva and went on to enroll at the Hebrew Academy of Lincoln Park, a religious high school in Westchester County. Every morning, she would wake up at 6:00 a.m., leave the house an hour later, and take three buses before arriving at school. There she was greeted by a largely uninterested student body, focused, as are high school students the world over, on grades and tests and boys and girls and sports and sense of self. Although it was a Jewish school with religious overtones, Sharon did not feel the same sense of wonderment that was prevalent in her old yeshiva; she did not feel inspired, was not moved by any member of the staff to discover her roots or ponder her tradition. She was overwhelmed by a multitude of secular studies, from math to physics to chemistry, which interfered with her passion for spirituality; for her, the secular subjects, while clearly important, seemed nonetheless devoid of any real value.

Feeling trapped, Sharon decided to change course. She decided she had to take her status as a leader among her peers seriously and create a vibrant and involved community of young Jewish activists where none was present. She put her blue jeans, her favorite article of clothing, back in the closet, vowing to adhere to the more traditional skirts for the remainder of her high school years. For the first time since entering the Hebrew Academy, Sharon felt consistency: here she was, leading a proper Jewish life, undistracted by the mundane nature of self-centered adolescence. Her excursions outside of her neighborhood grew few and far between, as did her interactions with non-Jews. Whereas she had once embraced contradiction, being a traditionalist Jew on the one hand and a universal humanist on the other, she was now chiefly dedicated to Judaism, determined to sweep others up in her enthusiasm.

And, gradually, she succeeded. The first to be infected by her zeal was her mother, who followed her daughter's example and exchanged pants for skirts. Sharon's mother also took to covering her hair, not a common practice in her immediate community. Her mother, Sharon noticed, seemed happier, as if her daughter's shift toward Orthodoxy allowed her to go back to her own roots, back to the life she had practiced before the Holocaust.

Sharon's peers were also influenced by her energy, struck by her good looks, her charisma, and her singular passion for the cause. Time and again, she convinced her fellow students to spend their Sundays not on the basketball court or in front of the television, but marching up and down the streets of Manhattan, demonstrating for a plethora of causes, petitioning against the Soviet government's treatment of that country's Jews or raising money for Israel. One morning in particular marked her ascension into a position of leadership; it was May 15, 1974, Israel's Independence Day, and Sharon arrived at school earlier than usual. As she was getting off the bus, a flock of visibly upset youth approached, surrounding her.

"Have you heard?" one asked. "About the massacre in Ma'alot?"

Earlier that morning, three terrorists, all members of the Democratic Front for the Liberation of Palestine, approached a high school in Ma'alot, a small and sleepy town in the north of Israel, not far from the Lebanese border. They entered the building, taking more than a hundred students and faculty members hostage. The terrorists also surrounded the school with explosives, threatening to blow themselves up with the hostages should their demands, consisting mainly of releasing fellow terrorists imprisoned in Israeli jails, not be met. Sayeret Matkal, the IDF's top counterterrorism unit, arrived at the scene shortly thereafter, and devised a plan: a sniper would shoot the terrorist guarding the front door, thereby leaving ground forces with a three-second window of opportunity during which they would break into the building, dispose of the remaining two terrorists, and rescue the hostages. The sniper placed himself for a few long minutes, aiming slowly before finally taking the shot. He hit his target, but not well enough: the terrorist guarding the door did not die instantly, and instead began firing, warning his friends. Panicked, the other two terrorists began detonating their explosives and shooting indiscriminately at students and soldiers alike. The soldiers entered the building, and a few moments later the battle was over, leaving twenty-two students dead and more than sixty wounded.

Transmitted throughout the world was one photograph taken immediately after the attack ended: a soldier, a look of shock on his face, running out of the school, carrying in his arms a young female student, blood trickling over her anguished face. The picture, a dreadful modern-day pietà, was a rare visual manifestation of a moment of abject horror, and it succeeded in galvanizing many in the American-Jewish community to raise funds and increase awareness in helping Israel combat Palestinian terrorism. Even before seeing it, however, Sharon didn't need more than the key facts, provided by her peers, to realize what she had to do; she had learned of an emergency demonstration, set for that afternoon in midtown Manhattan, against terrorism and in solidarity with Israel. The student body of the Hebrew Academy, she was determined, had to participate.

The school's principal, however, thought differently. First of all, he was not enthusiastic about allowing his students to skip classes, whatever the reason. Furthermore, the demonstration was in Manhattan, and allowing students to travel into the city, unaccompanied, was a responsibility he was reluctant to take. A diplomat, he offered Sharon a compromise; there would be a demonstration, but after school hours, and not in Manhattan but on Main Street in White Plains. Sharon looked at him and laughed in his face; it was, she said, all or nothing. Wincing at the thought of engaging in a conflict with his most active, most vocal student, the principal offered yet another solution: he would call an emergency meeting of the entire school, in which he and Sharon would present their opinions. Then there would be a vote, and whatever the students chose, he would endorse.

Facing the assembly of her peers, no more than several dozen of them, Sharon conjured all the impassioned spirit she could to convince her friends of the worthiness of the cause. Whether it was her charisma or the fact that endorsing her proposal meant missing a chemistry class she did not know, but the students overwhelmingly supported Sharon, and the principal, true to his word, allowed all who wished to participate to leave school at once and take the bus to Manhattan in order to join the demonstration. Leading a small, youthful band, all dazzled by her courage, Sharon left school triumphant. The demonstration itself almost didn't matter; what mattered was her own demonstration of power that morning in front of the student assembly, the passion and conviction, her ascendance to a true position of authority and influence in the service of a cause in which she wholeheartedly believed.

And it was in the service of this cause that she continued to work vigorously. She had been, of course, committed to the Israeli cause even before that incident, such as the year before, when she rushed from shul during Yom Kippur to listen to the radio for accounts of the surprise attack waged by Syria and Egypt on Israel, knocking on every door in her neighborhood to raise money for the Israel Emergency Fund. But as she grew older, her need for knowledge deepened, and she would spend hours reading about Israel's history, about the origins of Zionism, about the Jewish faith. The more she read, the more involved she became, desperate to know more, do more, feel more.

To that end, she joined the youth group Beitar. Formed in the 1930s by the so-called revisionist wing of the Zionist movement, the right-wing faction led by Vladimir Jabotinsky, the movement flourished throughout Europe before being curtailed by the Holocaust. The movement then found a home among the growing Jewish population in the United States, where Beitar members were mostly Orthodox, unabashedly Zionistic, and proactive to a fault. Whereas the mentality of the mainstream American-Jewish community, fearful of upsetting the rest of the country, called for mild-mannered responses and civilized discussions, favoring fund-raisers over demonstrations and backroom negotiations over direct action, Beitar was different in both style and substance. Taking a clear stand to the right on all matters pertaining to Israeli and Jewish politics, members would often find themselves on the fringes of what was considered acceptable behavior: they trained in self-defense, learned to maintain and operate firearms, and orchestrated highly visible stunts against perceived enemies, such as infiltrating official Soviet missions and creating havoc, or harassing high-ranking diplomatic officials who were continually unfriendly toward Israel's positions. Beitar members were also committed, at least on the surface, to the value of aliya, and swore to move to Israel at the earliest convenience and join the struggle there, defending the country's borders against malevolent enemies.

In the summer of 1975, Sharon graduated from high school. The Hebrew Academy had been a steady base of operations for her, and upon graduation she was left, like so many teenagers, disoriented and confused. She was dating a young man at the time, a member of her local Beitar chapter, and together they planned to get married and spend their honeymoon on a plane headed for Israel. For a while, Sharon propagated her position with her usual bravado, telling her parents and whoever else asked that she was moving, fulfilling the dream, making aliya. Deep inside, however, she was unsure: unsure about her prospective fiancé being the one with whom she wanted to spend a lifetime; unsure about moving, right at that time, to a foreign country, even if that foreign country was Israel; and, most important, unsure she could leave behind her parents, who were growing old rapidly. She waited, postponing a decision, doubting herself, all of which were unlikely traits for her. Finally, succumbing to uncertainty, she informed her boyfriend that she would not be marrying him and would not be moving. He left for Israel shortly thereafter, and she remained in New York City, hurting and hopeless.

To make matters worse, her parents decided to move away from Washington Heights. Her father, nearing retirement, had gone out of business when his luncheonette was razed in order to clear the ground for the World Trade Center; as a result, Sharon's parents decided to leave Manhattan for the suburbs, seeking more space and a patch of grass. They found a small two-story house in Forest Hills, Queens, and moved just as Sharon was graduating from high school. The move shook Sharon's confidence even further; she was a shepherd, but her flock was now in another borough, a long train ride away, for all purposes inaccessible. She was out of school, out of love, and out of ideas for her future. Reluctantly she agreed, at her mother's suggestion, to enroll at Queens College. Secular studies had always bored her, and she couldn't stomach the idea of going through four years of what she considered soulless drivel, being occupied by one mundane class after another. Yet, there was nothing else left for her to do, and so she found herself, in September of 1975, walking into the behemoth that was the college's campus, overwhelmed by the thousands of students rushing past her. No longer was she a firebrand, no longer was she even known; she was one among many here, a face without a name, indistinct.

Slowly, Sharon adjusted to college life. Her first move was to install herself in as many Jewish groups as she could find: she became involved in Yavneh, a modern Orthodox student group; she took Yiddish classes and learned to sing old Yiddish folk songs, often performing for the elderly, a young woman spiritedly singing tunes they had not heard for decades. Within months she had woven a web of friends for herself, all of whom were Jewish, most of whom were Orthodox. She was not interested, even on an ethnically diverse campus, in meeting other students from different backgrounds; she had been singularly involved in Jewish causes for too long to allow any foreigners, any gentiles, into her life now. Amid a student body so large, she felt, a yarmulke or a Magen David, a Star of David, was a great basis for an initial conversation. Once she became comfortable in her new environment, however, she revisited her closet, exchanging the skirt for the old, comfortable pair of jeans.

Her mother was shocked, dismayed, angry. Casually, Sharon explained that she felt like she had no reason to wear a skirt anymore. At the Hebrew Academy, she said, she had felt that wearing a skirt would make a difference, would set an example to the others, weaker of mind and of faith; at Queens College, no one was paying any attention, and therefore she could feel free to do whatever was most convenient. Still, her mother was perplexed; was this, she asked, Sharon's way of abandoning her faith? Confidently, Sharon laughed such allegations away. She was, she told her mother, just as adamant about her religious beliefs, her ideology, and her passion. She did not, however, think all these were somehow compromised by her favoring one garment over the other. The problem, she said, was that Orthodox Jews often favored motion over emotion, adhering to strict procedures of religious practice while neglecting the deeper, more meaningful feelings that were supposed to guide and govern one's spirituality. As part of this belief, Sharon also found herself a part-time job as an assistant in Manhattan's diamond district, an uncommon decision for an Orthodox girl at the time. In her spare time, she volunteered at a local Jewish community center in Queens, specializing in after-school programs and teenager outreach programs. Not so far out of high school herself, she was still very much the magnetic peer for local youth frequenting the center, and soon she was back in the position she was accustomed to, a leader.

She graduated three years later with a degree in communications and speech pathology, and found work as a Jewish educator at a local Queens community center. A year later, in early June of 1979, she was invited by friends to spend the holiday of Shavuot at Grossinger's, a once-popular resort in the Catskills. Built in the early 1900s by Selig Grossinger, a Jewish immigrant from Germany, the resort was considered one of the top vacation spots for Jews in the United States, featuring not only gourmet kosher food but also banquet halls, luxury rooms, and various sports facilities, including a year-round ski hill covered with artificial snow. In its peak, in the 1950s, the resort consisted of thirty-five buildings sprawling over 1,200 acres, housing more than 150,000 guests each year. By the time Sharon visited it, however, it was more of a monument than a living thing, as most of the customers who once frequented Grossinger's had either grown too old to travel or had passed away.

One Friday night, as most of the older patrons were already falling asleep, trying to overcome the gargantuan portions of food served for dinner, Sharon joined a group of younger men and women, all passing acquaintances, down at the resort's lake. They were singing *zmirot,* special songs sung only on the Sabbath, chatting and laughing, amicably arguing and enjoying each other's company. A few hours later, exhausted and all too aware of the *Shachris* prayer only a few hours away, the group headed back to their rooms, slowly strolling up the hill leading from the lake to the main guesthouse. As they were walking, Sharon was approached by a lanky, bespectacled young man with pointy features and high cheekbones, who presented himself as Danny Kalker. The two talked, and he told her of an incident from years back, when he worked as a water ski instructor at a summer camp, involving a snapping turtle and a handful of frightened children. She laughed. They exchanged some more anecdotes, each patiently listening as the other told largely mundane tales of fun and folly. Finally, they talked about ideology. To her surprise, Danny said that he intended to make aliya one day. It had always been his dream, he said, ever since he had spent a year in Israel, working and touring the land, immersing himself in Judaic studies, and learning the language. Sharon was enamored, the young man suddenly appearing in an entirely different light. She had been there as well, once, with her parents, for a brief stay, but had never lived there, had never worked there, had never become intimate with the people. As the two finally arrived at the guesthouse, they bid each other good night, promising to meet the next day.

The next morning, Danny and Sharon were ambling on their way up to the tennis courts, when they spotted Danny's parents walking toward them. "You're about to meet my parents," Danny said. "But don't worry, they like you."

Sharon was puzzled.

"How do you know that?" she asked. "They didn't even meet me yet."

Danny pointed at his father, asking Sharon if she noticed his smile. "Look at him," he said. "There's a special smile that he has only in *simchas* [a Hebrew word meaning happy occasions]. He has that smile now." The conversation with the parents proved to be pleasant, and the two spent some more time walking and talking and getting to know one another. When they left the resort a few days later, they were a couple.

Several weeks passed, during which Danny and Sharon tried to see as much of each other as they could. He lived in Brooklyn, she in Queens. She was an educator, he a computer programmer, then an underdeveloped field. Late in June, Sharon went to Israel for the second time in her life, this time to lead a group of teenage volunteers at a day camp in Jerusalem. After she departed for Israel, Danny was left by himself, realizing how much he missed her. He resigned from his job and bought a plane ticket. On August 1, 1979, he flew to Israel, meeting up with Sharon several days later. As they escorted Sharon's group on a trip to the old city of Jaffa, they were able to break away for a while.

One of the more magnificent remnants of historical Israel, the old city of Jaffa has been largely preserved as it was left by its Turkish builders several centuries ago. Walking through the narrow alleyways, tripping on the cobblestones and intoxicated by the fragrant breeze emanating from the nearby Mediterranean, the two were happy to be in Israel, happy with each other's company. They were young and awash in moonlight, standing, it seemed, within history itself, in a place where time had no power. It was there, near a tiny park overlooking the Mediterranean Sea, where renegade palm trees grew to unprecedented heights, that Danny knelt down and asked Sharon to be his wife.

Teary-eyed, she agreed. They would get married, she thought, and move to Israel, where one lived Judaism instead of merely talking about it.

CHAPTER TEN

Leaving Jaffa the next morning, Sharon and Danny boarded a crowded bus to Eilat, Israel's southernmost town and a bustling seaside resort which attracted Israeli vacationers as well as tourists from all over the globe. For the two New Yorkers, who took their vacations in the Catskills along with friends and family, the town was a revelation: bleach white sands stretching for miles and miles and fading into the Red Sea, which was so clear as to be almost translucent, with the stark skyline dotted with the occasional five-story hotel. More striking, however, were the people; the beaches of Eilat were packed with young men and women, tanning and swimming, as if there was no border several miles away, as if there was no mandatory military service in their immediate future or recent past. While the tourists and the older Israelis preferred the hotels, the younger Israelis simply camped out on the beach, starting fires and cooking food and playing guitars, setting up tents, or just sleeping out in the open air in sleeping bags. Sharon and Danny joined them.

Their return home to New York, however, was as taxing and depressing as the days spent on the beach were magical and carefree. They had a wedding to organize, a future to consider, plans to make. They had no money, few prospects, limited earning power. They were both more interested in ideology than in material goods; that was part of their mutual attraction. Yet, for the practical purposes of building a life together, material goods were necessary. Youthful and optimistic, they set the date of their wedding for December 22, 1979, allowing themselves just four months to plan the modest event. It came and went, and as 1980 dawned, Danny and Sharon found themselves as husband and wife. They briefly considered making aliya, as they had discussed during their first meeting at Grossinger's, but decided to postpone it for a few years. Their plan was simple: Sharon would finish her graduate degree in social work, Danny would continue to work, earning a nice salary in computers, and within five years or so, with the money other couples traditionally use toward putting a down payment on a house, they would pack their belongings, say their good-byes, and move to Israel, preferably to Jerusalem.

As their marriage rolled into its second year, Sharon became pregnant. Knowing that the apartment they had been renting would be too small for a family, and wishing to avoid the onus of never-ending rent, Danny and Sharon bought a small house a few miles away, in the Hillcrest section of Queens. In January of 1982 their first child, Shoshana, was born. She was followed in 1984 by Ari, and then again in 1987 by Rachel and in 1989 by Michael. The Kalkers enrolled their children in Jewish schools, keeping a traditional Jewish home yet never denying them any of the comforts the secular world had to offer, such as movies and music and television. Their self-imposed deadline for moving to Israel came and went, yet neither of them paid it any mind; they would move soon, they told themselves time and again, just as soon as Shoshana graduated from elementary school or Michael completed kindergarten. Yet, they were both enamored of the comforts of suburban life, with the security that comes with home ownership, with the stability that follows gainful employment.

As the years passed, the issue of aliya began seeping into the uncomfortable silences in the conversations Danny and Sharon had about the future. Both of them were spontaneous people, Sharon more so than her husband, and there would often be moments in which the decision was almost made, in which the house was almost sold and the children almost informed. Yet, a wall of harsh reasoning always stood in the way, built mostly by Danny. He was afraid, he admitted to his wife, afraid of having to struggle in order to find a job again, afraid that his Hebrew was insufficient to guarantee him employment in Israel, afraid of leaving behind everything he had ever known. Sharon responded with arguments that began on an earthly plane and then rocketed upward, touching on transcendental issues: she would assure her husband that, despite the difficulties, he was young and educated and skilled and there was no reason why he wouldn't be able to support them in a growing economy such as Israel's; then, she would talk about ideology, about religion, about how spirituality was not really possible outside of Israel.

Her answers reflected her own reservations about Jewish life in the United States. When she was growing up, it seemed to her, religiosity was a largely unregulated matter, each observant Jew allowed, within certain boundaries, to decide the scale, scope, and schedule of his or her own practices, just as she could take her blue jeans on and off yet feel, and be regarded as, equally Orthodox, equally Jewish. In the 1980s, however, she felt the cold wind of stringent Orthodoxy against her cheeks, was appalled to see certain practices that were once overlooked, such as women wearing pants, frowned upon by a growing majority of the community around her. She looked with dismay at what she perceived to be a gaping rift within the Jewish community, with the silent, secular majority waltzing toward assimilation, stricken by intermarriage and stripped of most elements of Jewish identity, and the religious minority setting stricter standards, building a higher wall, demanding more obedience and ostracizing those who failed to blindly comply. As skirts and prayers got longer and patience shorter, Sharon sought solace in her own Jewish endeavors, creating several educational programs for teenagers and spearheading a prayer group for women called Nishmat Nashim, Hebrew for Women's Soul, which was largely frowned upon by the Orthodox establishment, since women aren't allowed to participate as equal members in prayers.

Moving to Israel, she gradually became convinced, would save her from having to choose sides, rescue her from the creeping fundamentalism around her. There, she remembered with passion, every experience was a spiritual one, every stone a building block in the history of the Jewish people. The feeling of *kavanah,* or intent, perhaps the key factor in any prayer, came naturally there, penetrating one on every hilltop and in every house. There, she felt, one needn't wear one's best suits and sit through hours of excruciatingly painful ceremonies conducted in subpar Hebrew; it was enough to go outside and breathe the air. Sharon wanted to move there, to Israel, imagining her spirit would be freed from its quagmire once she made aliya. Danny, however, was more hesitant. He had already lived in Israel, and yearned to live in it again. His passion for the land was just as great as that of his wife, if not greater. Yet, he was a deeply rational, responsible man. Now wasn't the right time, he said. We'd know when the right time came, he said.

An opportunity came in 1991. Four years prior to that, the company Danny worked for merged with another company to create a synthesis, an insurance giant that was supposed to go public five years later. With one year to go, however, the merged company was purchased by a third party, called Cigna, and was being scrutinized in search of ways to streamline the company and the workforce alike. Danny was offered the chance to keep his job, but on the condition that he would move to Hartford, Connecticut, as the New York division was shutting down. The process of selling his home and buying a new one, of moving the kids out of their schools and into others, of leaving behind both his and Sharon's parents, all that was beyond what Danny and Sharon were willing to tolerate. It would have meant settling into a small community that could not even sustain a Jewish high school, which they would soon need for their daughter.

He declined the offer, and lost his job a year later. After a brief period of recovery and support, Sharon approached her husband with a concrete offer: losing his job, she said, might prove to be just the opportunity they had been waiting for; they should move to Israel right away, before Shoshana entered high school, before the kids grew too old to adjust to the new country. Still, Danny hesitated. With major corporate cutbacks, major life decisions were difficult to make. His confidence was affected as well in regards to finding employment in Israel, when it was difficult enough to find suitable work in his native country. But Sharon persisted. Finally, the two agreed on a compromise: they would travel to Israel in January and treat the trip as a candid exploration of the possibility of making aliya. If they liked it, they agreed, they would move instantly; if not, the question would still be open for discussion.

As the trip's deadline approached, Danny and Sharon fell into discord. Danny, it became clear, no longer wanted to go. He was in final negotiations for a new job in computers, and the concept of moving to Israel, while still appealing on a certain level, now seemed like an irresponsible and irrational thing to do. Deep in his heart, the fire of Zionism was burning, but when he looked at the facts everywhere else, none of them supported moving to Israel. To the usual calculations of liklihood of employment and adequate levels of income was added another, often unspoken, consideration: in January of 1991, when they had planned to go to Israel for a family Bar Mitzvah, an international coalition led by the United States attacked Iraq. Danny and Sharon followed the news reports of the war, shocked to see Iraqi Scud missiles fired at Israel. At the time, it served as a fresh reminder of the hostile and malevolent neighbors Israel was continually besieged by. They delayed their trip, letting the date of the Bar Mitzvah pass, realizing they could not take their four young children to Israel while men, women, and children were walking around with gas masks constantly at their sides.

Finally, in April 1991, the Kalkers went to Israel; as always, both Danny and Sharon found the experience inspiring, staying in the settlement of Efrat with Danny's brother over the Passover holiday. Yet, despite their renewed enthusiasm for Israel, the idea of making aliya slowly died down, all momentum lost. Perhaps it was the clear and growing difference between Sharon and Danny, one searching for stability and the other for adventure, or perhaps it was their mutual attachment to life in Queens or to their families or friends, that kept them from moving. Whatever the reason, the Kalkers decided to stay.

The question of aliya continued to resurface in nightly conversations between Danny and Sharon, each time in a quieter, less tenacious tone, each time more as a fantasy than as a reality. Pretending all was in order, Sharon was nonetheless growing restless and dissatisfied. All of her energy, her passion and dedication and commitment, were now channeled into her educational initiatives. Some of these projects were enjoying moderate success, but others met with resistance. In 1997, for example, the Va'ad Harabonim of Queens, a local organization of senior Orthodox rabbis that usually limited its authority to such religious duties as awarding restaurants with kashrut certificates, published a one-page announcement signed by almost all ninety members denouncing Sharon's women's prayer group. Such prayer groups, a rather recent innovation in Orthodox circles, were established in the late 1970s in order to allow women a communal forum for religious practice. Under Jewish law, women were banned from leadership roles in the community; they were not allowed to pray out loud, as their voices might distract the men; and they were not viable members of a minyan, a quorum of at least ten Jewish men required for any communal prayer. In response to the restrictions, Orthodox women across the United States, sporadically at first but with increasing steam, organized and formed the Women's Tefillah Network, tefillah being the Hebrew term for prayer. Organized by open-minded and egalitarian women such as Sharon, these groups would usually meet once a month, pray together, and study a portion of the Bible. By the mid-1990s, several dozen such groups were in existence.

The Va'ad Harabonim, however, disliked the initiative; instead of attacking her outright, their announcement tried to kill Sharon's initiative with kindness. The Va'ad recognizes, read the announcement, "the sincere desire of many women to express their devotion to G_D" and "highly commends this feeling, provided it is translated into action in the proper direction." In the mildest language imaginable for what was essentially a warning prior to excommunication, the Va'ad expressed its "disapproval of innovation" and distaste for "breaking the boundaries of tradition." In short, they disapproved of those who tread on what they considered the "slippery slope" of Judaism.

In the short term, the conflict infused Sharon with newfound joie de vivre. She realized that women's prayer groups, growing larger and more committed, would not disappear, regardless of what some clerics had to say. Always a fan of jousting with the establishment, she reveled in the opportunity to once again stand up to men in positions of power and assert her opinion, as she had done so many years before with her high school principal. The Va'ad's letter was widely reported in Jewish and local media, and Sharon was delighted by the sudden increase of interest in her group; Jewish women from across the neighborhood called or dropped by, asking questions and signing up for meetings. Pleased and defiant, she told a Jewish newspaper that her only reaction to the letter, following the increased interest in her group it had created, was to "hope she had enough chairs for all the women who wanted to attend." In the long term, however, the entire incident served as just an additional reminder of how unhappy she had become; thinking again of her favorite bit of wordplay, she couldn't help but feel that her family was simply going through the motions of life, having left the emotion somewhat unattended. Even more frightening than confronting her own lack of self-realization was observing her children growing up: she feared that they would inherit a fate similar to hers, passionate Jews trapped by the material comfort of American society on the one end and by the stifling, rigorous insistence on protocol of the Orthodox establishment on the other. She could see that some of her children, Rachel in particular, were already harboring a hidden resentment of religious rituals, which they considered hollow and meaningless. Sharon tried her best to broaden their horizons, but her imagination and creativity could go only so far. Slowly, she yielded to the thought of struggling to keep her spiritual balance and accepted the fact that she, already a middle-aged woman, would probably never make aliya.

Another year passed, and Shoshana graduated from Yeshivah of Flatbush High School in Brooklyn. The eldest daughter, she had inherited the largest dose of her parents' zeal for Israel and Judaism, and seized on her newly minted status as a high school graduate to announce that she wished to study in Israel for one year, to attend an enhanced program of Jewish studies at Michlelet Mevaseret Yerushalayim in Jerusalem. Sharon couldn't help but think about her own announcement, when she was Shoshana's age, that she was getting married and moving to Israel, smiling at the thought of her parents' panicky response and her subsequent change of heart. But whereas she herself had been rash and impulsive, her daughter was collected and calculating: she was not eloping with a man she had just met, not announcing her intentions to move to Israel for good, but rather planning on attending a reputable academic institution for the purpose of enhancing her Jewish education, limiting her stay to a reasonable and responsible period of one year.

While not in the least surprised, Danny was delighted with his daughter's decision. Even if the Kalkers never make aliya as a family, he thought, there was still the chance that a year of study in Israel would be the first step his children would take in making aliya on their own. Without hesitation, both Sharon and Danny gave Shoshana their blessings. Parting with their eldest was difficult, granted, and concern for her safety often troubled them both, but they were thrilled that she would at least have experienced living in Israel, formed a concrete bond with the country and its citizens, thereby strengthening her own Jewish identity in the process. And so off went Shoshana, away to Jerusalem, calling periodically with excited stories about someone she had met or something she had seen or somewhere she had visited, each story reminding Sharon and Danny of their own experiences of being in Israel for the first time, overwhelmed by the fact that everyone around was Jewish, taken with the sights and smells and sounds of the land they had previously known only from prayer.

Stateside, however, life remained uneventful. Ari transferred to the Benjamin Cardozo High School, a campus with verdant lawns and shady maple trees and four thousand students, not a single one of whom, at the time of Ari's attendance, was an observant Jew. Rachel, on her end, was spending most of her time on the basketball court rather than on her homework. Of all four children, she was the one closest to her mother in both figure and temperament. She was tall, blond and blue-eyed, agile and athletic, the kind of young woman one might expect to find in an advertisement for a trendy clothing company wishing to promote some undefined all-American look. Like her mother, she was quick to start a conversation, and possessed that mesmerizing ability to hold her listeners captive by the sheer force of her charisma. Still, she was a teenager, with emotional highs and lows, with a few friends and a few anxieties, with grades that could have been better and a life that was, overall, just fine. Finally, her younger brother, Michael, was growing up to be a well-mannered and clever child. He had decided, for example, that he wished to become a doctor when he grew up; unlike many of his peers, who make such decisions in the morning only to forget all about them by nightfall, Michael was persistent—he created a new e-mail account consisting of his first name followed by the letters MD, a self-reminder of his chosen vocation. He read up on the topic, devoting a considerable amount of time to developing a basic knowledge of anatomy. When he wasn't studying the human body, however, he was very much an ordinary fourth grader, playing video games, following sports, and engaging in fantasy games with his friends.

One day, however, Danny Kalker got a telephone call that would change the family's life forever. He was in his office early one afternoon when the phone rang. He answered, and was delighted to hear his daughter Shoshana's voice on the other end of the line. After a few moments of exchanging pleasantries, swapping stories, and talking about mutual friends and relatives, Shoshana paused, taking a deep breath. Danny already had a good idea of what he was about to hear.

"Dad," she said in a soft and hesitant voice, "there's something we need to talk about."

Danny's heart missed beat after beat. He began to smile. Trying her best to lend her shaky voice some depth and a ring of authority, Shoshana told her father the entire plan. After she finished her year at the seminary, she told him, mustering courage to utter each separate word, she planned on applying to Bar Ilan University, near Tel Aviv, in the hope of one day becoming a teacher of Judaic studies. She made it clear that after finishing her studies at Bar Ilan, she intended to stay in Israel. She made it clear, in short, that she had decided to make aliya. She conveyed all this to her father as gently as she could. Her father, she knew, had always wanted to move to Israel, giving her the sense, even as a child, that, for a Jew, residing anywhere else was far from ideal. His passion and commitment to the idea of aliya, she hoped, would strengthen her own conviction, giving her the support she—then merely a seventeen-year-old young woman—needed to take such a significant, yet frightening, step.

Nervous, she continued to enumerate all the reasons that propelled her toward her decision. Then, when she was done, a second of silence ensued.

"So what's the problem?" Danny asked his daughter.

"All my pros for staying in Israel are really strong," she replied. "And there are a lot of them. There's only one con."

"And that is?" he prodded his daughter, wondering what could possibly be in the way of her decision.

"My family," she said.

"Avraham Avinu left his family to go to Israel," Danny said, citing the biblical Abraham's decision to emigrate from his native Ur to Eretz Israel, the land of Israel.

"But Avraham's family were idol worshippers!" Shoshana said. "He needed to leave them anyway. You're good Jews, I don't have to leave you!"

Again, a moment of silence, this time longer.

"So go," Danny said, "and we'll follow you."

Shoshana couldn't see her father as they spoke, but Danny had a large smile on his face, the kind, he thought later, that his own father reserved for special occasions. Sitting on his swivel chair in his office, he clenched his fist, squinted his eyes, and muttered a silent but liberating *Yes!* He gave his daughter his blessings not once but thrice. He told her that he was far from shocked, that he had, in fact, half-expected her to make aliya. Overwhelmed, Shoshana thanked her father profusely. They hung up, knowing that they would talk again soon.

From that day forward, aliya was once again a viable option, a recurrent topic of discussion between Danny and Sharon. At first, Danny was afraid to raise the issue, concerned that his wife might have forsaken the idea entirely and would not be ready to reconsider. Sharon, however, had never entirely stopped entertaining the possibility. Soon there was new spirit burning within her, guided by the realization that if she and Danny chose to pursue aliya, it was now or never.

That Passover, the Kalkers traveled to Israel once more, for another nephew's Bar Mitzvah. This time, they did not stay with family but rented an apartment in Jerusalem, determined to live like Israelis, to get to know the land and the people. The family was particularly taken with Jerusalem's local cabs. Accustomed to New York City, where cabs are a utilitarian means of transportation, they were struck by the cab-riding experience in Israel. Here a ride was an adventure, as erratic and engaging and wonderful as the people who drove. To their delight, every cabdriver seemed to offer advice, amicably mock their accents, tell them his life story, and ask for theirs, curse other drivers, wave at friends, eat and drink—all the while driving the cab at breakneck speed.

As the vacation approached its end, Danny and Sharon had no doubt—they were making aliya. On the last day of the trip, the family drove to Hashmonaim, a small settlement halfway between Jerusalem and Tel Aviv, to look at a potential home there. Although the brand-new multilane highway to get to Hashmonaim had just been inaugurated, the drive seemed to the Kalkers to last an eternity. When they finally reached their destination, they were greeted by friendly neighbors who were more than pleased to show them around and offer information and advice. The Kalkers were taken in. A decision was made.

Thus reenergized, Sharon and Danny began making inquiries into the practicality of the move. Their first concern, obviously, was the children, and each child was a separate case. Michael, they realized, would be the one harmed the least by leaving the United States. He had friends, granted, but was still a child and would surely be capable of creating new friendships; also, he was only in sixth grade and could still easily adapt to Israel with little or no problems of academic continuity. His older siblings, however, would both be strongly affected by the move. Rachel would be planted in Israel for four demanding years of high school shortly after her arrival and would have to take her Bagrut exams—the Israeli equivalent of a New York Regents exam, only somewhat harder and all in Hebrew—during the end of the third year. Ari would be rushed to finish high school in Queens and expected, only a year later, to join the Isaeli army.

Then there were housing and employment issues and the other rudimentary basics of life that had been plaguing Danny for years, stopping him time after time from completing the process and moving. Sharon, for her part, also had to consider her parents: her sister, Hedy, had died several years before of ovarian cancer, and Sharon was now the sole living relative the elderly couple had. Faced with so many concerns on the one hand and their increasingly strong yearning to make aliya on the other, Danny and Sharon realized that they had come to a crossroads, and needed to choose one path and forever ignore the other. They chose to make aliya, and set about informing the children of their decision.

And, just as Sharon and Danny had anticipated, the children each reacted according to character. Ari grew pale and morose, asking endless questions about the army, concerned about not being able to complete his high school requirements in the short time he had left before the designated departure date a year from the following summer. Rachel, incredulous at first, screamed and hissed, threatening to stay behind. "You can't just do this to me," she told her parents again and again; "it isn't fair." Finally, Michael listened and nodded, asking a few questions but expressing his consent and contentment. The Kalker household, once an organic entity revolving on the mundane goings-on of daily life, became the headquarters of a single-issue army, overwhelmed and understaffed. Plans were made, lists were drawn up, timetables composed and adhered to zealously. Danny and Sharon met with Jewish Agency officials, as well as with representatives of Tehilah, Hebrew for glory, a nonprofit organization founded in the 1980s that focuses on facilitating the aliya of young Orthodox and mostly American Jews. They inquired about a new house, new jobs, new schools. Through a contact at the Jewish Agency, who wrote a powerful letter to a friend of his on the board of education, they managed to arrange with Cardozo High School that Ari be allowed to take all his remaining courses at once, earning a regent's diploma after only three years of high school; then, they thought, he could move to Israel with the rest of the family, study in a Yeshiva for a year, and go to college, deferring his army service for several years, so he could get acclimated before becoming a soldier.

While Sharon was busying herself arranging for a quick and

smooth departure, Danny was entrusted with setting the foundation for the family's future in Israel. The Jewish Agency provided enormous assistance, guides helping to explain the aliya process, informing the new immigrants of their special rights and of the numerous forms they needed to fill out in order to enjoy them. Tehilah, on the other hand, provided everything the Jewish Agency did not: information sessions delivered in plain, coherent terms; assistance with career placements in Israel; and organized pilot trips, sending prospective immigrants to several communities with large populations of American-Jewish *olim,* the Hebrew term for those who made aliya, and helping them get acquainted with the country and find affordable housing.

Danny signed up for such a trip. As he was packing, he thought that the two most important things he was taking with him were not physical objects, but spiritual concepts—*emunah* and *bitachon,* Hebrew for faith and confidence. The trip presented many challenges, but Danny thought that by moving to Israel he was doing God's will, and he was certain that God would help him be successful in the process.

In May of 2001 he flew to Israel, by then having sent his résumé to several potential employers. Unlike most of his peers on that trip, he had family in Israel—his brother Joe had immigrated almost twenty years before, in 1981, and was now living in Efrat, a Jewish settlement behind the Green Line.

Any discussion of the settlements is, from the first word onward, tainted by one's ideological convictions. Even the term is controversial: while to most people the small Jewish towns located in the midst of a Palestinian population in the West Bank or the Gaza Strip are known as settlements, to their inhabitants, as well as to the Israeli Foreign Ministry, they are simply known as "Jewish communities," making no distinction between what lies east and west of the Green Line. The line itself, referring to Israel's borders prior to the 1967 war, is also controversial: eastern Jerusalem, taken by Israel during the same war, was officially annexed, yet the West Bank and the Gaza Strip were not. They, in turn, came to be known as the Territories, a definition whose mere vagueness attests to the disinclination of all involved in the conflict to give names to places; giving names is an act of ownership, and ownership is what the conflict is all about. Through a bizarre turn of events, the West Bank was never really owned by any sovereign nation: In 1947, when the UN passed Resolution 181, it was a part of discombobulated Palestine, destined, under the partition plan, to become part of the nascent Arab state. The Arabs, however, rejected the plan, and when they attacked Israel in 1948, the West Bank was captured by Jordan. However, because the Arab invasion stood in direct contradiction to the UN Security Council's bidding, no countries save for the United Kingdom and Pakistan recognized Jordan's sovereignty over the land when, in 1950, it declared ownership of the West Bank. In 1967, then, Israel won over a swath of land that was historically ownerless, and could therefore not be returned to anyone.

Awash with the triumphant zeal of the 1967 war, some religious groups began plugging the victory into what they understood as the heavenly ordained plan designating the Jewish people as the sole owners of the biblical Land of Israel. Under the guidance of a rabbi named Yehuda Tzvi, a handful of activists began campaigning for Jewish resettlement of the West Bank. The Arab riots of 1936, which had resulted in the deaths of dozens of Jews, had eradicated Jewish communities in Hebron and elsewhere across the West Bank. The most prominent among them was a young rabbi named Moshe Levinger, whose wife, Miriam, was an American-Jewish immigrant from New York. In April of 1968, less than a year after the war, Levinger led eighty followers into Hebron, where they checked into a local Palestinian hotel and celebrated Passover. By September, construction of Kiryat Arba, a Jewish settlement just outside of Hebron, was complete, and Levinger moved there with several of his students. In the meantime, the Israeli government treated the first settlers lightheartedly, perceiving them as a fringe group bound to disappear if not nurtured. Levinger, however, managed to capture the imagination of many modern Orthodox Jews, and a camp became organized on the outskirts of what was traditionally the politically moderate National Religious Party, a camp calling for more settlements, citing the Bible as a Jewish lease on the entire land.

As additional settlements were built, Israeli governments, on both the left and right, were largely receptive to the new concept. First of all, they realized, the more settlements there were "on the ground," the harder it would be, in any future negotiation with the Palestinians, to dispute Israel's ownership of the territory. Second of all, the settlements were a convenient housing solution, as the government was able to offer newly arrived immigrants as well as impoverished Israelis new, spacious houses at moderate prices, alleviating the crises of density and the high cost of living in Israel's major cities. Therefore, the Jewish population of the West Bank changed dramatically, transforming from small religious settlements into more diverse communities comprised of political devotees, new Israelis, and young couples seeking suburbia at more affordable prices.

Young, modern Orthodox Americans found a comfortable zone in the exact center of that scale. On the one hand they were mostly attracted to the religiosity that inspired the settler movement's original creation, and on the other they were attracted to the relatively high quality of life the communities had to offer: there they could live together, within walking distance of their shul, a tightly knit community, with each member enjoying a large house and a breathtaking view of the naked curves of the cream-colored hills of Judea and Samaria, the historic biblical names for the two regions making up the West Bank. In 1983, Rabbi Shlomo Riskin, the renowned leader of Manhattan's Lincoln Square Synagogue, jolted the American-Jewish community when he, followed by several dozen of his congregants, made aliya and founded the settlement of Efrat, several miles to the south of Jerusalem. Danny's brother Joe joined Rabbi Riskin in the mid-1980s.

During his pilot trip to Israel, Danny and his brother were

seated in a car en route to Efrat. As they approached the Tunnel Road, named for the numerous tunnels on the main road that connects Jerusalem to a host of settlements in Gush Etzion—Efrat, with a population of twelve hundred families, being the largest—Joe stopped the car along the side of the road and handed Danny a bulky object.

"Here," he said nonchalantly. "Put this on."

Danny took the object, drawing a sharp breath as he realized it was a bulletproof vest. He stared at his brother for a second, trying to determine whether Joe was joking or being serious. His brother's blank stare answered the question.

Silently, Danny put on the vest. It was the first time since he and Sharon had decided to make aliya that he stopped to think about the one topic previously obscured by the immediate concerns of finding a house and a job: the security situation, the terrorist attacks, the potential danger to his family. More intrigued by the experience than the actual idea of wearing the vest, Danny slipped the vest on. It was the first time the reality of the situation hit home.

But the issue refused to disappear. On May 29, 2001, the last day of Danny's pilot trip, a fifty-three-year-old, recently arrived Jewish immigrant from New York named Sarah Blaustein traveled on the Tunnel Road from Jerusalem on her way back to her home in Efrat. With her in the car were her husband, Norman; her son from a previous marriage, Samuel Berg; a young Jewish woman by the name of Ester Alvan; and three other passengers. Norman Blaustein had initiated the trip; he was flying to New York the next day to attend to some business he still had there, and it was his habit to pray at the Western Wall before each trip. Halfway down the road, their car was attacked by Palestinian snipers. Sarah Blaustein and Ester Alvan were killed on the spot; Norman Blaustein and Samuel Berg were wounded.

At the same time, Danny and his brother Joe were seated at Angel's Bakery in Jerusalem's industrial zone, about to close the deal on a rental house Danny had seen in Hashmonaim. Just as pen was being put to paper, Joe got a call on his cell phone. He nodded his head, said a few words, excused himself and left. He was a member of Zaka, an all-volunteer organization whose members, mostly religious men, take it upon themselves to arrive at the scene of an attack and try to locate all human remains in order to bring them to proper burial. Danny was moved. All the feelings he had suppressed came gushing back, washing him with warm dread. Just several days before, he had traveled on the same road. Just several days before, he had come to Israel to finalize his family's aliya. Soon, they would move to Israel, travel its roads and board its buses and frequent its public places, all potential targets for deadly terrorist attacks. Danny extinguished those thoughts as soon as they arose. If Israelis can handle it, he thought, the fear and uncertainty and unbearable loss, so could he, so could his family.

He took some time, however, to reflect on the rampant violence that had ravaged Israel for as long as he could remember. He recalled the events of 1987, when a vehicle driven by a Jewish settler struck and killed several Palestinian passersby. Their funerals turned into protests, which inspired the intifada, Arabic for uprising; for the first time in twenty years of Israeli governance, the Palestinian population took to the streets in demonstrations that often became violent, throwing rocks and Molotov cocktails. The Israeli army, certain at first that the demonstrations would die out within a few days, quickly came to its senses, and reacted with great force. Many Palestinians died, most of whom, despite their often active participation in violent demonstrations, were never classified as combatants. Fundamentalist Muslim terrorist organizations such as Hamas and Islamic Jihad gained power and prominence, launching suicide attacks against targets inside Israel proper as well as constant shootings and bombings against Jewish civilians in the West Bank and the Gaza Strip. A peace accord, signed in 1993 by Israel's prime minister Yitzhak Rabin and the Palestine Liberation Organization's Yasser Arafat, led to the creation of the Palestinian Authority, a transitory body slated to one day govern the sovereign state of Palestine. The accord faltered, however, and Palestinian terrorism continued. Claiming the issue of settlements was never meant to be discussed until the final stage of negotiations, sometime in the distant future, one Israeli prime minister after another endorsed the construction of more settlements and the expansion of existing ones. In 2000, several months after a risky bid by Israeli prime minister Ehud Barak to finalize the peace process and create a Palestinian state over the lion's share of the West Bank and the Gaza Strip, the intifada erupted anew, with the Palestinians blaming the violence on a visit by Ariel Sharon, then a hawkish member of Knesset, to a holy Muslim site on the Temple Mount, sacred to both Muslims and Jews. The violence that ensued claimed the lives of hundreds, with a spate of suicide bombings driving the Israeli population to despair. Ariel Sharon was elected prime minister in February of 2001. For most Israelis, there was no longer a difference between the settlements and the rest of Israel; everywhere, violence was rampant. Sharon set in motion a plan to erect a fence around Jewish communities in the West Bank, enclosing most of them on the Israeli side, at least temporarily.

A mile or two from the site of the future fence, in a tiny community called Hashmonaim, just outside the Green Line, Danny found a house. He was also offered a contract for a full-time job in computers. This was rare, as most other emigrants on pilot trips were given, at best, nothing more concrete than a promise for another meeting once they had moved to Israel. As he left Israel, Danny smiled; he had traveled, he reflected, with faith and confidence, and he left Israel with a job and a house. This, he thought, was *Yad Hashem,* the hand of God helping him along.

CHAPTER ELEVEN

The day Danny returned to New York from his pilot trip, he picked up a copy of the *New York Times*. In Israel, where he had spent the previous two weeks, the news was treated not as entertainment but as ritual. This was especially true of radio news broadcasts: every hour, every radio in every house and every car would emit a series of long, shrill beeps, marking the time, like church bells did in other countries. Then the news would come on, delivered in an austere tone by baritone-voiced announcers, with no spirited background music or intermittent jingles to interrupt the solemn stream of mostly bad tidings. In New York, he thought, the news consisted of weather and traffic and the stock market and the Yankees; in Israel, it was about life and death and war and peace, a life where the personal was so heavily influenced by the national. Israelis, he had noticed, used their news broadcasts not as almanacs but as travel guides; if the news announced that a suicide bomber had blown himself up on a certain street, for example, most Israelis simply crossed that street off their mental maps, avoiding the area if possible. Thus they protected themselves from living in the constant and debilitating shadow of tragedy and memory. They also protected themselves against the horror of the sheer randomness of terrorism; if a bomb went off in a certain street, most Israelis told themselves, contrary to reason, that if one just avoided that particular street from then on, one was likely to be safe. Danny held in his hands the familiar format of the *Times*. He scanned a few headlines pertaining to violence and crime: here a young woman had been raped, there a youth stabbed, and in the Hudson River bodies were being dredged up.

At that moment, all the incoherent tension he had felt while in Israel, all the anxiety that had been building up in him ever since his brother handed him the bulletproof vest, all the fears concerning security and shooting attacks and suicide bombings, congealed, resurfacing in the form of one lucid thought: in Israel, violence happened for a reason. He looked again at the grisly stories in the newspaper. For nothing, he thought, these people had died for nothing. They died for greed, or anger, or just for being unfortunate enough to stand in the wrong place at the wrong time. That, it struck him, was senseless, almost incomprehensible. In Israel, on the other hand, where violent attacks were more frequent and devastating, he, ironically, felt safe. There, he knew, he was not targeted at random; he was hunted as a Jew. I would rather, he thought, be shot for being Jewish than be mugged and murdered on the streets of New York for a few dollars and some loose change. From a strictly statistical point of view, he was well aware, he was far more likely to come in harm's way in Hashmonaim than he was in increasingly crime-free Queens; yet his logic, seemingly counterintuitive, comforted him. I would rather, he told himself again, die as a Jew. With that thought, his pilot trip was truly complete, the last unconscious hurdle now dissolved. He was ready for the move, anxious to exchange the leafy avenues of Hillcrest for the primordial beauty of the settlement.

Returning home, he shared his experiences with the rest of the family. He told them at length about Hashmonaim, about the view and the breeze and the soothing silence. He told them about the community, consisting predominantly of like-minded people, modern Orthodox American Jews, many of whom were recently arrived immigrants, who shared the same values as the Kalkers. He was elated; he spoke not as one does of a place, an earthly composition of hills and houses and trees, but as one does of an idea, complex and abstract. The main thing he wanted to convey to his family was the feeling he got, standing on a raised plateau at twilight, looking to the west and realizing that the hills surrounding him had hosted the battles of the Maccabees, the ancient Hebrew warriors, and that all around him Jewish kings had once roamed. He spoke of the senses and the spirit, but, save for Sharon, who had experienced such transcendental moments on previous trips to Israel, none of the others seemed to share his passion.

Rachel, in particular, was growing increasingly dispirited as the deadline for departure drew nearer. For her, the move made little sense. It was a result, she thought, of her parents' stringent Orthodox emotions, a direct descendant of all the tedious Sabbath ceremonies she had had to bear, all the uninspired lessons she had had to sit through. What other reason, save for religious zeal, did one—as an American—have to move to Israel? In Queens, there was ample Jewish life, a vibrant Jewish community, a multitude of stores and services. But there was also more, an entire secular world inhabited by interesting people and fascinating things which, she was certain, did not exist in Israel. In Queens, she could be spared the embarrassment of being constantly Jewish, that perpetual ethnic label she resented so much; she could be Jewish when she chose to, and at other times be just like everyone else walking down the street, indistinct, inconspicuous. She couldn't help but compare, time and again, the trajectory of her immediate future with that of her peers. They, she thought, her eyes dampening with self-pity, would graduate from high school, move on to college, remain together, stay friends, embark on careers, enjoy life. She, on the other hand, would be alone, in a country—of what? Orthodox people? Single-minded Jews? She would study and then maybe join the army and remain forever stuck in a culture that wasn't her own. Even if she managed to avoid the army, she thought, returning to Queens several years from now, she would have missed the sweetest years of adolescence with her friends.

And so she resisted. She cried a lot, dramatically pointing out every last disadvantage of her parents' decision, questioning much, mocking often. Her behavior tested, and often crossed, the lines of what is considered acceptable teenage gripes, and what had begun as a quarrel over aliya seemed to unearth deeper undertones of familial discord. Finally, Rachel gave up. Realizing that no amount of histrionics would convince her parents to remain stateside, she took to sulking, spending time in her room, and making the final arrangements necessary before leaving.

Finally, the day of the flight arrived, and the turbulent energies that had swirled around the Kalker household for months died down; they were now in the eye of the storm. The flight, more than ten hours, passed in a dizzy whirl. All four Kalkers (Ari had already moved to Israel awhile before) were preoccupied by one object, the plane ticket that Danny had given each, a one-way ticket. Oddly, the ticket, a seemingly insignificant item, did what hours of conversation and days of pondering could not: it made abundantly clear the finality of the Kalkers' decision.

The landing in Israel was a moment of elation. After years of dreaming of this, it was now becoming a reality. Immediately upon arriving at Ben-Gurion Airport, several miles southeast of Tel Aviv, the Kalkers were confronted with representatives and officials. They had to fill out forms and sign papers and track the copious amounts of luggage they had sent. They were greeted by local representatives of Tehilah, some of whom Danny had met during his pilot trip to Israel, as well as by Shoshana and Ari. It was late summer in Israel, and the Kalkers were also welcomed by a balmy Israeli afternoon, with heat and humidity competing for prominence, each doing its best to smother every living thing with a heavy, wet blanket of stifling exhaustion. As veteran New Yorkers, they were, of course, no strangers to excruciating summers, but the Middle Eastern sun was different, more tenacious and unremitting.

In spite of the modern cars and shiny glass buildings, the airport could not have been mistaken for any of its American counterparts. While in New York's JFK Airport the chaos was mitigated by lines and signs and uniformed people to guide one through the arrival process, Ben-Gurion's modern exterior housed a pandemonium that was, the Kalkers thought, distinctly Israeli. The conveyor belt spitting out suitcases, for example, was crowded by hordes of travelers, each jockeying for a better position, inching closer and closer to the luggage at the expense of others, yet showing delight in helping elderly travelers with their bags. Outside, in the taxi pickup zone, two metal railings had been set up to designate a specific waiting area for passengers; despite the clear markings, however, there were people everywhere, shouting into their cellular phones, striking up conversations with complete strangers, combusting into arguments and, just as quickly, breaking into smiles. The Kalkers were fascinated; this was clearly unlike their hometown, the city in which strangers were best left unapproached. This was Israel.

Leaving the airport, they drove up to Hashmonaim. As their house was still to be occupied by the current renters for another week, they drove to the home of a fellow Hashmonaim resident, a total stranger to them, who agreed to let them use an unoccupied apartment. Exhausted as they were from the flight, Michael immediately began to explore their new surroundings. Neighbors arrived to wish them well, one even bringing them a prepared lunch. And so the Kalkers finally got some rest; they would need it, they knew, for the bureaucracy that lay ahead.

Many who had made aliya had warned them about Israeli bureaucracy. It was, most agreed, one of the most time-consuming aspects of moving to Israel, and the least welcoming manner of absorbing ideologically committed and enthusiastic Jews into the country. The Kalkers had heard stories of people spending weeks pursuing the bureaucratic necessities. For all her love of the country and its people, Sharon, accustomed to spotting the weak points of major organizations, was quickly able to get a rather accurate picture of the Israeli bureaucratic mechanism. It was born, she knew, along with the state, and, true to the zeitgeist, had been infused with rich socialist overtones. Customer service—in both the private and public sectors—was a foreign concept, as relegating one man to the status of customer and another to that of server meant breaking the basic bonds of equality, cherished and nourished by Israel's founders, most of whom were ardent socialists. Rather than satisfaction, clerks and sales representatives alike were required to bestow upon their clients a fraternal sense of communality, to serve out of a sense of obligation rather than aspiration for profit. This paradigm, pressured by a burgeoning economy, soon collapsed, leaving civil servants in the unique and covetous position of being protected by progressive regulation while at the same time being spared the scrupulous scrutiny of quality control. Hence were born two-hour lunches, half-day vacations, and a petulant approach to customers that made civil servants infamous among the uninitiated community of American-Jewish immigrants.

Sharon soon experienced the maddening system firsthand. One morning she went to Misrad Harishui (the Israeli equivalent of the DMV). The task ahead, she thought, was simple enough: she needed to obtain an Israeli driver's license, and, having her American license with her, the process should be a quick and painless one, a mere formality. After she had been sitting for many minutes on a cracking plastic bench in a tiny room which defied all the laws of air circulation, it was finally her turn to speak to the clerk. She approached and began to explain her request in the polite and long-winded way she was accustomed to. Abruptly, the clerk interrupted her and told her that in order to obtain the license, she needed an eye exam; to schedule an exam, she needed a form; the form, alas, was nowhere to be found. Still, the clerk assured her, she should get her eyes checked, and when she was done, she should return, fill out the form, and receive the license. Obediently, Sharon went to another office, eager to get the eye exam, a technicality in her mind, out of the way. Another wait in another stuffy office, and Sharon's turn to take the exam finally came. The clerk, however, refused to allow her to see the doctor: without the form, he said, she couldn't take the eye exam. Sharon returned to Misrad Harishui, fuming. A different clerk spoke of a different form, without which no license could be expected to materialize. Incensed, Sharon knocked over a cup of steaming coffee she was drinking, scalding her skin and staining her dress. Finally, she wised up to the unwritten rules of the game, and angrily demanded to see a manager. One was summoned and told her that no forms whatsoever were required: all the information was computerized, and all she had to do was ask and the coveted license was hers.

Having been told of the bureaucracy in advance, Danny was able to head off the ennui. He was calm, he felt, well prepared to deal with anything. Besides, he could not stop marveling that, for all the bureaucratic nonsense, all of his affairs—identification cards, driver's license, the container of possessions he had shipped to Israel via the ocean—were all resolved within exactly two days, a sliver of the time it took his brother, some twenty-odd years before, to go through the same thing. He also felt grateful for the guidance he had received from the aliya officials in New York who had, he felt, helped him overcome the overwhelming moment.

After a few days of *sidurim*, a Hebrew word meaning arrangements and which, they quickly learned, encompassed everything from obtaining a driver's license to shopping for vegetables, the Kalkers were tired. The boisterous and direct Israeli nature, so charming upon first encounter, had, they realized, its darker sides; sometimes, all they wanted was a drop of order, a bit of uneventful quiet, all of which, for better or worse, were hard to come by in Israel. They were finished, however, with most of the formalities of immigration, and were now free, for the first time since arriving at Hashmonaim, to explore their new environment.

The nature of Hashmonaim becomes clear by simply observing

the road leading up to the community. To arrive there, one must drive on major highways, most likely Road No. 1, which connects Tel Aviv and Jerusalem. At some point, however, one must get off the highway and steer the car toward a block of smaller towns, recently constructed communities erected between Israel's two largest cities and serving mainly as sleepaway suburbs for professionals working in either place and seeking a better quality of life than is offered by the undersized, overpriced apartments in Jerusalem or Tel Aviv. Then one must turn once more to a smaller, one-lane road that leaves the Green Line behind and heads into the West Bank.

To the uninformed driver, the Green Line doesn't exist. It is not visible, and no clear demarcation is there to distinguish Israel proper from the West Bank, uncontested land from what is arguably the most heavily disputed swath of territory in the world. Rather, the nonexistent border traverses a small valley a mile or so from Hashmonaim, where quick entrepreneurs, eager to serve the swelling population of the nearby Jewish communities, have established a greenhouse, several shops, and a café named after the sixteenth-century prophet Nostradamus. Crossing the valley toward the east, one gradually becomes aware that a certain boundary, unannounced though it may be, has just been crossed. The surrounding hills are dotted with Arab villages and Jewish settlements, the former recognizable by the minarets of their mosques and the latter by their guarded gates and barbed-wire fences. Another turn in the road, and one reaches the front gate of Hashmonaim, a large contraption colored bright yellow, where an armed guard inspects each vehicle before allowing it into the community. It was from that gate that the Kalkers began their excursion.

The first thing that struck them was the emptiness. Unlike New York, where everywhere they looked the skyline was obstructed by buildings, Hashmonaim offered a panoramic view of the surrounding hills and the valley below. Everywhere nature set the tone; the houses, the roads, the telephone poles, all seemed to spring out of the dusty earth, organic and unobtrusive. The color palette was different, too, the city's grays and blacks and whites replaced by the creamy hazel brown of the hills, the pale yellow of the stones, and the deep, dark green of the shrubbery.

From the gate, they walked up Hashmonaim's main road, some of it paved and some not. The occasional car would drive by, slow down, the driver nodding his head or waving hello. Once inside the perimeter of the community, they realized, the fastidious discreetness of suburban life in the United States was no longer applicable; here, many knew each other and each other's affairs. To their left, they could see the community's nerve center, a quadrangle of buildings temporarily housing the secretariat, security office, post office, and two large synagogues. The secretariat, they noticed was housed in a ready-made building. As communities were rapidly growing, expanding, and rezoning, the demand for additional housing units often far exceeded the supply. Until permanent structures could be built, temporary ones, made primarily out of Sheetrock, were trucked in, dropped on an empty lot, and hastily connected to the water pipeline and the electricity grid, ready for usage overnight. This, the Kalkers were told, was how one could tell where a settlement had started; as public facilities were usually the first to arrive on the ground yet the last to be replaced by brick-and-mortar buildings, one could easily spot the epicenter of any given settlement simply by looking for the clunky, beige temporary units that usually stood long after most of the residents were happily ensconced in more lavish houses. In Hashmonaim, they could tell, those buildings were placed at the very center of the community's geographical area, so as to be equidistant from most houses. One day, they assumed, as the community's population and budget grew, those buildings, too, would be replaced by the stony architecture that dominated most of Hashmonaim's homes.

On a raised plateau just up the road, a small court was paved with gray concrete tiles, upon which the synagogue, an unassuming cubical construction, stood. Nothing, apart from a few humble stained-glass windows, differentiated the building, the community's spiritual center, from the other houses surrounding it. While it was much larger than other neighboring houses, it remained undecorated and dimly lit. In Queens, the Kalkers were used to lavish synagogues where comfortable cushioned seating was provided and a lush, velvety curtain in hues of violet and wine covered the ark. Here, however, they saw nothing but plastic seats and bare cement walls, with none of the familiar ornamentations—such as sentences in Hebrew scrolled over the walls or artwork representing biblical scenes—that they were accustomed to in American shuls. Most striking, however, was the way the men who came to pray were dressed; recalling his own displeasure at donning a suit and a tie each time he went to shul, Danny looked with amazement as his new neighbors, wearing simple work pants and a T-shirt or a button-down shirt, ambled into the sanctuary, their knitted yarmulkes on their heads. The women were casually dressed as well, in plain blouses and skirts. No one seemed interested in the others' outfits, an important aspect of communal life in most New York shuls. Some of the men, however, carried with them an unexpected accessory: a slick, metallic, long-barreled, black and oily M-16 automatic rifle. In Israel, they knew, where everyone served in the army, guns were common; in a community surrounded by an angry sea of Arab villagers, such as Hashmonaim, they were almost necessary. The Kalkers' previous experience with guns had been mainly limited to those they saw on television and in the movies, not including Sharon's scant firearm training in Beitar and Danny's military training during his year in Israel as a teenager. They had seen Israelis carrying guns before—the sight was common on the streets of Jerusalem, where young men and women, soldiers on a short leave from the army, meandered, seemingly unaware of the weapon, a new part of their anatomy. But the Kalkers' neighbors in Hashmonaim were, for the most part, American-born, just like them, men who, up until several years before, had held nothing more deadly than a kitchen knife in their hands. Yet, they seemed remarkably comfortable with the long weapons slung from their shoulders by black nylon straps. When they entered the shul, the men would simply place the guns beneath the seat and pray; as they got up to go, they picked up the guns again, as if it were nothing more unusual than a hat or a coat left hanging on a rack. Despite the acute differences in style, Danny's heart warmed at the sight of the shul, was touched by the sense of camaraderie bubbling in the stuffy room. He felt instantly welcomed.

Just below the shul lay the main playground, connected to the two local schools. One of them, the high school, comprised a group of long and narrow buildings, of the same variety as those which housed the secretariat and post office. The classrooms themselves, serving a population of slightly less than one hundred children in the community, were bare, containing little save a blackboard and several posters of scenic landscapes. The school also doubled as the local chapter of the Bnei Akiva religious youth movement, and featured, on its outer wall, a mural, painted by the students, of young men and women in yarmulkes and skirts, smiling, walking, dancing, and having fun. Adjacent to it was an outdoor basketball court. The court even had bleachers, capable of seating several hundred spectators comfortably, to watch basketball games as well as various events put on for the community throughout the year, from Yom Hazikaron ceremonies to the festive annual flag presentation staged by Bnei Akiva.

On the court, a group of young men were playing basketball. They were wearing Gap T-shirts and Levi's jeans, Nike shoes and caps with logos of NBA teams emblazoned on the front. Some had tzitzit, fringes attached to the corners of their shirts that Orthodox Jews wear under their clothes, peeking from their shirts, clinging to their sweaty bodies. They laughed and shouted at each other, effortlessly switching from English to Hebrew and back again. Beside them, on the ground, a boom box spurted out the most recent American pop music. As night fell, the music blended in with the calls of muezzins, the Muslim criers summoning the faithful for prayer, from the surrounding villages, hip-hop beats syncopating with praises of Allah.

The triangle consisting of the shul, the school, and the secretariat stood at the heart of the community. Around it, spiraling in widening circles, were the streets, most of which were named after the fruits of the land. After the Kalkers' had stayed within the temporary apartment for a week, their empty new house was finally ready. It was located on the main circle of the community, bordering on the dusty valley. Therefore, it was awash with gentle breezes, each arriving at a different time of the day, each distinct from the others: the brisk, crisp morning breeze; the gentle, caressing wind of the afternoon; the robust whirls of the night. Danny stood outside the house, took a deep breath, and smiled.

The house itself was larger than their old home in Queens. In front it had a tiny porch, a parking space, and a basketball hoop, erected primarily for Rachel's sake. Inside, the house had four levels. The lower level contained a room designated for use as a bomb shelter, as well as a storage area. The main level housed a spacious living room, kitchen, and dining area, as well as a spare bedroom, while the upper level had three bedrooms and three bathrooms. The uppermost level contained a large recreational area, where the Kalkers set up a Ping-Pong table.

Energized anew by finally having a space of their own again, the Kalkers set about decorating their house. The pictures went up, the piano came in, pots and pans were arranged in cabinets, and food was purchased and placed in cupboards. When it was all done, Sharon was struck by an eerie feeling. This, she thought, is my house now, but I don't feel like I live here; I am surrounded by all of my familiar possessions, but this still doesn't feel like a home. Not yet.

Their paperwork in order, their house decorated, and the initial shock of immigration having slightly subsided, the Kalkers were ready to begin living life in Israel. Danny commuted every day to his new job in southern Tel Aviv, a mile or two from the park where, twenty-two years earlier, he had asked Sharon to be his wife. Initially concerned about his capability to work and communicate in Hebrew, he quickly discovered that his colleagues, most of whom were native Israelis, all spoke English well, some better than others, and that his own Hebrew was much better than he had suspected. He was most impressed, however, with his colleagues' approach to work. In the United States, he often bemoaned what he considered to be the overbearing prominence of the capitalist work ethic, prompting people to spend most of their waking hours at the office, away from family and friends. In Israel, he felt, priorities were arranged differently; here, where longer workdays were the norm, a job was just a job. Astonished, he learned that Israeli employers and employees alike were allowed, almost expected, even, to take time off for a variety of reasons. First of all, there was *miluim,* approximately one month a year of army reserve duty, which men have to serve until they are nearly forty-five. Employers, themselves soldiers in the reserves, understand that, and it is not uncommon to see a colleague bid farewell and disappear for a few weeks of training or guard duty. Then there were prayers; Danny left work at midday each day to pray *Mincha,* the middle of the three daily prayers Jews are required to recite. As there was no synagogue nearby, he and a group of coworkers congregated in a clothing factory across the street, converted by its owner for fifteen minutes a day into an impromptu shul and frequented by a small crowd of regulars and a wide array of passersby. For Danny, this was worship at its best—communal, spontaneous, brimming with intent. Most days, he left the office at around five, arriving at Hashmonaim a half-hour later, happy to be able to spend the rest of the day with his family.

Sharon, on the other hand, was not as fortunate with her career prospects. A veteran Jewish educator, she had hoped to continue her work, teaching youth about Jewish values, history, and philosophy. Wherever she went, however, employers saw an entirely different potential, offering her a position as an English teacher. The important stuff, she thought with dismay, is only taught by Israelis; Americans are relegated to teaching English. At first, she, the girl who hated secular studies and found her fulfillment only by exploring and propagating Judaism, was resentful and uncompromising. She hated being considered an Anglo, a term most Israelis used to bundle together all Jewish immigrants from English-speaking countries; it had, she was well aware, its share of negative connotations, as the Anglos were considered gullible, overly polite, nebbishy milquetoasts, not entirely compatible with the bravado of the Israeli national character. Slowly, however, she became resigned, taking on a string of jobs as a teacher and private tutor of English. She tried to harness her spirit into explaining grammar and administering reading-comprehension quizzes, but the more she did, the clearer it became that her quest for spiritual completion, her primary cause for making aliya, was at odds with her new career. Still, she had no choice; she needed a job and felt grateful to have found one.

If teaching English did not agree with Sharon's sense of vocation, teaching Israeli students tested her patience. In Queens, her students were sometimes raucous, but rarely disrespectful. They called her Mrs. Kalker and usually deferred to her authority. In Israel, a country disdainful of ceremonious behavior of any sort, students called teachers by their first name; hers called her Sharon, which, pronounced with their Israeli accents, became a foreign, unfamiliar name, the *a* stretched and emphasized, the *r* rolling, the *n* brusque. They talked back to her, unimpressed by her title or seniority. When she threatened to fail one particularly inept student, the child told his mother, who in turn called up the principal, protesting the gross injustice and threatening action. The principal yielded, and the student, to Sharon's utter amazement, was awarded a passing grade. She could tell that for her students she was nothing but a *frayer,* Hebrew for sucker or dupe, the least flattering thing one could be in a society that revolved around its citizens' desire to get ahead, scam the system, shun authority, pay less and earn more. With her soft-spoken demeanor and her smiling eyes and her unmitigated enthusiasm for Judaism, Zionism, and Israel, she was not one to exert control or set boundaries; she had expected boundaries already to be in existence. She also felt like an outsider: the students and their parents and the other teachers all had the same points of reference, all shared similar experiences, all spoke the same language. She, on the other hand, was the American, the English teacher, the Anglo.

Frustrated, Sharon nonetheless invested most of her free time in improving her Hebrew and in gaining a better acquaintance with Israeli culture and society. She borrowed popular Israeli fiction from the library, spending Sabbath after Sabbath reading, slowly, sometimes not more than several pages a day, learning new words, getting accustomed to Hebrew grammar, Hebrew sentences, Hebrew vernacular. Through the books, she would also learn of contemporary events, of the recent zeitgeist of the country. But no matter how hard Sharon tried, a part of her continued to feel lost. This feeling was often manifested and magnified by small things, such as American foods that she could not find in Israel. True, every item in her local store was kosher, eliminating the need to look for the special seal of approval on each product, but good lasagna, for example, was nowhere to be found, nor were most deli-style meat cuts she had grown accustomed to. American snacks, such as chips and candy, normally a source of comfort in trying times, were now unavailable. Sharon's spirit soured; she was a citizen, she felt, but not an Israeli.

Sharon's frustration, however, was dwarfed by Rachel's. Far from having found her niche, Rachel grew more bitter by the day. Unlike her brother, who was fortunate enough, because of his young age, to attend the local Hashmonaim school, located directly across the street from their house, Rachel commuted to nearby *modi'in,* where she sat and stared at teachers speaking Hebrew at a staccato pace, firing words that were utterly incomprehensible to her. Whereas she had once been a good student and a popular kid, she was now struggling academically and socially; she was allotted more time for each exam she took, as she read Hebrew slowly and with effort, but she still found most tests difficult. At home, she would spend most of the time alone in her room, thinking of what was going on at that moment in the parallel universe she had left behind, that of her friends in Queens. While she was stuck on the barren hills of the West Bank, she imagined, her friends were probably doing something interesting in some wonderful place. She had made a few friends in Israel, most of whom were adolescents her age who lived in Hashmonaim, but none were enticing enough to compel her to forget her old friends, the friends she had left behind.

Her sulking dismayed Danny greatly, and he would try to talk to her, to explain once again the merits of their new home. She thought, as probably every teenager does at one point or another, that her father didn't understand her; but, unlike most teenagers, she had extenuating circumstances, having been separated from all that she knew and loved. After another dismal conversation one Friday afternoon, Rachel stepped outside to the backyard. Gazing at the hills and the valley and the sky, she shut off. She began screaming as loudly as she could. Her parents tried to intervene at first, trying to approach her. But Rachel needed to scream, needed to come undone. So her parents went back into the house, and with their hearts breaking watched their child standing on a rock, screaming at the hills.

Rachel's behavior, however, was just one component of the general malaise in the Kalkers' new home. Danny and Sharon found themselves growing apart. Their marriage, they were both aware, had always had its problems, emanating mainly from fundamental differences in personality: Sharon was sprightly and spontaneous, Danny rational and collected. They had both hoped that the move would bring them closer together, that at least some of their personal conflicts would be cleansed away by the fresh Israeli air. They had hoped that in the tightly knit community of Hashmonaim, surrounded by like-minded expatriates and able to weld a clear, strong spiritual identity for themselves, they would discover that they were more similar than they had realized, that they were, after all, compatible. Instead, they grew apart. In Queens, living in a small Jewish enclave and pressed to practice their Judaism actively or risk losing their identity, they were introverted, drawing on each other for meaning and support. In Israel, on the other hand, everyone was Jewish, and there was no need, in an Orthodox community situated on the biblical hills, for any rituals or distinctions to prove it. Therefore, they could afford to continue to draw on one another while at the same time opening up their horizons to new directions, new thoughts, new people. Free to self-explore, each of them was welcome to test just how far his or her heart would go if released from its shackles. They discovered that the differences between them were irreconcilable.

A year and a half after making aliya, Danny and Sharon separated. She stayed in Hashmonaim, while he moved to a community, a few miles away, inside Israel proper.

CHAPTER TWELVE

The Kalker family found itself in a state of dissonance, dispersed all over the country. Just as they were making important strides toward building a home in Israel, it seemed, that home was disintegrating. Alone in her house, Sharon spent many afternoons thinking about her condition. Perhaps, she thought, it was now time for a reality check. She was in her midforties, and her career in Israel was stumbling over hurdle after hurdle. The major source of satisfaction she had had in Queens, interacting with youth, establishing educational programs, being constantly active in her community, was gone; in Israel, the only community she felt genuinely a member of was that of her immediate friends and neighbors, themselves immigrants, themselves politely ignored by mainstream Israeli society. What, she wondered, was the value of living in a Jewish state, if she was labeled an Anglo? How would she ever master Hebrew, when every time she struggled to ask someone a question, with her small vocabulary, they would answer her—whether from impatience or misdirected kindness—in equally broken English? She could still, she realized, go back to Queens. Her family was moving in separate directions, like tectonic plates, tearing up the ground beneath her feet. Shoshana was on the verge of graduating from Bar Ilan University and would doubtless stay in Israel; she planned to be a Jewish educator, and with her college training and more profound experience in the Israeli system, Sharon thought, she stood a much better chance than she herself did at succeeding. Ari, while he had not yet found a suitable framework for himself, was nonetheless happy with the host of opportunities that came with being eighteen, alone, and unsupervised. He, too, Sharon thought, would probably prefer to stay in Israel. As for her two youngest children, Sharon assumed that they wouldn't mind moving back. Rachel would undoubtedly be thankful, and Michael, even if ambivalent, would not sustain any serious social injury, as he would be returning just in time for high school.

With a heavy heart, a clouded mind, and Rachel in tow, Sharon flew back to Queens for a short visit with her parents. They, she realized, were another, major reason to contemplate returning to the United States. For two weeks Sharon did as little as she could. She enjoyed her mother's cooking, comforted herself with snacks and visits from old friends, and tried to imagine what life would be like if she was to return to Queens.

No lightning bolt hit her, no major epiphany offered itself, nor was any revelation unveiled. As she boarded the plane back to Israel, Sharon knew that returning to New York was out of the question for her. She didn't know why, or knew but couldn't articulate it. It was something she felt in Hashmonaim when she opened the door every morning, something that tingled at the back of her neck every time she traveled to Jerusalem, something that was extracted from her, like precious drops of amber, with every Hebrew word she spoke and with every Hebrew word she learned. One day, she hoped, she would be able to give that feeling a name; in the meantime, she decided, she was content simply to do its bidding. She returned to the house in Hashmonaim full of resolutions.

The following week, she informed Rachel and Michael that she had new ideas in mind. Until now, she told her children, they had all celebrated the Sabbath in a certain way, singing the same songs and reciting the same passages. For the coming Friday night, she told them, she wanted each of them to prepare something that he or she deemed appropriate for the Sabbath ceremony, be it a favorite song, a speech discussing that week's Torah portion, or even general reflections on any given topic. Her children looked at her, stunned. They were used to the rigid order of the traditional ceremony, exact and unchanging. They had never considered themselves partners in the process, and told their mother that they didn't know what to do. Softly, she insisted that they give the matter some thought and, come Friday night, say whatever was on their minds.

When the moment finally arrived, the children sat silent at first, unsure of the validity of their ideas. Then, slowly, they spoke. Rachel suggested several *zmirot,* special chants for the Sabbath, which the family usually shunned. These, she said, may not be as traditional and meaningful, but they meant something to her; she loved them and would love to sing them with her mother and brother. Michael had some *zmirot* of his own, as well as a studious speech providing a biblical spin on contemporary events. Uneasy at first, the three sat at the table, hesitating, like a comedian trying out a set of jokes for the very first time, always fearing the jeers of his crowd. As weird as it was, however, doing something else after years of routine felt wonderful. By the end of that evening, Sharon, Rachel, and Michael were relaxed and comfortable, extemporaneously bursting into song, telling jokes, and sharing memories. As the evening finally came to an end and the children ran off to meet with their friends on the basketball court, Sharon lay in bed, thinking about what she had done. She had established, she thought, a partnership of sorts with her children, and yet had not compromised her position as the adult, the authority. This was the kind of silent confidence that she could never conjure in the classroom, yet around the Sabbath table, with her own children, it felt natural. Maybe, she thought with a satisfied smile, the air was getting to her after all; maybe with every breath she took she became a little more Israeli.

The same applied to both Michael and Rachel. For Michael, always enthusiastic about the move, the major moment of transformation occurred several weeks after their arrival in Israel. As he and his peers approached the age of Bar Mitzvah, the Jewish rite of passage marking a boy's ascendance into manhood, they were taken on a class trip to Jerusalem, the highlight of which, they were told, would be a visit to the Western Wall. The wall, or Kotel as it is known in Hebrew, is the only surviving remnant of the ancient, biblical temple which was destroyed in 70 CE, and Judaism's holiest of places. Therefore, as Israeli boys prepare for their Bar Mitzvahs, many schools organize trips to the Kotel, seeking to provide their students with a spiritual experience to enhance their religious studies.

Walking up to the Kotel, Michael and his classmates were struck by how underwhelming the path leading to such a monumental place was. They crowded in narrow alleyways, no wider than nine feet, with foot traffic in every direction and pandemonium around every corner. At the end of the path was a small post of the border police, manned by a bored-looking soldier, just a few years older than Michael, who inspected their bags, searched for metallic objects, and then nonchalantly waved them through. For Michael, the wall was primarily a tourist attraction at that stage, and as such he thought it weird that he had to be searched and scrutinized before being allowed into the perimeter. But this, he remembered, was Israel, and just above the soldier's post, directly on top of the Kotel, he could see the Temple Mount, where the golden dome of the Muslim Rock Shine shimmered in the sun. This, he was aware, was where the recent spate of violence had started, with Palestinians at the mosque hurling stones down at Jews praying at the wall. Under such circumstances, a security check was a small price to pay.

As he entered the plaza in front of the wall, viewing it for the first time, an odd thing happened to Michael; one by one, emotions he had forgotten, and some he didn't know existed, climbed up to his throat and lodged there, challenging him to come to terms with the way he felt. He looked at the Kotel; it was so different from what he had expected. In all the illustrations he had seen, the Kotel was always a magnificent monument, portrayed as awash in golden sunlight, the emblem of fortitude. In front of him, however, stood a wall, made of the same familiar Jerusalem stone, covered with mold and bursting with rumpled paper notes that worshippers, following an old custom, tucked between its stones in the hope that the message would be received by God. The stones, each one of which was, on average, four feet high and ten feet long, were arranged in the shape of a slightly slanted descending terrace, and the whole wall was less than sixty feet tall, three or four stories by New York standards. Men and women prayed apart, separated by a makeshift divider running down the middle of the plaza. Looking around the men's side, Michael noticed a wide array of characters: there were elderly religious men in black hats and long black coats, caressing the stones with their hands, as if the wall were the cheek of a beautiful woman; there were soldiers, brought to the wall on the occasion of completing their basic training, there to pledge to protect not only the state of Israel but the entire Jewish people; there were tourists and paupers and people praying for everything from health to wealth to love.

Then it hit him.

He was standing, he realized, in the nearest place now left on earth to the Holy of the Holies, the site of the ancient temple where the Ark of the Covenant had stood, a place from which, it is believed, the Divine Presence never departed. He was standing in the place to which Jews the world over, himself included, turned as they whispered their daily prayers. He was standing at the site of destruction, at the point from which the Jewish people were scattered across the earth, doomed to nearly two millennia of perpetual yearning for Zion, of longing to be able once again to pray at the wall, of hoping that the Divine Presence still hadn't departed from the city of Jerusalem, hadn't forsaken the Jews. This, he realized suddenly, was what Jews were saying each year at Passover when they concluded the Seder with the blessing "*Le'shana haba'ah be'Yerushalayim,*" Next year in Jerusalem. And here he was, in Jerusalem, at the Kotel, praying; here he was, a young Jew who, unlike generations of his forefathers, had had the chance to act on the collective yearning of his people and return to Jerusalem, move to Israel, make aliya.

The emotions swirling around his throat threatened to explode. He was overwhelmed, realizing for the first time since he had arrived how far away he really was from New York. He was happy because he had learned, in the few short weeks he had lived there, to love Israel, to enjoy its climate and its people. He was thrilled by the thought that there were so many things for him to discover here, so many nature reserves to explore and so many biblical sites to visit. For the same reason, he was frightened, unaware of what the future held, petrified by the ominous presence of the unknown. He was sad, thinking of the people he had left behind in New York, his friends and his teachers and his grandparents. Again, he looked at the wall.

"I moved here," he said to himself. "It's done."

And with that thought in mind, he began to cry.

Whereas Michael was immersing himself in religious practice and spiritual searches, Rachel was preoccupied with the more mundane elements of everyday life. Her first moment of clarity occurred as she was waiting outside Hashmonaim's gate for the bus to Jerusalem, where she now attended high school; it dawned on her that here she was, a suburban kid, allowed to travel by herself to the city, where she could stay for an hour or two after school before returning home in the afternoon. She juxtaposed this thought with her memories of Queens; if, she recalled, she wanted to travel to Manhattan alone, she needed a very good reason and much pleading. Otherwise, it was forbidden. In Queens, each one of her steps had to be reported back to her mother, who insisted on knowing in advance exactly what her plans were. In

Israel, she was free to move more or less as she pleased. When she went out at night to hang out with the other teenagers in the community, she could return whenever she was tired, unburdened by curfews. More than once she had come home as late as two in the morning. In Queens, it was unthinkable to be out at such an hour; in Hashmonaim, her mother didn't even stay up to make sure she got home safely.

That, she realized, was the great paradox of living in Israel. On the one hand, with the security situation in a permanent state of high alert, parents went through life feeling perpetually paranoid, arming their children with cellular phones for security purposes and sending them off with ample words of caution. On the other hand, the random threat of terrorism notwithstanding, there was little in the way of harm to worry about, as crime in most cities was negligible, and therefore children were granted liberties far greater than those given to children in the United States. It was also, Rachel understood early on, a society very much centered on its youth: it was young men and women, she had read, who had paid with their lives to guarantee the establishment of the state; it was young men and women who ran the army and defended the borders and continually risked their own safety for the greater good. Therefore, it was young men and women that Israeli society idolized. Like her mother, she noticed a concrete difference between American and Israeli schools; but whereas Sharon, the teacher, was dismayed by the nearly infinite freedom allowed to Israeli children, Rachel, the student, was elated by it.

Sitting in class, she felt freer to chat, doze off, tune out. As her Hebrew, and consequently her grades, improved, she was once again on top, once again unfazed by quizzes and exams. She had more time and more presence of mind to socialize. Some of her friends were American-born, and they shared with her the same frustrations and fears, and others were Israeli-born, Sabras, and they charmed her with their fearless and easygoing manner. It was, she thought, a perfect way to be, candid and sometimes crude but mostly sweet and caring. Better than the cliquey mentality of her American high school. Better than caring about nothing else but boys and makeup and MTV. The friends she now had could hold political discussions with her, could talk about life and love and loss. They would all be soldiers soon, and therefore had no choice but to mature rapidly, before it was too late. She was also noticing how different her girlfriends in Israel were from most of the young women she knew back home. In Queens, she was often shocked by how much of their souls and their bodies girls were willing to offer in order to be considered popular. In Israel, her friends appeared to be more focused, less gullible, more respectful of themselves and of others.

Commuting to Jerusalem each day on the bus, Rachel had time to think about the vast physical and emotional distance she had traversed in a little over a year. She was also forced, however, to think about another, more gripping topic: suicide bombings. Since the outbreak of Palestinian violence in the fall of 2000, Jerusalem's buses had become a primary target for terrorists. Time after time, Palestinians strapped with explosives would board the city's crowded buses and detonate their charges, killing scores of Jews. As a result, the buses had become a forbidden territory for all but those who had no other means of transportation, a large number of whom were children and teenagers commuting to school. To counter the sordid randomness of suicide bombings, to balance the horrible knowledge that there was little that anyone could do to predict, let alone curtail, such an attack, some Israelis developed elaborate methods of observation, reading the deepest of meanings into the most seemingly mundane elements of human behavior.

One day, as Rachel was traveling on a bus on her way back from school, a woman got on and sat not far from her. Applying the aforementioned method of observation, Rachel was immediately suspicious: the woman was dirty, her hair unkempt, her clothes ragged; worst of all, she was carrying a large duffel bag, a major warning sign in the collective Israeli consciousness because such bags can hold a great amount of explosives. In her mind, Rachel evoked all the other warning signs she was aware of, examining the woman carefully for each one. First of all, she looked at where the woman was sitting. More often than not, she knew, suicide bombers chose a strategic place on the bus, usually the seats right above the engine, located roughly four or five rows into the bus. That was where the woman was sitting. If suicide bombers succeeded in detonating themselves in that particular spot, the damage would be greater because the charge often caused the gas tank to explode, turning the whole bus into a burning ball of flames. On to the second sign: the woman's eyes. Rachel was looking for dilated pupils. She had often read profiles of suicide bombers in the Israeli media, and knew that before being dispatched to their death, the terrorists were given a sedative of some sort, or a rolled marijuana cigarette, preventing the possibility of last-minute hesitations and changes of heart. Dilated pupils, therefore, often meant the person was stoned, which brought the woman on the bus a step closer to being a potential terrorist. Other measures of verification were needed; Rachel looked for stains. Stains were said to be a common result of carrying an explosive device, as the lubricants and oils used in preparing the device often seeped out, leaving their print on the terrorist's clothes. The woman's clothes were certainly stained, but considering her overall disheveled condition, Rachel could not tell if the stains were the result of motor oil or simply poor personal hygiene. Was, then, the woman looking around, a behavior often attributed to suicide bombers wishing to improve their position so as to ensure maximal damage prior to blowing themselves up? Yes, she was, but again, her entire demeanor was jumpy and incoherent. Rachel was anxious; she had to make a choice.

On the one hand, she instinctively felt like alerting the driver. The risk she was taking by not informing anyone, in case the woman indeed proved to be a terrorist, was too great. On the other hand, the woman could very well turn out to be a poor, innocent soul, wrongly suspected because of her shabby appearance and deeply insulted by being branded with the worse stigma of all, that of a mass murderer. Fear guided her to tell, civility to remain silent. Somewhere in the back of her mind a third option began to congeal, that of simply getting off the bus at the next stop and leaving the others on board to meet their own fate, whatever it might be. She remained in her seat, paralyzed, unable to make a decision, her eyes locked on the strange woman. She called her older brother for advice, keeping her voice as calm as she possibly could. Finally, the time came for her to get off the bus. The raggedy lady may have been many things, but a suicide bomber wasn't one of them. This time, Rachel was lucky, she thought. There would be other times when she would have to play the same gruesome game of identifying a potential bomber before he or she blew him- or herself up; that was a part of living in Israel.

While they were concerned about Rachel's safety, Danny and Sharon considered the issue from their own perspective: they had been accused, while still in Queens, of being irresponsible parents for dragging their children into the line of fire, to Israel, to a settlement of all places. They countered this accusation with two major arguments. First of all, they said to their concerned colleagues and friends, you're wrong about what Israel is really like. While the threat of terrorism certainly is a concrete and recurrent one, Israel is still, statistically, safer than some of New York City's neighborhoods. Furthermore, as Orthodox Jews, they accepted the idea of a preordained divine plan; of course one had to take precautions and use judgment and common sense, but in the larger scheme of things, the Lord would call to Him whomever He wanted at whatever time He deemed proper. It was the latter argument that they repeated to themselves, like a mantra, every time they couldn't reach one of their children's cell phones, every time the radio beeped and the news came on and spoke of another attack, of more victims.

Yet, the Kalkers were lucky; the random order of killing skipped them and their acquaintances. They were aware of the carnage around them, yet they never had to give it a face or a name. Until June of 2003.

That month, Sharon was coping with a minor surgery she had to undergo. The procedure itself, she quickly realized, was not going to be the most difficult part of her experience; even more daunting a task was navigating the bureaucratic labyrinth of the Israeli medical system by herself. She felt confident enough; the novels she had been reading provided her with a better, livelier grasp of the language, and her speech was approaching the speed at which Sabras spoke, her accent sufficiently clipped so as not to sound too foreign. She also continued to draw on the support of her sheltered community in Hashmonaim. One woman in particular, an American immigrant named Judy, provided her with the warmth and assistance she deeply needed. Immediately after Sharon's surgery, for example, Judy picked her up from the hospital in Jerusalem, waited for over an hour while Sharon filled out an avalanche of forms necessary to secure her release, and then drove her back home. On the way, Judy told Sharon with unbridled excitement that she was looking forward to the following weekend, as a major family event was planned. One of her sons was recently married, and his wife—Judy's newest daughter-in-law—had a nice young brother. That coming Wednesday, Judy said, the brother was getting married in Jerusalem, and the whole extended family would come together for two or three nights of celebration. Sharon was happy; her friend, she thought, was a good soul, and deserved all the joy that came her way. Sharon even knew the groom's family; his parents were Tzvi and Michal Goldstein, a nice young couple who, like herself, had emigrated from New York, and who were living in Eli, a settlement several miles to the northeast of Hashmonaim.

The wedding came and went. The day after, on a Thursday night, Tzvi and Michal Goldstein, both in their late forties, were driving from Eli to a hotel in Jerusalem, where their son's *sheva brachot,* a traditional postwedding ceremonial celebration, was scheduled to begin the next day and last the entire weekend. Also in the car were Tzvi's parents, Eugene and Lorraine Goldstein, who had arrived in Israel several days earlier from their home on Long Island in order to attend their grandson's wedding. All were excited: the next day they would celebrate not only the wedding, but also Eugene and Lorraine's fiftieth wedding anniversary and Tzvi and Michal's twenty-seventh wedding anniversary.

The quickest way from Eli to Jerusalem was to travel on Route 60 to Ofrah, a large settlement just outside the major Palestinian town of Ramallah, and then take the Ramallah bypass road around the city and into nearby Jerusalem. A few miles north of Ramallah, the Goldstein's car was ambushed by Palestinian gunmen. There was a short shower of bullets. Looking into the backseat, Tzvi Goldstein could see that his wife was lightly wounded, but his elderly parents were badly hit, bleeding, fading out of consciousness. Then he himself was shot, a single bullet penetrating his chest. Acting on instinct, he pushed his foot to the gas pedal, driving as fast as he could, eager to extract his family from the infernal shooting range in which they were now targets. Slowly, his wound sucked away his life force, drop by drop. Yet, he sped away, aiming for the bypass road, where, he knew, he was likely to come across an Israeli patrol, likely to get help for his wife and parents. Just as he reached it, he collapsed, the car crashing on the side of the road and flipping over. He had managed, despite a fatal injury, to drive over six miles. Shortly after that, he died of his wound.

Avi Zohar, a spokesperson for Magen David Adom, the Israeli equivalent of the Red Cross, told the New York *Daily News* the next day that Goldstein's act was noble. "After six miles," he said, "he lost control and the car flipped over. He drove so far to save his parents, to get them to the hospital. He was a good son." The parents, meanwhile, were rushed to Hadassah Ein Karem hospital, both in serious condition. So was Goldstein's wife. Sharon's friend Judy, who had planned on a weekend of celebrations at the hotel, was called to the hospital to serve as a translator from English to Hebrew.

Hearing of the attack, Sharon was overcome by a fierce rush of debilitating sadness. She sat down in front of her computer and, in one stream of emotion, wrote an e-mail to her closest friends back in Queens. It was titled "The Night I Became an Israeli":

In August of 2001 I made Aliyah, and at Ben Gurion airport was told I was now an Israeli. I even received documents to prove it! In truth, however, I was not an Israeli, I was merely an American living in Israel. During my first year here I couldn't have felt less Israeli if I had tried. Living in a largely anglo community, I never needed to speak Hebrew and hardly heard it. . . . During that first year I still relied heavily on American food products and bemoaned the differences in things like lasagna noodles, meat cuts etc. Israel was my national home and I was a legal citizen but I was not Israeli.

Year two brought with it a greater comfort zone. I knew what to expect at events such as Yom Hazikaron, Yom Ha'atzmaut and Yom Yerushalayim. I learned how to drive in and out of Jerusalem with ease and even ventured to Beit Shean and Natanya with a greater confidence. I attended professional development seminars in Hebrew and voted in my first Israeli election. This year brought with it the celebration of a daughter's [Shoshana's] engagement, the trials and tribulations of a divorce, preparing with my child [Rachel] for her first bagruyot, and finally navigating the medical system completely in Hebrew due to some surgery. As a result I felt more competent and informed, but not more Israeli.

That all changed last night. Shabbat began in a relatively routine way. After Michael left for shul, I was reading a quick article in the paper before I too planned to go to daven. A friend dropped by with a big bowl of salad and inquired as to how I was feeling as I was still just one week post-op. Having had a most productive day, I excitedly told her how grateful I was to be feeling stronger and healthier and then politely inquired as to her mood. She told me how she had been yelling at everyone and dropping things all afternoon. I was understandably concerned, and upon further probing learned that since I hadn't read the yishuv [community] email or listened to the news all afternoon I had missed very significant informa-

tion. There was a shooting piguah [Hebrew for terrorist attack] on the road near Ofrah. The driver was killed, his parents from America, who had come to celebrate their grandson's wedding, were in matzav kasha [critical condition] and so was his wife. Piguim always bring out the sense of areivut [mutual responsibility] we feel for one another here, but I had never known a victim personally, until now.

Last Friday, my friend Judy picked me up from the hospital and kindly waited well over an hour until I could get the paper work done. She is one of those kind souls who always does what has to be done, helps everyone everywhere, and does it all with a smile. In the last year and a half she has married off three sons and became a grandmother twice. Nothing fazes this woman and she appreciates every small blessing in her life. On our ride home she eagerly told me how she was looking forward to celebrating the sheva brachot of her newest daughter-in-law's brother. The wedding was to be this past Thursday night and the family would be together the following night as well. The family was indeed together, in Hadassah Ein Karem where she [Judy] served as the English communicator for her deceased machuten's [in-law's] parents. From what she told me, the family was given an entire ward and they managed to have sheva brachot for the young couple on the hospital floor. On motzei Shabbat [Saturday night] a bus came to the yishuv and we attended Tzvi Goldstein's funeral on Har Hamenuchot [where the largest cemetery in Jerusalem is located]. A mere 12 hours after marrying off his son he was gunned down in cold blood en route to their sheva brachot. His 19-year-old married daughter and widow will sit shiva [a Jewish custom calling for seven days of mourning the dead] here and his son will begin after sheva brachot ends on Wednesday night. Judy will be everyone's caretaker and the entire community will be there to support her.

This marks the first funeral I have ever attended in Israel. It is the first time I have a personal connection to a victim of a terrorist act. My innocent days of being an American living in Israel are gone forever. In its place is a connection permanently burned into my heart through tears on the one hand and hugs on the other. Israel is not a place for the frail and the weak among us. Living here requires one to adjust to life-changing events in a second. It forces one to live to the max; to share in each other's joys completely and to weep in their sorrow as one. It's about being connected—to the past, the present and the future—to the land, the people and G-D. It's about living a meaningful life, not just achieving benchmarks and setting new ones. It's about making history, not just reading about it. It's about coming home.

I am an Israeli.

And with that, she felt, her spiritual quest was over. The fleeting feeling, the elusive reason that made her come to Israel and stay there even in the face of great difficulties, that emotional drive which had no name, was finally captured, put down in writing. The murder of Tzvi Goldstein, and the shock it delivered, herded together all of the fragments of understanding that Sharon had been acquiring since arriving in Hashmonaim. She was no longer the starry-eyed, naive immigrant, charmed by every morsel of what she considered authentic behavior; neither was she raging at all the little idiosyncracies that made no sense to her. Her eyes were open now: she realized what Israel was really about, had experienced the chaos and bureaucracy and the creeping fear of living in the shadow of constant threat. Still, there was much love in her heart. Walking in streets named after Jewish prophets and kings, after majestic mountains and biblical sites, made her spirit soar. She was living, as Danny was fond of calling it, on "Jewish time," according to the Hebrew calendar, in a country whose heart beat according to Jewish tradition. There was no one driving on Yom Kippur, and on Passover everyone celebrated the Seder; this was a stark difference from life in New York, where she had led, she felt, a double life, being a Jew in the privacy of her own home but, out on the street, just a member of one of many ethnicities. In Israel, there were also many ethnicities, but one shared religion, one shared nationality, one shared fate.

Three years after moving to Israel, the Kalkers have all settled in. Sharon married a high school sweetheart with whom she had reconnected while on vacation in New York; he followed her to Hashmonaim. Danny, in the meantime, remarried as well and moved to Jerusalem. His Hebrew, while not yet perfect, has improved tremendously. As his Hebrew became better, and as he integrated more and more with his neighbors, he realized the one crucial difference between Israel and the United States. In New York, it seemed to him, while he took religion to be the main focus of his life, most of the other Jews took their religion as secondary, trying to fit their observance into a full and robust secular life. In Israel, on the other hand, he found that many more people took their Jewishness—be it religiously or culturally—to be the primary focus of their lives. And he loved that. Despite the occasional tensions between secular and religious, between left and right, he felt as if there was more acceptance among the various factions than he had ever seen in America.

The move, he observed proudly, was good not only for him but also for the whole family. His children have each settled into Israeli society successfully, speak Hebrew fluently, and have many Israeli friends. The eldest daughter, Shoshana, married a young man whose family made aliya twelve years before. They are both educators and plan to serve as *shlichim*, or emissaries, helping to spread Jewish education and culture in the Diaspora. Ari is currently serving in the army; he has trained to be a sniper and continues to excel in other areas. Rachel is completing her final exams, and has already earned a certificate from Wingate Sports Institute, a prestigious Israeli college, qualifying her to coach basketball, which she is currently doing in Hashmonaim. She is in the process of testing for various units in the army. Michael is studying at an esteemed high school in Jerusalem. He has become indistinguishable from any of his Israeli counterparts.

After all the legitimate fears, anxieties, hesitancies, stresses, and obstacles, the Kalkers have all come to successfully integrate into Israeli society. They often enjoy trips in the countryside, where they are awed to imagine the stories of the Bible come to life, thrilled to recognize that they are walking in the very paths their ancestors once tread. The Kalkers have truly come home.

EPILOGUE

It's May of 2003, and all throughout Israel ceremonies are held, and people listen to the same songs on the same radio stations. Like most Israelis, Marlin and Betty, Mike, and the Kalkers mourn, but gradually a soothing calm envelops their minds; soon, they know, Yom Hazikaron, Memorial Day, will be over, and at that exact moment Yom Ha'atzmaut, Israel's Independence Day, will begin, a magical transformation.

The official transition from mourning to merriment is the ceremony on Jerusalem's Mount Herzl. It begins with a spectacular military parade, which most Israelis tune in to watch, year after year. There is something pleasant about watching soldiers—on every other day rugged, muddy, and occupied by combat—dressed in frilly, festive uniforms, marching with flags and drums and trumpets; for one day, the Israeli army resembles a European royal guard, largely ceremonial and mostly ineffective. That is the true value of the parade. Moments ago, the television broadcast images of fallen soldiers, heroes with bloodied faces, real men of valor. Now the soldiers on television are marching around, smiling and saluting, as if their biggest concern was successfully executing a left turn or switching their weapons from one hand to the other at the right time.

Marlin enjoys the ceremony very much. He still remembers Israel's first Independence Day, remembers taking photographs of soldiers in their brand-new uniforms, marching around with whatever meager weaponry was left after the long, gruesome war. This, he thinks, is the blessing of the old-timers: perspective. The Jerusalem in which he hungered and in which he was bombed has turned, over the course of the years, into a different city. Arabs still live in east Jerusalem and ultra-Orthodox Jews in neighborhoods such as Mea Sha'arim, but around them are malls and McDonald's restaurants, Parisian-style sidewalk cafés and Mideastern dives, where steaming tea is served in small copper cups to guests slouched on oriental rugs and ornamental pillows. There is still violence, but it is of a different kind. Whereas he once feared Jordanian snipers and Arab militiamen, he is now wary of Palestinian suicide bombers. But never afraid: he has lived here too long to be afraid.

For many years, when their marriage and the state were still new, Betty and Marlin would gather, along with thousands of other Israelis, in the city center, singing and dancing and tapping, as is the Israeli custom, little plastic hammers on the heads or shoulders of passersby. Watching the colorfully lit triangle formed by Ben Yehuda Street, King George Avenue, and Jaffa Road, where the festivities took place, Marlin would remember other times, times when he and Agron ducked an artillery attack, times when the now-jubilant streets were covered with corpses.

As the years passed, concern over terrorist attacks moved the party inside, from the streets to people's homes. The Levins have an annual tradition of hosting a party in their garden, a gathering of a small group of old friends, some of whom came with them on the *Marine Carp*, many of whom are American-born. It is no ordinary party, but a *mangal*, a Hebrew word connoting a more unruly kind of barbecue; Marlin and a friend get the logs ready, and then sit in garden chairs, watching the burning wood. One by one, the guests arrive, each carrying some food—potato salad, baked beans, some fruit. Marlin puts meat on the grill, hamburgers and hot dogs and Buffalo wings. They chat, in English peppered with Hebrew or vice versa, about everything, but not about politics; after so many years, there's nothing left to say about politics that they haven't already said. Someone comments that, the pita bread and hummus aside, their get-together looks suspiciously similar to any Fourth of July celebration in the United States. There's still a tiny bit of America left in all of them, even after so many years in Israel, and they all laugh. "We have two loves in our lives," Marlin tells the guests, as he often does. "Our fatherland, America, and our motherland, Israel."

In Misgav Am, Mike is busy. After having operated the siren, he is now in charge of the most important part of the Yom Ha'atzmaut celebration: the fireworks display. He has preparations to make. He has already applied for all of the necessary permits, from the Ministry of Labor, the police, the fire department, and Magen David Adom. Even after so many years in Israel, he is still overwhelmed by the bureaucracy. Now he checks the kibbutz's grounds for the perfect launching site, taking into his calculations the direction of the wind and the changing of the temperature. The main ceremony takes place on the lawn in front of the *heder ochel,* the kibbutz's dining hall, an elevated gray building standing on four cement legs. The kibbutz's teenagers, thrilled by the sanctioned opportunity to play with fire, prepare *ktovot esh,* thick wires bent into the shapes of letters, wrapped in oily rags, and set on fire, so as to provide sentences spelled in flames. The flag is raised again. The *ktovot esh*—a Star of David, a menorah, a catchy slogan—are lit. Then one of the teenagers informs Mike via the walkie-talkie that it's time for the main attraction.

From more than a hundred feet away, Mike sends firework after firework into the heavens. Each firework has a fuse, and each is launched from a small cardboard stand. For fifteen minutes Mike, the warrior, becomes a choreographer of light and color: he fires a firework which explodes in the shape of a palm tree, then shoots some that leave a blue and red trail, launches starts and streamers and sparklers. He recalls with a smile the good old days, when the kibbutz was too poor to spend hundreds of shekels on fireworks, and Mike and his friends had to steal emergency flares from the army and use them instead.

By the time Yom Ha'atzmaut rolls in, Mike has already received his lecturing schedule for the summer. In the coming months, he'll meet with more than two dozen groups, consisting mostly of American-Jewish teenagers. Talking to them, with his profanity and gun and baseball cap, he'll tell them that he, too, was once like them, a confused American kid. Sometimes, he'll even forget some of his English, pausing for a moment, searching his mind for the right word, laughing about his misuse of his mother tongue. Every few years, he sees a familiar face wearing an IDF uniform, and a soldier comes by and tells him that once upon a time he, too, was an American kid, who heard Mike give his lecture and decided, right then and there, to make aliya. Mike loves these moments, takes great pride in them, even though he doesn't think it's absolutely necessary for every Jew to move to Israel. The most important thing, he tells anyone who will listen, is to make the Jews united, in the United States and all over the world, to make them united in their support of each other and in their love for Israel. That, he says, is what he lives for.

After he launches the fireworks, he looks around him. In the villages a few miles to the north, he knows, Hizbollah is watching the festivities, firing shots in the air to remind Mike and his colleagues that despite their joy they're still surrounded.

The Kalkers know they're surrounded as well. From their window they can see the entire Israeli-Palestinian conflict, can see their small settlement, the Arab villages, the army bases. The children are outside, playing with friends, enjoying the sun. Sharon is watching *Chidon Hatanach,* the same international Bible quiz in which she participated as a high school student so many years ago. Now, however, she is living in the biblical land, and the questions in the quiz all pertain to events that took place in the hills surrounding her house. Such a different experience, she is thinking, from living in Queens and studying Judaism.

Soon, she knows, the summer will come, and she will, most likely, travel back to New York, visit her parents, amazed that once, not so long ago, she used to live there. Her son is now a soldier, and she, too, shares every Israeli mother's fate of sleepless nights, waiting for him to call, anxious for a sign of life. Soon, maybe, she will also have grandchildren, and they, despite their American lineage, will be Sabras, will know no other home but Israel. Soon, but for now she sits on the couch while her children play outside.

All over Israel, families are celebrating, and those who wept for the dead in the morning are gleeful by nightfall. For Marlin and Betty, Mike, and the Kalkers, this is no longer an odd transition. They are used to it now, accustomed to this crazy pace, to this mad place, to feeling everything with such intensity. They, and approximately one hundred thousand American Jews like them, made aliya at different times and for different reasons. Yet, when Yom Hazikaron makes way for Yom Ha'atzmaut, their hearts skip a beat. They feel, as Danny Kalker is fond of saying when asked why he made aliya, that Israel, both as a state and as an idea, is the past and the future of the Jewish people; for them, it is also the present.

AFTERWORD

In the course of researching and writing this book, the history of Israel came to life for me in a way it failed to do while I was a student in that country's classrooms. The courage and determination of the men and women—Sabras and immigrants alike—who fought for Israel's independence and, later, for its well-being never felt so concrete, their burden so meaningful. And Israel, I learned, teetered on the edge of total devastation more times than I'd ever realized. This book reminded me of what many natives of Israel, such as myself, often tend to forget, which is never to take anything for granted.

My education, however, didn't stop there. I learned of the motivations that propelled Marlin and Betty to come to Israel—their fierce Zionism; their belief, inspired by having witnessed the aftermath of the Holocaust, in the importance of a Jewish state; and the zeitgeist that allowed them, as the first or second generation of American-born Jews in their families, to immigrate once again, this time to Israel. I learned of Mike's reasons, his youthful enthusiasm, set against the backdrop of the tumultuous sixties and their emphasis on identity politics and soul-searching, and illuminated by Israel's glorious victory in the 1967 war. Finally, I learned about the Kalkers and their melding of spirituality and ideology, of religion and Zionism.

But the one answer that I was seeking, the one key to the question locked up in the heart of this book, continues to elude me. Why did these Americans, living in comfort and security, choose to leave it all behind and move to Israel? Each of them, as I have mentioned, had his or her own motivations for making aliya, but simply enumerating what they are doesn't entirely finish answering the question. A man can give as many reasons as he wishes when asked why he emigrated from America to Israel, but the real answer simply isn't available to the cognitive faculties. It must be felt. It is sensed when one walks down the streets of Jerusalem, realizing that one's ancestors walked those same streets centuries ago. It is present when one experiences the depth of spirituality in Israel, the sort of spirituality that relies less on texts and ceremonies and prayers, and more on the air and the hills and the sea. This, I suspect, is the true motivation that brought all the men and women depicted in this book to Israel, the real reason they have stayed there for all those years.

Finally, while writing this book, I have had, of course, to come to terms with my own choices. Having traveled the path opposite to that of the individuals I wrote about, I was forced to wonder whether or not my decision to live, at least for now, in the United States constitutes a betrayal of the same values for which Marlin and Betty, Mike, and the Kalkers sacrificed so much. This is a question with which I continue to grapple; the best advice I've received on the matter, however, came from none other than Mike. Quoting his favorite mantra, he told me, over steaming black coffee in his overly air-conditioned office, that I must remember one thing. "The main goal," he said, "is not for every Jew to come to Israel. The main goal is to make the Jews—in Israel, in the United States, everywhere in the world—united, to make them support each other and love Israel."

That, he told me, was what he lives for. Aliya was his path, but it is not the only one. Whether my fate carries me back to Israel, where my family has lived for nine generations, or keeps me here in the United States, where my wife and I hope to raise a proud Jewish family, remains to be seen. This, however, hardly changes the fact that the larger goal, the benefit of Klal Israel—the whole of Israel—is not limited in space or time. And it is a goal that is accessible by many paths; it can be pursued, with equal diligence, in New York and in Jerusalem. This book, I hope, is a first step in this direction.

NOTES

x The National Jewish Population Survey 2000–2001 is available online at http://www.ujc.org/njps.

xi For more on the sociological aspect of aliya, see Chaim Waxman, *American Aliya: Portrait of an Innovative Migration Movement* (Detroit: Wayne State University Press, 1989).

xi The article I refer to regarding Kobi Mandel's death is Dan Uri, "Stoning of Two Israeli Teens Shocks World," *New York Post,* May 10, 2001, p. 20.

xii Rabbi Shimon Hadarshan, *Yalkut Shimoni* (Jerusalem: Mosad Ha-Rav Kuk, 1973).

xiii Ben Halpern, *American Jew: A Zionistic Analysis* (New York: Alfred A. Knopf, 1983).

xiii For more about the 1761 delegation from Safed, see Waxman, *American Aliya.*

xiv Ezer Weizman's comment quoted in Steve Lipman, "Breaking Away: Now More Than Ever, American Jews and Israelis Are Strangers. What Does the Growing Rift Mean for the Future?" *Jewish Week,* July 7, 1994.

xiv For Sharansky's op-ed, see Natan Sharansky, "Papa Knows Best," *Jerusalem Report,* July 14, 1994.

xv For Ben-Gurion on the Diaspora, see David Ben-Gurion, "Letter to Zionists," *Jewish Frontier*, February 1954.

13 For a fictionalized account of Harrisburg in the mid-1940s, see John O'Hara, *A Rage to Live* (New York: Random House, 1949).

20 The British White Papers of 1922 and 1939 are both available online through Yale University's Avalon Project, at http://www.yale.edu/lawweb/avalon/20th.htm.

22 For more on the Hallicrafter SX-42 two-way radio, see http://oak.cats.ohiou.edu/~postr/bapix/SX42.htm.

28 For a firsthand account of Marlin's encounter with the British officer aboard the *Marine Carp*, see Marlin Levin, "30 Years Ago: Reminiscences of an American Correspondent in Jerusalem," *Israel Focus*, May 1978.

34 For more on Jerusalem's architecture during the British Mandate and Richard Kaufmann, see Lili Eylon, "Israel's Architecture of Hope," *Architecture Week* 13 (December 2000), p. C4.2.

45 For Marlin's article on Betty, see Marlin Levin, "Life for a Young Housewife Isn't Fancy, But It's Pleasant," *The Brooklyn Eagle*, June 23, 1948.

46 For more on UNSCOP, see Peter L. Grose, *Israel in the Mind of America* (New York: Alfred A. Knopf, 1983).

60 For more on Fawzi el-Kutub, see Esther Hecht, "Stronger Than TNT," *Jerusalem Post Magazine*, January 30, 1998.

81 The description of the attack on Ben Yehuda Street is composed mainly of interviews with eyewitnesses and Miriam Amdur's unpublished memoirs. Additional sources include Zipporah Porath, *Letters from Jerusalem: 1947–1948* (Tel Aviv: Cherikover, 1998), and oral histories.

84 For more on the attack's aftermath, see Hecht, "Stronger Than TNT."

88 The best history of the IZL, including a detailed account of Deir Yassin, is Yosef Kisoter and Shimshon Feder, eds., *Irgun Zvai Leumi (I.Z.L.): The Story of Israel's Underground Movement*

for National Liberation (Tel Aviv: Israel Ministry of Defense Publishing House, 2000).

100 For more about Jewish life in Brooklyn, see Ilana Abramovitch and Sean Galvin, eds., *Jews of Brooklyn* (Lebanon, NH: University Press of New England, 2001).

101 Kaufmann quoted in Abramavotich and Galvin, *Jews of Brooklyn*.

120 The young Jewish woman's letter quoted in Nancy Weber, "The Truth of Tears," *Village Voice*, June 15, 1967.

120 For more on the American-Jewish reaction to the war and its aftermath, see Lucy S. Dawidowicz, "American Public Opinion," in M. Fine and M. Himmelfarb, eds., *American Jewish Year Book 1968* (New York: American Jewish Committee, 1968).

134 For more on the Black Panthers in Israel, see Sami Shalom Chetrit, "30 Years to the Black Panthers in Israel," available online at http://www.mec-film.de/black/EnglishArticles.htm.

149 For an excellent account of the 1973 war, see Abraham Rabinovich, *The Yom Kippur War: The Epic Encounter That Transformed the Middle East* (New York: Schocken Books, 2004).

209 For a report on Sarah Blaustein's murder, see Matthew McAllester, "A Victim of Violence: Ex-LI Woman Among 6 Dead in New Fighting," *Newsday*, May 30, 2001, p. A7.

242 For a report of Tzvi Goldstein's murder, see Ruth Bashinsky and Corky Siemaszko, "Deadly Ambush: NY Family's Car Attacked in Israel," *New York Daily News*, June 21, 2003, p. 7.

BIBLIOGRAPHY AND SUGGESTED READINGS

Abramovitch, Ilana, and Sean Galvin, eds. *Jews of Brooklyn*. Lebanon, NH: University Press of New England, 2001.

Bashinsky, Ruth, and Corky Siemaszko. "Deadly Ambush: NY Family's Car Attacked in Israel." New York *Daily News*, June 21, 2003, p. 7.

Ben-Gurion, David. "Letter to Zionists." *Jewish Frontier*, February 1954.

Biale, David. *Power and Powerlessness in Jewish History*. New York: Schocken Books, 1986.

Cohen, Rich. *Tough Jews: Fathers, Sons, and Gangster Dreams*. New York: Alfred A. Knopf, 1999.

Dawidowicz, Lucy S. "American Public Opinion." In *American Jewish Year Book 1968*, edited by M. Fine and M. Himmelfarb. New York: American Jewish Committee, 1968.

Eylon, Lili. "Israel's Architecture of Hope." *Architecture Week* 13 (December 2000), p. C4.2.

Freedman, Samuel. *Jew vs. Jew: The Struggle for the Soul of American Jewry*. New York: Simon and Schuster, 2000.

Golan, Mati. *With Friends Like You: What Israelis Really Think About American Jews*. New York: Free Press, 1992.

Goldberg, J. J. *Jewish Power: Inside the American Jewish Establishment*. Boston: Addison-Wesley, 1997.

Goldin, Milton. *Why They Give: American Jews and Their Philanthropies*. New York: Macmillan, 1976.

Gordis, Daniel. *If a Place Could Make You Cry: Dispatches from an Anxious State*. New York: Crown Publishers, 2002.

Gorny, Yosef. "The 'Melting Pot' in Zionist Thought." *Israel Studies,* Fall 2001.

Grose, Peter L. *Israel in the Mind of America*. New York: Alfred A. Knopf, 1983.

Halpern, Ben. *American Jew: A Zionistic Analysis*. New York: Alfred A. Knopf, 1983.

Halpern, Ben, and Jehuda Reinharz. *Zionism and the Creation of a New Society*. New York: Oxford University Press, 1998.

Hecht, Esther. "Stronger Than TNT." *Jerusalem Post Magazine,* January 30, 1998.

Hertzberg, Arthur. *The Jews in America: Four Centuries of an Uneasy Encounter*. New York: Simon and Schuster, 1989.

Horovitz, David. *A Little Too Close to God: The Thrills and Panic of a Life in Israel*. New York: Alfred A. Knopf, 2000.

Kisoter, Yosef, and Shimshon Feder, eds. *Irgun Zvai Leumi (I.Z.I.): The Story of Israel's Underground Movement for National Liberation*. Tel Aviv: Israel Ministry of Defense Publishing House, 2000.

Kosmin, Barry A., et al. *Highlights of the CJF 1990 National Jewish Population Survey*. New York: Council of Jewish Federations, 1991.

Levin, Marlin. *The Birth of Israel*. Jerusalem: Gefen, 1998.

———. "In a Battlefield Newsroom." *Jerusalem Post Jubilee Supplement,* December 1, 1982.

———. "Life for a Young Housewife Isn't Fancy, But It's Pleasant." *Brooklyn Eagle,* June 23, 1948.

———. "30 Years Ago: Reminiscences of an American Correspondent in Jerusalem." *Israel Focus,* May 1978.

Lipman, Steve. "Breaking Away: Now More Than Ever, American

Jews and Israelis Are Strangers. What Does the Growing Rift Mean for the Future?" *Jewish Week,* July 7, 1994.

McAllester, Matthew. "A Victim of Violence: Ex-LI Woman Among 6 Dead in New Fighting." *Newsday,* May 30, 2001, p. A7.

Milstein, Uri. *History of Israel's War of Independence.* Lanham, MD. University Press of America, 1996.

O'Hara, John. *A Rage to Live.* New York: Random House, 1949.

Porath, Zipporah. *Letters From Jerusalem: 1947-1948,* Tel Aviv: Cherikover, 1998.

Rabinovich, Abraham. *The Yom Kippur War: The Epic Encounter That Transformed the Middle East.* New York: Schocken Books, 2004.

Sharansky, Natan. "Papa Knows Best." *Jerusalem Report,* July 14, 1994.

Tyle, Larry. *Home Lands: Portraits of the New Jewish Diaspora.* New York: Henry Holt, 2002.

Waxman, Chaim. *American Aliya: Portrait of an Innovative Migration Movement.* Detroit: Wayne State University Press, 1989.

———. *America's Jews in Transition.* Philadelphia: Temple University Press, 1989.

Weber, Nancy. "The Truth of Tears." *Village Voice,* June 15, 1967.

ACKNOWLEDGMENTS

For a long time I wanted to be a writer. Sometimes, when I would put down a particularly crafty sentence on the page, my eyes would close and I'd imagine a time when the burden of proof was no longer cast upon me, when the title "author," like a military rank or a mark of nobility, would be bestowed upon me. Writing this book, my first, I realized how inadequate were my aspirations, how myopic my vision of my chosen vocation: there were no moments of epiphany, no swirling spirits, no divine revelations. There were nights of coffee and cigarettes and alcohol, torrents of despair over a sentence gone sour or a paragraph collapsing under its own rotting structure. I learned that no matter how ambitious my aspirations, I would never be able to compose a work that embraces all the elements of a given subject. I doubt that anyone could. I therefore had to learn to forgo that desire and try merely to do the best I can. I also learned that even if it is my name appearing on the cover of the book, the names of others play no less important a role in bringing this endeavor to life.

First and foremost, I wish to thank Professor Samuel Freedman, under whose tutelage at Columbia University this book grew from a brief e-mail, to a proposal, and, finally, to the volume before you.

It is with no small degree of sorrow that I realize how inadequate any attempt to properly thank Professor Freedman is doomed to be; his mentorship provided me with both the sharp tools of language and structure and the soft warmth of reassurance. I am proud to have him as my teacher, my literary rabbi, and, I hope, my friend. Milton commented that "a grateful mind by owing owes not, but still pays, at once indebted and discharg'd"; this book is my payment to him, the first, I hope, of many.

While at Columbia, I have also had the good fortune of coming under the instruction of Professors Carole Agus and Kevin Coyne. Each taught me to hone my craft and free my mind. Their support, exceeding any measure of my expectations, will not be forgotten.

As this book took its first steps into the concrete world of publishing, it was met by an extraordinary array of people, to whom I owe a great debt. First among them is my agent, Anne Edelstein. I could not have asked for a better companion on this arduous journey than Anne, in whom are manifested the best virtues of the advocate, the consultant, the good friend, and the fierce protector. My deep appreciation and blind trust in her freed me from all earthly concerns, and for that I am enormously thankful. Completing the joy of great agentry is Emilie Stewart, whose knowledge, ease, and patience helped calm me down and send me back to my desk with gusto.

When the book was acquired by St. Martin's Press, I was fortunate to come across a gallery of goodly figures. First, Jane Rosenman, who believed in this book enough to bet on a nobody emigrant from Israel, gave me hope; although she has moved on to other pastures, her shepherding is much appreciated. George Witte, St. Martin's editor in chief, was unfailing in his support for this book, even as editors came and left; his resolve, his faith, and his fine manner in approaching this book and the hardships it had incurred are greatly treasured. To Surie Rudoff, who provided me not only with masterful legal advice but also with passionate and splendidly well-informed comments about grammar and content alike, above and beyond the call of her duty, I am very thankful.

The talented Adam Goldberger, whose extraordinary attention to the manuscript far exceeded mere copyediting, refined this work greatly.

Finally, and most important, is Ethan Friedman, my terrific editor, who emerged like a knight in shining armor from the shadows to sweep this book off its feet. His insightful eye and analytical mind carried the book from the plateaus of unfulfilled potential to much greater heights. He is a master of both style, structure, and story; his contribution to the book is very great, as is my gratitude.

My parents, Iris and Moshe Mindlin and Rony Leibovitz, and my grandmother, Rivka Greller, deserve glowing words of gratefulness as well, whether for their logistical support, furnishing me with a loving base of operations on my many reporting trips to Israel, or for their interest, their attentiveness, and their encouragement. I am truly blessed to have such a family and greatly cherish their love.

A word of thanks also to Molly, a great friend and companion, for her patience and love.

To Lem Motlow and the people at Jack Daniel's, many thanks for providing the fuel that makes the machine run. To the folks at R. J. Reynolds tobacco company, my gratitude; your Camels carried me to shore. To the ghost of Marcel, I have not forgotten.

As this list draws to an end, it is time to thank the people at the true heart of this book: Marlin and Betty Levin, Mike Ginsberg, and the Kalker family. I hope this humble book does justice to their spirit, their achievements, and their lives. All were magnanimous with their time, their knowledge, and their experience; all welcomed me, a perfect stranger, with great generosity; and none hesitated to travel even to the most painful corners of recollection in search of the stories that constitute this book. I am honored to have met them.

Finally, to Lisa, my stunning wife, I am forever in your debt. You are my muse, my editor, my joy, my best friend, and my love. Without you this book would never be. I will gladly spend a lifetime trying to tell you how grateful I am.